LEWISTON COUNTRY

An Armchair History

by

Margaret Day Allen

Edited, with a Foreword and additional chapters,
by
Ladd Hamilton

Illustrated by Anthony C. Venbrux, M.D.

Nez Perce County Historical Society, Inc.
1990

Library of Congress Catalog Number: 90-060181
ISBN 0-9626050-0-X
© Copyright 1990

Margaret Allen and Ladd Hamilton

Printed in the U.S.A.
by Steeley Print & Binding
Lewiston, Idaho

Published by the Nez Perce County
Historical Society, Inc.
assisted by
a grant from the Idaho Centennial Commission

Second Printing

LEWISTON COUNTRY

An Armchair History

CONTENTS

THE ORDER OF THINGS: A Chronology

1836 — Spalding establishes his mission on
Lapwai Creek.

1852 — Captain E.D. Pierce arrives at Lapwai to trade
with the Indians.

1855 — The Nez Perces and the government agree to
establish a reservation.

1857 — Captain Pierce returns to the Clearwater,
looking for gold.

1860 — Pierce and party strike gold in Canal Gulch.

1861 — The rush is on, and a town rises at the
confluence.
Gold is discovered in Florence Basin.

1862 — Badman Henry Plummer arrives in Lewiston.

1863 — The Hotel De France becomes the best in the
north country.
Lewiston becomes the capital of a new
territory.
Lloyd Magruder is viciously murdered, and a
manhunt begins.
A new treaty shrinks the Nez Perce
Reservation.

1864 — The law executes Magruder's murderers.
The first school opens, briefly, at Lewiston.
The "Boise Gang" wrestles the capital away.

1865 — Boise officially becomes the new capital.
The Colonel Wright is wrecked in a final
attempt to climb the rapids of the Snake
River.
The first Chinese arrive in the mining camps.

1867 — Congress ratifies the Treaty of 1863.
Father Joseph Cataldo builds a church for
Lewiston Catholics

1870 — The steamboat Shoshone makes a wild trip
through Hells Canyon.

1872 — John Silcott starts building the Uniontown
         Grade.
1873 — Lewiston gets its first real school building.
         Water flows through the Lewiston ditch.
1874 — Lewiston becomes legal at last.
         The Uniontown grade is completed.
1877 — War breaks out between non-treaty Nez Perces
         and the U.S. Army.
1878 — J.P. Vollmer installs the first telephone in the
         Pacific Northwest.
1879 — A Frenchman builds the Raymond
         House.
1883 — Fire ravages Chinatown.
         Asotin County is created.
1884 — Lewiston gets its first parochial school.
1893 — The Annie Faxon blows up.
1895 — The first Salvation Army troops arrive.
1896 — The Salvation Army sets up its first Lewiston
         headquarters.
         Lewiston State Normal School opens.
         The first white child, Maurice Van Arsdol, is
         born on the Clarkston Flat.
         Clarkston ditch starts delivering water.
1898 — The railroad reaches Lewiston, finally.
1899 — The first interstate bridge spans the Snake.
1902 — Lewiston abandons its ditch.
1910 — First taxicab rattles up to Normal Hill.
1912 — Lewiston proudly presents the first Northwest
         Livestock Show.
1913 — The 18th Street Bridge puts Silcott's
         ferry out of business.
1916 — Work begins on the Spiral Highway.
1927 — Clearwater Timber Co. builds a
         "colossal" lumber mill in east Lewiston.
1931 — Northern Idaho lumber companies merge to
         create Potlatch Forests, Inc.

Foreword

The reader may argue that this "armchair history" is less a history than a collection of historical sketches. The authors will accept that. We intend it as a look back at our town and region as it was before any of us knew it, and at the frontier forces that helped shape the lives and attitudes of the people who preceded us here.

Some of these people were transplanted Europeans, some were Nez Perce Indians, some were Chinese. All are a part of the history of this place and therefore a part of us. "History is merely gossip," wrote Oscar Wilde, to which Henry Ford added, "History is bunk." But history is neither; it is what we were and thus a part of what we are.

That is one of the reasons, I am sure, why Margaret Allen undertook to write this book. It was not only to define the place but to identify herself as a lifetime part of it — and, in the process, to identify us, too. This place's past still lives in those who have been here for a time, and affects the way we think and act and respond to events. To understand that may help us understand ourselves a little better, to secure our sense of place and of belonging to these mountains and prairies. This is not a definitive history of the Lewiston country. That has not yet been written and perhaps will never be. We have not tried to cross all the t's, only to record some of the events of the past that have made this the kind of place it is. To do even that much has not been easy. The Nez Perces kept no written record for historians to draw upon; the earliest white people — with a few notable exceptions — were far too busy exploring, mining, planting and surviving to take notes, much less publish them. What we have are the Journals of Lewis and Clark, a few personal memoirs — by William A. Goulder, Captain E.D. Pierce and Joaquin Miller, for example —and some interviews that tap old memories. Even these are not completely trustworthy.

Captain Pierce, the man most responsible for the founding of Lewiston, did not dictate his memoirs until long after he had left the region for good. Joaquin Miller came through here as a young man and wrote about the place later, striving less for truth than for literary effect (note his description of Lewiston in Chapter Two). As for the early-day newspapers, they were edited by men whose personal stake in the outcome of things made them far from disinterested chroniclers of their time. Alonzo Leland's announcement in the *Teller* that the railroad would reach Lewiston before Christmas — eight years before the fact — was typical. Yet we probably have no better mirror of their times than those yellowed columns of news and opinion, hurriedly and often extravagantly written.

There is much we can learn from a study of our past, including this: Some awful things were done by rather nice people. General O.O. Howard's treatment of the non-treaty Indians at the council of May, 1877, was outrageous, and yet later, when the surrendering Nez Perces were doublecrossed by the government, it was Howard, together with Colonel Nelson Miles, who tried to get justice done. The Indian Wahlitits made war inevitable by leading a bloody assault on white settlers, but it was the same Wahlitits who earlier had shown compassion for the elders of the band and who later fought heroically beside his wife at the Battle of the Big Hole. The missionary Henry Harmon Spalding drove Indians into forced labor to build his mission, using the whip when necessary, but this indomitable man also inspired a fierce and lasting loyalty among many of the Nez Perces.

Also worth noting, I think, is the almost nonchalant courage and hardihood of the first white people in the Lewiston country. People like Israel Cowan, the club-footed former school teacher who carried the express on his back through the snow between Lewiston and Pierce City. Or Warren P. Hunt, who packed gold out of the mountains in his saddlebags for ten years and never lost a bit of it. Or Susan McBeth, the frail and crippled missionary teacher who carried on her work at Kamiah when she could barely hobble between the rooms of her tiny house. Or Captain Sebastian Miller, who spent weeks in the wilderness searching for his steamboat, then rammed her through Hells Canyon to Lewiston. As for the Nez Perces, their bravery in war is no less remarkable than their patience in adversity.

We are the heirs of these extraordinary people, for we have inherited the place they had some part in making.

This narrative begins with the discovery of gold in Canal Gulch near the present town of Pierce and carries the story into the 1920s. In a few cases, as in recounting the history of the French hotels and of the timber industry, it seemed necessary to extend it past World War II. Most of the research and much of the writing is Margaret Allen's. The organization of the material is mine, and it is admittedly arbitrary. It was my decision, for example, to devote a separate chapter to two hotels, the Raymond and the De France, while making only passing reference to the Hotel Lewis-Clark (because it came along later). Just as arbitrary, perhaps, was our selection of what to include; enough interesting material has been left out to make another book, and I hope someone will write it. Meanwhile, this is, as far as I know, the only general history of the Lewiston country in book form that was written with the casual reader in mind.

History buffs may question the spelling of some of the names in the chapter about the vigilantes. Although Hill Beachey's name is sometimes spelled as *Beachy,* it is Beachey in his own handwriting on several documents. One of Lloyd Magruder's murderers spelled his last name at various times both as Romaine and Romain. Another of the murderers sometimes called himself Lower and sometimes Lowrey or Lowry. The man who called himself David Renton was known to many as "Doc" Howard. In this book they are Beachey, Romain, Lower and Renton.

A personal word: Most of us who worked at the *Lewiston Morning Tribune* with Margaret Allen — who was a reporter for many years and for many more a librarian — knew she was gathering material for a book about Lewiston. We wondered sometimes if she would ever get around to finishing it, and her answer was always the same: There was still a mite more research to be done. Finally, in the early spring of 1989, she asked me to finish it for her and get it into print. Her eyes were bothering her and she was running out of steam. She turned over to me several hundred typed pages in a half dozen big envelopes, and those pages are the basis of this volume. To round the narrative out, I have added chapters on the War of 1877, the Chinese, the development of the timber industry, statehood, and the opening of the reservation.

Dr. Anthony Venbrux, the illustrator of this book, is assistant professor of radiology and surgery at Johns Hopkins Hospital in Baltimore, Maryland. He is a graduate of Lewiston High School and the University of Idaho, and in these pictures he has combined his interests in history and art. At Margaret's request he began making the drawings, based on old photographs, in the mid-Seventies, and finished the last one in the final week of 1989 while visiting at Lewiston with his family.

Margaret and I are indebted also to the Idaho Centennial Commission, which helped to finance the publication of this book; to the Nez Perce County Centennial Commission and its director, Sharrol St. Marie, for both moral and material support; to the Nez Perce County Historical Society for many services; to the *Tribune*'s librarian, Phyllis Collins, for her help in finding things; to other helpers including Larry Carter, Michael Sullivan, Carole Simon-Smolinski, George Day, Robert Weatherly, Richard Morgan, Johnny Johnson, Robert Wing and Lora Feucht; and to my wife, Pauletta, who read and corrected the manuscript.

Ladd Hamilton

1

Gold!

It was Wilbur F. Bassett, many believe, whose gold pan changed forever the Clearwater country of Idaho. Bassett, a member of the prospecting party of E.D. Pierce, panned out his bit of gold in Canal Gulch near the present village of Pierce on or about September 28, 1860. In the words of Captain Pierce, "I never saw a party of men so excited." And no wonder: The color in Bassett's pan would come near to emptying the placer diggings of California and start a new stampede to the creek bottoms of northern and central Idaho.

Bassett didn't discover Idaho gold; others had known it was there, but kept it to themselves. The Rev. Pierre Jean DeSmet, the Catholic missionary who passed through the region in the 1840s, mentioned only the conversion of the Indians. Road builder John Mullan, enroute from Fort Benton, Montana, to Walla Walla, Washington, in 1858, forbade his men to prospect. Jean de Lassier let nothing so trivial as gold dust interrupt his trapping; but he carried a bit of dust with him for more than a year, from 1857 to 1858.

Elias Davidson Pierce, a former Army captain and the leader of that first handful of prospectors, said later he had known there was gold in those mountains as early as 1852. That was the year he first ventured into what is now northern Idaho in order to trade with the Nez Perces.

He put up his tent near the home of the Rev. Henry Harmon Spalding, the Presbyterian missionary, on Lapwai Creek, and began to do business. "The Indians came in swarms," he recalled later, "all anxious to trade. I had at first to depend entirely on my interpreter but in a short time I could speak the language and make the Indians understand me in all business transactions." Pierce bought horses from the Indians for $10 to $12 each in goods, branded them, and corralled them for sale later "back in the states" for $100 each. He found the Indian ponies "well broken and kind under the saddle." He bought altogether on that trip 110 head of horses. In February of 1853, Pierce gathered his stock and left Lapwai for The Dalles and his home in California.

Things did not go well for him in California, however, and in April, 1857, he was back at Lapwai, ostensibly to do more trading. Here he discovered that the Indians were not as friendly as before. Major Edward Steptoe and Colonel George Wright had been waging a vicious war against the Yakimas in what is now eastern Washington and slaughtering their horses. (On one occasion Wright's troops had driven a thousand Indian horses into a narrow canyon and methodically shot every one of them.) The Nez Perces were so angry with the whites that they had advised their great and good friend, William Craig, to leave the reservation. However, they would do Pierce no harm, they assured him, because they were eager to trade. Pierce himself was less eager to trade than to hunt for gold, since he had seen signs of it in 1852. He decided to stay on for a while as a trader and wait for a chance to slip into the mountains.

After a few months at Lapwai, Pierce returned to Walla Walla convinced there was gold in the Clearwater country and determined to do some prospecting later. In February, 1860, he was on his way back to the Clearwater with a companion, Seth Farrell (or Ferrell). Hidden in their packs were prospecting tools which they later told the Indians were to be used for farming and building roads.

On February 20, Pierce, Farrell and a friendly Nez Perce chief went up the Clearwater to a low bar, where Pierce washed out a pan and found some specks of "floater" gold. The gold itself didn't amount to much, but it told Pierce there must be a feeder vein somewhere upstream in the mountains. The next day, Pierce and Farrell took a stroll up the Clearwater about ten miles, prospecting along the way, and, according to Pierce, "found gold in every place we tried." When they returned to camp they confided in the Nez Perces there but told them to say nothing to anyone else. And they made plans to go to Walla Walla soon with several of the Indians to buy mining supplies.

At Walla Walla, the Indian agent, A.J. Cain, told Pierce he could not go prospecting in the Nez Perce country because it might start a war. Pierce did not pay much attention to Cain, for shortly after that he was in The Dalles buying equipment that was unavailable in Walla Walla. When Pierce and the Indians returned to Lapwai (apparently without Farrell, for Pierce does not mention him again), they were met by the Indian sub-agent, Charles Frush. Frush told Pierce he couldn't pass through the reservation without a written permit. Pierce didn't have one. He said he didn't expect that to stop him, whereupon Frush offered to write him one on the spot, and did. Pierce continued up the Clearwater but he had not gone far when a couple of strange white men caught up with him. Fearing they might be claim jumpers, Pierce made some excuse and turned back to Lapwai. He told the Indians there what had happened and said he would go to Walla Walla and return later when the coast was clear.

According to Pierce's account, people in the Walla Walla region were clamoring for a chance to return with him to the Clearwater, but he was in no hurry. According to some other accounts, Pierce had trouble organizing a party because of widespread fear of the Indians; the Whitman massacre of 1847 was still fresh in memory, and the Yakimas and Cayuses were known to be hostile. At any rate, Pierce got some people together and assured agent Cain that he wouldn't set foot on the Nez Perce reservation but would stay to the north of it. Cain replied that since the Indians had no rights outside the reservation, he would not concern himself any longer with Pierce's venture.

Pierce and his party of eleven, including Wilbur Bassett, reached the mouth of the Tucannon on August 12, 1860, and there "procured a guide who was familiar with the country." There is no mention in his memoirs of Jane, the daughter of Chief Timothy, but she was probably that guide. There is no mention of Timothy, either, or of the help Timothy and his Alpowa band of Nez Perces gave the Pierce party in preparing it for the trek into the mountains. But Pierce did not dictate his version of events until almost fifty years later, after his memory perhaps had dimmed.

The Pierce party crossed to the north side of the Snake River near Timothy's camp at a place now known as Silcott. Jane, then 18 years old (her Christian name had been given her by Spalding at his Lapwai mission school), led the prospectors out of the Snake River valley onto the Palouse, traveling north. They turned eastward just south of present day Moscow and crossed Potlatch Creek near what is now the village of Kendrick. Then the going became hard, according to Pierce: "15th. Wound our way through heavy timber and chaparral; had to cut a trail for our animals, about sundown could see the north fork, a clear sparkling stream; could see it meandering through deep walled canyons. . . We had to build bridges in many places before we could pass. At one place, it took us all one day to build a bridge to be safe to cross with our animals. The country was so extremely rough and having to make a trail most of the way, some days did not make over three miles. I am quite confident there never had been a human being in the country before."

It took them well over a month to reach the Lolo trail, which then connected the Nez Perce Nation with the

Flathead country to the east. There Pierce and his party rested for two days and on about September 28 they reached "a nice place, a nice stream of water," and camped. They found gold there, "in every place in the streams, in the flats and banks and gold generally diffused from the surface to the bedrock." On October 2 the party moved down to another stream, which Pierce named Oro Fino ("fine gold" in Spanish), because there seemed to be better prospects there. The men laid out a townsite and named the place Pierce City. They organized a mining district, established its boundaries, and drafted a set of mining laws. Within a short time the prospectors had $100 in gold dust, enough to establish the district's credibility, and on October 12 the party left for Walla Walla by a shorter, easier route.

At Walla Walla, Pierce assured all who would listen that there was enough gold in the Clearwater to keep five thousand men busy for ten years.

Bassett couldn't wait to take the good news to his friend, Alonzo Leland, at Portland. Leland, then the editor of *The Portland Times*, would later join the rush himself, but in the meantime he wrote for his newspaper a series of articles describing the riches to be found on the Clearwater—all perhaps based on his conversations with Bassett. Leland's pieces were so glowing and so persuasive that they enticed thousands of prospectors away from the stripped-out placer mines of California and caused some of the locals to suspect that he was secretly working for a riverboat company.

The Pierce party, now about 30 strong, returned to the Clearwater and spent that winter building log huts and whipsawing lumber for sluice boxes, meanwhile mining under the snow—but without Captain Pierce. He had gone instead to Olympia to ask the Territorial Legislature for a charter to build a wagon road, together with the necessary ferries and bridges, from Walla Walla to the mines. He got the charter, but he didn't get back to Pierce until the following March and he never did build the wagon road.

After three months at Pierce, he left for the Powder River country of Oregon where he and a couple of associates hoped to do some road building and prospecting. A year later, in the fall of 1862, Pierce was poking about in the Boise Basin. He visited Lewiston briefly in May of 1863, apparently for the last time. As for the Clearwater, he said later, he had done what he set out to do there and he had no more interest in it.

*   *   *

Reports of new strikes continued to trickle in to Walla Walla throughout the winter of 1860-'61, filling the city with restless excitement. One of these reports was carried by three prospectors who had returned to Walla Walla for provisions. They had been lost and without food for three days and had finally stumbled upon the ranch of a Nez Perce chief who fed them and directed them on their way.

Miners coming out of the Clearwater reported finding up to $40 in gold per pan, and with every report the excitement grew. Travel through the mountains was still by foot, since pack horses couldn't penetrate the deep snow.

On March 4, 1861, one of Pierce's original party wrote from Walla Walla: "Times are good here now. There is great excitement about the mines. . .The valley will be deserted in a few days. . .The town is full of pack animals. There is not a pick, gold pan or any quicksilver to be had at any price."

As early as February, the first wave of prospectors started moving from Portland and the Willamette Valley eastward even though the trails could not yet be opened. By March, some 500 gold-hungry prospectors were pushing for the Clearwater diggings from western Oregon. Later that month, miners from western Washington and California began converging on The Dalles and Walla Walla.

"All Willamette Valley seems to be here," a San Francisco correspondent wrote. "I don't know who will care for the crops in Oregon when so many have deserted.

There must be four thousand here. Most came here flat broke, but in Oregon we learn to manage without money.''

So they came that spring, in wagons, on horseback, astride mules, walking under heavy packs. Many came without blankets or warm clothing, mining tools or even food. Those who could afford it paid fancy prices to ride in comfort on the Colonel Wright, the first steamboat to plow up through the rapids of the Snake River and into the Clearwater.

The Colonel Wright had been specially built for swift, uncharted waters by the Oregon Steam Navigation Co., which wanted a boat that could get as near to the mines as possible. One of the passengers on this maiden voyage was Seth Slater, not a prospector but a businessman hoping to relieve the prospectors of some of their gold. Slater had brought along between ten and fifteen tons of equipment and merchandise, announcing that he would establish his store as close to the mines as the boat would carry him. That turned out to be not very close. Once out of the Snake and in the Clearwater the going was slow and the steamer had to be lined, or winched, over occasional rapids by ropes fastened to trees or boulders on the shore. About 20 miles upstream, the boat met an obstacle it could not pass, a wide, churning eddy. Two attempts at lining failed; the engine could not even hold the boat in the channel.

It was the end of the line. And there on the north bank, near what is now the village of Lenore, the prospectors debarked with their gear and went on by land. Slater set up his store on the spot and named the place Slaterville. It consisted of two tent dwellings, two larger tents designed as store and storehouse, and a fifth, a saloon tent with a bright blue and red canvas top. At one side of it, Slater printed the word ''Whiskey'' in charcoal. The saloon was simply equipped, with a barrel of whiskey, two bottles and two glasses.

Slater sat and waited for customers who seldom came. The water level dropped, ending navigation in the Clearwater, and the pack trains that passed by usually paused only for water and a brief rest. Slater gave up and moved his store down to the meeting of the waters, a place the Indians called "Tsceminicum," which was to become the city of Lewiston.

2

Ragtown

Seth Slater arrived at the confluence of the Snake and Clearwater rivers to find that he was not the only merchant there. The Colonel Wright had returned to the Clearwater, this time stopping just upstream from the confluence and tying up at the south bank near the present site of Twin City Foods. There she had deposited the would-be merchants, miners and hangers-on who would form the first white population of the future capital of the new territory of Idaho. Tents went up quickly and within days this little camp became a hive of commerce, the supplier of goods to the Clearwater, teeming with the bustle and excitement of miners passing through on their way to wealth and adventure.

The earliest arrivals remembered it vaguely as irregular rows of tents illegally squatting on Indian land. Because of treaty restraints, authorities outlawed permanent buildings, but it didn't much matter; there was little thought of permanency in those first years. With some exaggeration, and depending mainly on hearsay, Nathaniel Pitt Langford described early Lewiston this way in *Vigilante Days and Ways*, published in 1893:

"In less than three months from the time the first immigrants commenced to establish a settlement there, several streets of more than a mile in length were laid out. These were thickly covered, on both sides, with dwellings, stores, hotels and saloons, chiefly constructed of factory cotton. The frame was of light wood . . . or poles and the cloth in most cases fastened to it with tacks. Seen from a distance, the town had the appearance of being built of white marble . . . At night, when lights were burning in these frail tenements, a stranger would think the town illuminated . . . The sound of the violin, which struck the ear on entering the street was never lost while going through it and at many of the saloons the evidence of bacchanal orgies, which were in progress inside, was often apparent in the eagerness exhibited by the crowd.''

Lewiston grew, without plat or plan, with no city government, no tax money and no jail. It was a mining camp without a mine; a "rag town" of tents with a small aristocracy of log cabins. Illegally but with supreme confidence, stealthily yet uproariously, with all the abandon of a frontier town, Lewiston grew.

As the weeks passed, more and larger pack trains left daily for the mines. Those packers grew wealthy who made the best guesses, and each packer aimed to be the first trader to enter a new camp, each looking for a camp where the gold dust was more plentiful than flour, bacon or beans. The town soon adopted the habit of paying with gold dust, already much preferred to Civil War continentals. Every miner carried his buckskin bag and every merchant his scales.

This "ragtown" had other characteristics of the mining camps: an open-front store at almost every house, a saloon at least on every corner and dance halls in the largest tents. Its population fluctuated like the tide. Estimates of Lewiston's head count in its first three years ran as high as twelve thousand and as low as 365.

The community acquired its name sometime in early 1861—probably in May; the city considers May 13 its birthday—when some settlers, including Tom Beall and Vic Trevitt, were sitting around wondering what they ought to call the place. According to Beall, it was Trevitt who suggested Lewiston to honor Captain Meriwether

Lewis, the explorer. Trevitt was the representative of a Portland firm, Ladd & Tilton, who had come to open the first store in the new town. (It was never clearly decided whether his or Slater's was the first.) Trevitt's proposal made sense to the others, and Captain Lewis had a city named after him.

In August of that year, an old California sourdough named Peter Baboin, or Babaire—accounts vary—made a rich gold strike in the mountains of the Salmon River country, but the news of "Old Baboon's" discovery was kept secret by him and his companions until early October when the prospector came into Lewiston and gave the news, and directions to the mine, to an old friend, the express agent, Joaquin Miller. He apparently told others as well, for almost immediately the city was swamped under another rush of miners to the Salmon.

The city's future seemed secure. One R.G. Stuart, a law student and novice prospector, described the Lewiston of early fall, 1861, in a letter to his sweetheart.

"Lewiston is to be a place—it is to be Stockton, Sacramento and Marysville combined. It is the trading point for all these miners, the Oro Fino and Salmons . . . I would have went back of the present laid out places and fenced in some acres of ground, but I had no money and the nearest fencing has to be brought some 20 or 30 miles. There is scarcely a shrub in sight of Lewiston. After Lewiston commences growing and gains importance and the town lots become valuable, as they will this coming season, it is going to be a grand good place for law. There will be such a diversity of title jumpers, pre-emptors, Indian agency and all that, and to facilitate the thing, court costs are not more than one fourth what they were in California."

The place made a different impression on William A. Goulder, a miner and newspaper editor who passed through Lewiston at about the same time. Goulder expressed doubts about the city's future, wondering, as he wrote later, whether the "little hamlet of Lewiston . . .

could be imagined to have a future'' in the face of its handicaps.

And there is Joaquin Miller's description of the place. Miller, who was later to become famous as the "Poet of the Sierras," arrived at Lewiston in the fall of 1861 to be the resident agent of Isaac Mossman's pony express line, and years later remembered the town this way:

"Lewiston, built of boards and canvas, looking sickly and discouraged, stood shivering in the wind of October . . . and winced under volleys of pebbles that struck the sounding houses with such force you might have thought an unseen army was bombarding them. The town looked as if it had started down from the mines in the mountains above, ragged and discouraged, and, getting to where it then was, had sat down in the forks of the river to wait for the ferry. The town looked as if it ought to go on—as if it wanted to go on—as if it really would go on, if the wind kept blowing and the unseen army kept up the cannonade.''

Miller had experienced the first blasts of one of the worst winters on record in the region east of the Cascades. Wood must have been the only fuel available to heat the tents, and woodsmen had to trek forty miles, round trip, from Lewiston to reach the nearest forests. Stuart was right when he spoke of "scarcely a shrub" nearby. There would have been fuel dealers, and they would have been preparing for cold, but no one could have known what the miners and merchants were in for as the winter of 1861-'62 approached.

3

Roughing It

Of all the mining camps where men endured the difficult winter of 1861-'62, none suffered more than Florence, high in the Salmon River country of central Idaho.

Millersburg was the first name given to this mining settlement, but its residents quickly renamed it Florence—some say in honor of the foster daugher of Dr. George C. Furber, one of the first arrivals there. Some others insist that the Florence so honored was born in the camp, the daughter of James Hunt, who operated a store and hotel in the community. Joaquin Miller later claimed that it was named originally for him by his friend Peter Bablaine, or Baboin, who discovered gold there and laid out the town. According to Miller, Bablaine was charging $1,000 to $5,000 for lots in Millersburg, a sum so outlandish that Dr. Furber led the population a few hundred yards away, laid out a new town and named it after his eldest daughter. It is more likely that Millersburg took its name from Joseph M. Miller, who made the first gold strike on Miller Creek, and most historians now believe the place was renamed in honor of Florence Hunt.

Although the Florence gold strike was made in August, 1861, a secrecy agreement kept the news from reaching Lewiston until early October. Within days, miners began leaving the diggings of Pierce and Oro Fino.

A stream of men, many on snowshoes and carrying heavy packs, were off through the snow-covered mountains on a trek of more than a hundred miles. By November there were some two thousand men in the camp, many of them poorly equipped and unprepared for the rigors of a wilderness winter. More than half the horde had brought little food, no warm clothing or adequate bedding. November and December were mild enough, but on the day before Christmas it turned bitterly cold. On New Year's Day of 1862 the Columbia River was frozen and the Snake had congealed into a winding block of ice. The more cautious of the prospectors read the signs and made hasty exits, braving the snow and cold in a desperate gamble. Many of them arrived at Oro Fino and Pierce on frozen feet and some would not have made it at all but for the help of Indians. Hundreds of others stayed on at Florence, however, and soon found themselves facing starvation.

Heavy snows continued to fall in the Florence basin, shutting down most mining. For no work, the miners got no money. There was little enough food for those who could pay, and none for those who could not. Half-starved men dug down through several feet of snow, trying to pan enough of the yellow dust to keep alive. Some of the more resourceful miners found that flour boiled with snow water and the inner bark of an evergreen tree would relieve hunger pangs. By the time G.A. "Doc" Noble brought the first pack train of supplies into Florence later that January, there was nothing left in the stores except flour at two dollars a pound. Noble had spent ten agonizing days and nights struggling through drifts to cover the distance from Lewiston to Florence and made it only because at one point, when he became lost and desperate, some Indians had come to his aid.

By March, other pack trains were trying to get through to the besieged camp. The snow continued to fall. Alonzo P. Brown, brother of Idaho County pioneer Loyal P. Brown, said he had recorded 113 almost consecutive days of falling snow. (Even in the following summer there were daily morning frosts at Florence; a blinding snowstorm fell all day on July 3.)

Deep drifts and fallen trees prevented the pack animals from going beyond Mountain House, a cluster of storage tents some fifteen miles from Florence. From there, all supplies had to be carried in on human backs. Weakened men, some ill with scurvy, carried the loads through snow trails. At first they received forty cents a pound, then fifty cents, for their efforts, then more. The glare of the sun on the sparkling snow was as cruel as the snow itself. Many of the packers went snow-blind on the trails and could no longer see where they were going. To keep moving required desperate and pathetic measures. The group would place a seeing member in the lead and follow in single file. The leader would hold the blade of a long-handled miner's shovel under one arm, so the man behind him could grasp the end of the handle. The next man in turn would grasp the blade of another shovel for the guidance of the man behind him. "In this way a dozen or more snow-blind men would often be seen marching single file, all loaded down with their blankets and provisions," wrote William A. Goulder in his *Reminiscenses of a Pioneer*. Goulder spent part of that winter at the horse ranch of Mr. and Mrs. Theodore Poujade, a sort of way station on the Weippe Prairie some fifteen miles from Oro Fino. Goulder reported that one day during his visit a file of blinded men came struggling through the snow to the house, their faces blackened with a mixture of ground charcoal and bacon grease, most of them utterly helpless under their loads. "They had to be led around and taken care of like so many helpless infants. In addition to being blind, they all suffered from severe pains in the eyes, which made the house for the time being a veritable hospital. Mrs. Poujade devised a remedy of poultices of tea leaves from the steeping of the tea, to be bound with light bandages over the eyes. When the tea leaves gave out, we used cloths saturated with tea, which proved an excellent substitute. The remedy proved to be all that could be desired, and in a day or two the patients were all restored to their normal condition and ready for another battle with the snow."

For many others, recovery was less complete. Joaquin Miller suffered a case of snow blindness while packing into Florence on foot that winter and it affected his vision for the rest of his life.

Nowhere in the mining camps was there enough food, especially vegetables, and scurvy was rampant. When the illness became particularly bad at Oro Fino, someone remembered that a store of potatoes in gunny sacks had been buried by packers the autumn before on the Weippe Prairie. These were dug up and transported on men's backs for some fifteen miles to the mining camp and distributed to the sick. They were eaten uncooked, sliced and soaked in vinegar.

Captain E.D. Pierce, whose party had made the first big gold strike on the Clearwater in 1860, later recalled the winter of 1861-'62 in these words: "The miners ran short of supplies. Every possible means were used to reach them with provisions. Men would shovel snow and try to get through with their pack animals loaded with 200 to 300 pounds while others would harness themselves to hand sleds, trying to skim along through the surface of snow that was from ten to twelve feet deep. Hundreds of men strung along on snow shoes with from 50 to 75 pounds on their back. A Frenchman who made a regular pack train of himself would push the distance of twelve miles through a rough country. He would load himself with 200 pounds and make it through in one day, for which he would receive one dollar per pound. A nice little sum for each day's labor. The suffering in the mountains from hunger and frozen limbs was indescribable."

That winter in the camps was not all struggle and suffering. There is this account of life at Oro Fino in Goulder's *Reminiscenses*:

"The long winter evenings were devoted to the

reading of the few books that could be found in the camp and in overhauling the old newspapers that had accumulated in the cabins while the express had been able to make regular trips. A man named Harris kept a little newsstand in Oro Fino that winter and among the treasures on his shelves was a nearly complete set of Scott's novels. My comrades in the cabin agreed to buy and pay for the books if I would agree to read them aloud evenings while they rested in their bunks and did the listening. To this I very willingly agreed, with the condition that they should keep duly awake and attentive. When all was arranged and ready, I would begin to read, throwing into my voice all the mellifluous tones and soporific effects that I could muster. Very soon they would be both sound asleep and snoring in perfect rhythm and harmony with the voice of the reader. Then I would cease reading aloud, and enjoy for an hour or two a session of intense delight and profitable reading. At the first sign of their awakening, I would resume my sleep-compelling style of reading, which would soon again produce the desired effect. These exercises would be finished to the satisfaction and delight of all concerned, when we would be ready to take up another series of stories. I thus read for the first time all of Scott's novels except *The Fair Maid of Perth* . . ."

A lot of chess was played in the camp on those long winter evenings, and there were weekly meetings of the Oro Fino Lyceum and Debating Club.

Daytimes, the men kept busy stowing fuel and whip-sawing lumber for next spring's sluice boxes. And the packing from place to place never ceased despite the snow.

One young man who packed into Florence that winter later recalled with some amazement the terrible loads that were carried by men on foot. In a letter to Joaquin Miller, Joshua J. Walton wrote:

"I remember well the circumstances of meeting you when we—Father and myself—were going into Florence, carrying our packs on our backs. You were coming out with the mail—in fact carrying the letters and mail from the camp of Florence to the Slate Creek station . . . I remember that all the provisions and supplies for the camp were carried in on men's backs, over the snow from five to ten feet deep, and that, too, over those huge old mountains that seemed almost perpendicular and especially when a fellow had from seventy-five pounds to one hundred and fifty pounds on his back! I saw with my own eyes men with three fifty-pound sacks of flour on their backs at one time, which they had carried over that snow-trail—over those big mountains! I saw one man carrying a large blacksmith's anvil on his back, one with a large bellows, and a great many with ten-gallon kegs of liquor on their backs! Everything was carried on men's backs until the snow melted off of the mountains so pack mules could travel."

When spring finally came, the rush to the Salmon River mines resumed and by the summer of 1862, the population in the Florence basin had jumped to some five thousand. A visitor, coming upon the place at twilight, later said he could see in the distance a thousand cooking fires, reminding him of an army in camp.

A single steamer unloaded seven hundred California sourdoughs and their packs into Portland, all heading for the Salmon River mines. It was the richest placer field thus far discovered in Idaho, and while it lasted it may have been the richest ever found in the United States.

4

The Golden Age

The deep snows of winter finally melted into a torrent of spring floods, and by April of 1862 the mule trains were moving out of Lewiston almost daily enroute to the mines. It was to be a most auspicious year for the town between the rivers.

We know a great deal about the Lewiston of 1862, because of two sources: the first issue of the town's first newspaper, *The Golden Age*, which appeared on August 2 of that year under the editorship of A.S. Gould; and a photograph taken at about the same time from a bluff overlooking the town.

Near the center of the photo is the leading hotel, the Luna House, a long log building covered with a canvas roof. The streets are empty strips without signposts or sidewalks. A magnifying glass reveals two wavering building signs—the "Assay Office" and "Holman Bros. Hauling Done."

What became the town's main street was an afterthought. When the hordes of squatters swooped in, they favored two areas. Boating companies and innkeepers sought sites along the rivers; the merchants preferred slightly higher ground. Atop the bluffs, on what is now called Normal Hill, was a dry plain of sagebrush and jackrabbits, considered useless land. The town's first merchants built their frame and canvas stores facing north, toward the hills across the Clearwater and well away from the bluffs, which they feared might crumble at any time (they haven't.) Thus the stores and saloons lined up along D Street, facing the river, with their backsides facing the bluffs. Within a short time, people were using a shortcut from one end of town to the other that took them back of the stores and saloons, and the path they beat there, a meandering one, became so well traveled that the merchants found it prudent to display their merchandise at both the front and back. Snake Street was the first name applied to this accidental thoroughfare, but that caused some confusion because another street was being developed southward along the Snake River. Then the more dignified name of Montgomery was chosen. Later it became E Street and finally Main.

During the summer of 1862, as the population swelled, more buildings crowded between the river and the bluff and a street grid developed with the Luna House dominating the center. The streets were numbered from west to east and lettered from north to south with A Street—later to be washed away—running along the Clearwater River and E Street following the path that later would become Main.

In the advertising columns of *The Golden Age* that August were the offerings of thirty-two local businesses. They included Ross & Dempster, "dealers in groceries, provisions, Miners' and Hotel Stores;" Crawford, Slocum & Co., "groceries, clothing, blankets, medicines and dye stuffs;" Yates & Lane, "groceries, drygoods, liquors," and the drug stores of Dr. I.S. McIteeny and L. Terry ("Large stock of patent medicines. All orders from the mines to be attended to").

There are no ads in these columns for the businesses of Seth Slater and Vic Trevitt who, only fourteen months before, were competing to establish the first store in town. But J.D. Baldwin and Jagger & Co. had goods on sale. Kaufman & Rosenthal advertised "Groceries, Provisions, Hardware, Boots, Shoes, Hats, Yankee Notions, etc."

and D. Fleischman offered "Packers' and Miners' Outfitting Supplies," plus "Fancy & Dry Goods, Prints, Lawns, Shawls, Embroiders, Silk Hose, and Lace and Silk Mantillas, Window Shades and Carpets." This appears to have been the only store catering to the women in the mining camps.

Two boat lines were using the advertising columns of *The Golden Age* to promote business. They were the Oregon Steam Navigation Co. and Ephraim Baughman & Co. It was one of the few times the OSN lost its monopoly on river transport in that period, but the loss was short-lived. Baughman and his partner, A.P. Ankeny, sold their boat, the Spray, to the OSN for roughly twice what they had paid to build it.

There is intriguing evidence in *The Golden Age* of a circus having passed through Lewiston that summer. A second hotel, the What Cheer House, had been opened by J.R. Marshall, "late of Lee & Marshall's Circus," offering "accommodations for families." And the first classified ad in the paper reads: "For Sale, Cheap, For Cash: One large Circus Tent, 48 feet in diameter, 144 in circumference. Inquire at Idaho Saloon, John H. Scranton." Mrs. Elizabeth White, one of Lewiston's earliest pioneers, recalled years later that at one time Lewiston had a gambling tent with tables that could seat five hundred men. John Scranton was a real estate agent and the editorial writer for *The Golden Age*, and before coming to Lewiston had operated boats on Puget Sound.

Two express companies were offering to carry gold dust, among other things: Wells Fargo & Co., and the Mossman Co., with headquarters at Portland. Mossman advertised its "newly extended services" to the Nez Perce, Salmon, Elk City and Powder River mines. The town had two commission companies, George E. Cole and W.C. and F.A. Holman. Linville and Schank operated a saddle and harness shop opposite the Bank Exchange. Thomas J. Moore had a livery stable and a bakery.

Meals were available at the hotels and at least two

restaurants—the Barnum, which claimed its chef, one Cascabel, was "long known as the best Cook in California," and the Pioneer at Second and D Streets. Connected to the Pioneer Restaurant was a lodging house, Nolan & Co., where a transient could sleep for fifty cents a night. The Pioneer charged twelve dollars a week for "full fare," both meals and lodging. The Barnum advertised "a good meal for 75 cents"—roughly three times the cost of a hotel meal in most towns "back in the states."

Among the professional people hanging out their shingles were William F. Smith, possibly Lewiston's first established lawyer; Dr. F.C. Clark, a dentist; E.P. Stone, justice of the peace; and John Scranton, real estate agent, journalist, businessman and civic leader. Some dentists, engineers, photographers and physicians rotated their services among the various small towns and mining camps of the region.

As for *The Golden Age* itself, it stood for law and order in its editorials, opposed vigilante justice and unfair business practices. The paper backed Senator J.W. Nesmith of Oregon in his efforts to solve the Indian problem by moving the Indians "somewhere else." Publisher A.S. Gould announced in capital letters, "WE ARE FOR THE UNION, UNDER ALL CIR-CUMSTANCES, WITHOUT QUALIFICATION OR RESERVATION"—a stand that drew fire, literally, from Confederate sympathizers who one day shot 21 holes in the U.S. flag that flew over the newspaper's office. Gould's patriotism apparently cooled, because he did not remain long in Idaho and on the following January 8, *The Golden Age* reported a sheriff's sale of Gould's combination office and home.

In the making in that summer of '62 were postal routes from Walla Walla to Pierce, Oro Fino and Florence by way of Lewiston and from Walla Walla to Coeur d'Alene. The mails were to be carried by pony express, and an energetic promoter, Mason H. Haggard, was working at Lewiston to get the service started. From the mountains to the east and south came continuing reports of new gold strikes and from the west, by river and by land, came new immigrants to work the mines or serve the miners. It was a season of great expectations.

5

Rich Diggings

According to the reports from Florence, the first hole dug on Miller Creek brought $25 in gold. Joseph Miller panned out $100 worth that same afternoon in the summer of 1861. On another stream, five men working one rocker took out $700 in ten hours. Sylvester "Three Finger" Smith averaged $300 a day from his rich claim in Baboon Gulch. A single pan once brought him $600. Smith also claimed to have weighed out $697 in gold from a hundred buckets of pay dirt. One man, whose name is unrecorded, washed out 600 ounces of gold in four days. At a time when a laborer's wage was about $1.50 a day and gold was worth $15 an ounce, the total take was a fortune of $9,000.

Baboon Gulch, named for Peter Baboin, who discovered it, was said to have produced $500 from a single pan. The story is that Baboin made his exit leading three mules loaded with gold dust and never was heard from again. Another miner in Baboon Gulch, Jacob Weiser, was reported by Alonzo Leland to have washed out $6,600 in gold in four days; another report has it that he did it in only one day.

Many of these reports no doubt were exaggerations, born of the exuberance of a heady time, but the Florence diggings were in fact incredibly rich. By conservative estimates, the Florence placers produced ten million dollars in gold in their three good years and some other estimates range as high as thirty million. With such riches pouring forth, there was bound to be waste, and it was enormous. J. Ross Brown, a former U.S. Commissioner of Mines, has estimated that some $300 million in gold was lost beyond recovery during the Idaho gold rush.

Even in the richest years, for most of those who did it, mining was hard work. In summer, a miner's day began before daylight and continued until the approach of darkness. After sundown and sometimes well after dark, the miner returned to his cabin and prepared a dinner usually of beans, bacon and strong coffee. For breakfast he probably would eat sourdough flapjacks, more bacon and more coffee. If his cabin happened to be near the center of the camp, he might pay three dollars in gold dust for a meal less tasty than he could buy back home for a quarter.

His cabin typically was a log hut about ten by twelve feet with an extended shake roof, furnished with a bunk, a table, a chair and a box nailed to the wall to hold his cooking "traps"—kettle, coffee pot, frying pan, tin cups and knives.

All early gold mining, in Idaho as elsewhere, was by placer. That is, by water carrying sand and gravel over a device—usually a sluice box—designed to catch anything heavy moving slowly along. Panning for gold is the most primitive form of placer mining and the gold pan was used only to check for the presence of gold, not to collect it. For that, the most useful early-day tool was the sluice box. It was a wooden trough perhaps ten feet long with narrow slats or "riffles" nailed to the bottom. Water was diverted from the creek, by flume or bucket, into one end of the box and sand or gravel was shoveled in at the same end. As the water washed the material down, the bits of gold would fall out and the riffles would catch them. The sluice box required lots of water. When water was scarce, miners might resort to a cradle-like wooden structure called a rocker. This was a two-level device consisting of a sheet of perforated metal, which was set on an incline and then rocked with quick jerks. One man would rock the thing while another shoveled sand into it, both of them hoping that some gold would drop through into the lower level. Whether using a sluice box or rocker, the miner needed to separate the gold from other heavy material that

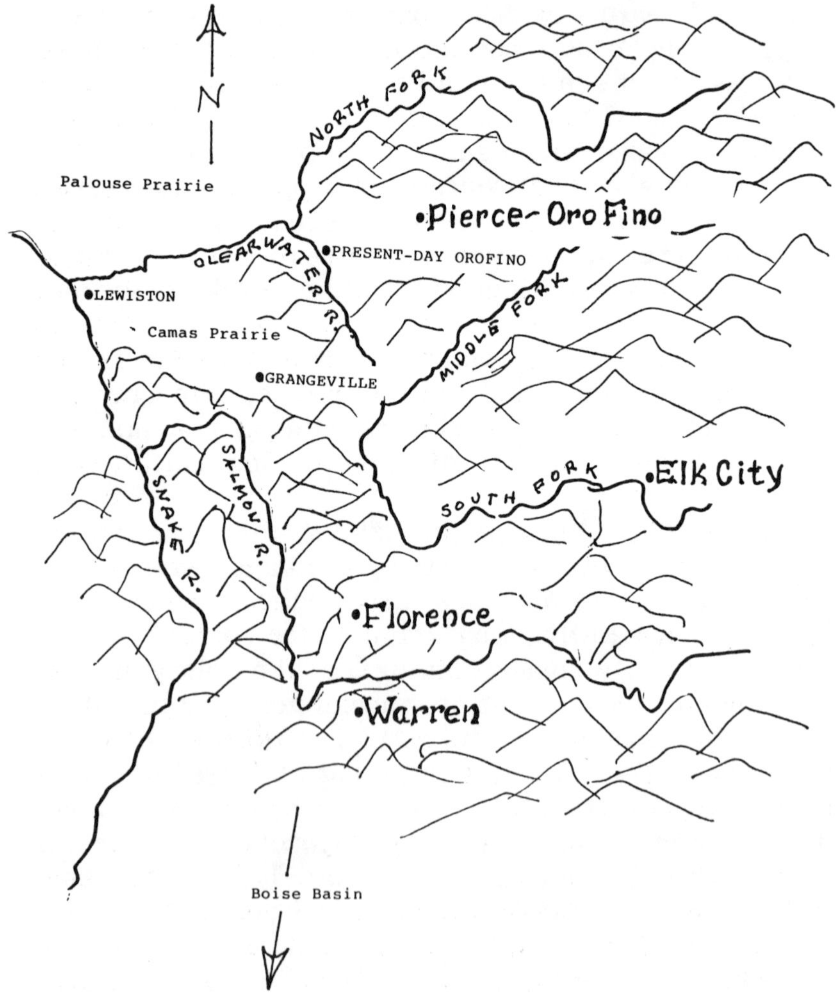

The important early mining camps in northern and central Idaho.

might fall into it. To do this he sometimes used mercury, often called quicksilver, to form an amalgam with the gold, or he simply jiggled the gold particles free of the less heavy rock and sand.

One man who owned a claim might hire as many as a dozen other men to help him work it, since that kind of placer mining is labor-intensive. Many of the people who worked the mines of the Florence and Oro Fino regions were day laborers, hired to build sluice boxes, hoist buckets and shovel gravel. Most of them probably were one-time prospectors whose own search for gold had been fruitless.

William S. Goulder and his associates operated two strings of sluices at Oro Fino, employing twenty-four men divided into day and night shifts. The workers were paid $5 a day, meted out at the end of each week in the form of two ounces of gold dust worth $15 an ounce. There was no work on Sunday. That was the day set aside for resting and repairing worn tools, and Goulder recalled later that on Sunday mornings Oro Fino would be crowded with miners coming in from the surrounding gulches and ravines, carrying tools to the blacksmith. At noon, the express would arrive from Walla Walla and since there was no post office in the camp, the expressman would deliver the mail to the Wells Fargo representative, W.A. Atlee. Atlee, standing behind his counter, would call out the names of the addressees and deliver letters, packages and newspapers to the waiting men.

The miners tended to be a rough lot and yet many historians have praised their honesty, hospitality and generosity. A miner seldom locked his cabin even though he might leave boxes and cans of gold dust standing about. One miner might shoot another and get off on a plea of self-defense, but to steal another's gold or rob his sluice box was unpardonable. When a Florence miner in Bear Track Gulch reported to Bill Moomau, president of the Miners' Meeting, that his sluice box had been robbed, the whole community was aroused. Moomau alerted all to watch for Bear Track dust, for the dust from each gulch could be identified. At a gambling table, a man known only as "Fat Jack" put out some Bear Track dust and soon was fleeing for his life under a threat of "never return." Unfortunately for Jack, he did, and he died.

If the miners were a generally honest bunch, the sharks who preyed on them were not. The news of the Idaho gold rush, which rivaled in interest the reports from the Civil War, lured not only prospectors to Florence but thieves and gamblers as well. As storekeeper Alonzo Brown wrote, "The saloons and gambling houses were wide open night and day and a man was killed nearly every night."

There was much quarreling of Union and Confederate sympathizers, and the main street of Florence became a sort of dividing line between them. As Brown described it later: "Men had a habit of getting drunk at the saloons and shooting into stores and tents as they went by. I slept in the store, on the floor, and to protect myself from stray bullets fired by drunken men, I piled up a stack of flour sacks as wide as my bed and about four feet high and made my bed behind the flour."

Did Brown exaggerate the violence or was Florence really that much different from the camps of Pierce and Oro Fino? Joaquin Miller, who spent some time at Oro Fino in 1861, wrote later that he had planned to practice law there but found the camp so orderly that he threw away his law book and bought into an express route instead. But the Pierce-Oro Fino district wasn't as rich as the Florence diggings and didn't attract nearly as many people of various kinds. Brown's description of Florence may not be far off the mark.

Brown had come from Roseburg, Oregon, to try his luck and decided there was more to be made serving the miners than being one. He and D.W. Stearns formed a partnership, bought the freight of a large pack string and started a store. They found a just-built log building, paid $2,500 for it, and were in business that evening. Brown and his partner took turns packing into Lewiston for new supplies and while one was away, the other minded the shop. Business was so good they couldn't handle it all with their own pack string and they had to start buying, in addition, the goods brought in by others. In one week that summer, Stearns and Brown took in $7,000 in gold dust.

By the fall of 1862, they had an inventory worth $20,000 and high hopes of making it big the next summer. They couldn't have known that gold would be discovered in the Boise Basin then, at the very time the mines of Florence were beginning to play out. But it was, and most of the people in the Florence district suddenly were on their way south, leaving twenty stores in Florence with stock ranging from $5,000 to $40,000. In the early fall of 1863, Brown and Stearns closed the store and sold the building for $25. In the Salmon River mountains and on the Clearwater, people would continue to work the mines for many more years, but the gold rush was over.

6

Call It Idaho

By 1862 it was becoming clear that the growing numbers of people in the inland Northwest would require a more workable government and that Washington Territory, which then included Idaho, would have to be divided. It no longer made sense to try to govern this vast region from Olympia. That summer, the mining camp of Florence had a larger population than Portland. The city of Lewiston had more people than Portland, Olympia and Seattle combined. Shoshone County, which had been formed by the Washington Territorial Legislature in 1861, cast the largest vote in all the territory in the election of July 8 that year. The present state of Idaho, which had virtually no white settlers in early 1860, had become the population center of the Northwest by 1862.

The question was not whether the territory would be divided, but where the lines would be drawn and where the capital of the new territory would be. Every settlement of consequence in the region was in the running, or thought it was, and each was scheming to win the prize. Not that it mattered much: Although the rivalry was in the Northwest, the decisions would be made in the East, at Washington, D.C., and Washington was too absorbed in saving the Union to concern itself seriously with anything happening in the far-off western wilderness.

When the Oregon Territory was established in 1848,

two years after the U.S.-Canadian border was decided upon, it included everything from the Pacific Ocean to the continental divide—all of the present states of Oregon, Washington, Idaho, most of Wyoming and part of Montana. It was an expanse roughly one-sixth the entire area of the continental United States. The Washington Territory was carved out of this in 1853.

Geography did not favor a rational division of Oregon, Washington and Idaho. The Cascade range, roughly paralleling the coast, blocks precipitation from the Pacific Ocean, creating a wet, rain forest environment in the western third of both Oregon and Washington and a desert-like climate in much of the eastern two thirds of both states. A branch of the Rocky Mountains cuts Idaho in two from east to west, dividing Idaho between north and south. If Oregon had not been so quick to demand the lower Columbia River as its northern boundary, the Northwest territories might have been carved from roughly similar areas. But the Columbia cut the coastal forestry and fishing region in two. It gave Oregon no place for expansion except into the arid east and virtually guaranteed that Oregon would remain a one-city state, subservient throughout to metropolitan Portland.

Olympia, which had been founded as Smithfield in 1847, was considered the most promising city in the new Washington Territory, and became the capital; Seattle was a tiny village on a wooded hill, inspiring no one. Vancouver, nicely situated on an important waterway, hoped to wrest the capital from Olympia (and in fact almost did). When it came time to divide the Washington Territory, Olympia responded to the Vancouver threat by at first advocating the north-south dividing line at the Cascades. That would give the Puget Sound counties a population advantage over Vancouver and render irrelevant Vancouver's claim to be the gateway to the eastern mines. Then the thinking in Olympia changed; its leaders now wanted to set the line as far to the east as possible so that Washington Territory would still include the mining regions. At Lewiston, John Scranton, the editor of *The Golden Age*, said no. He argued that the new territory should stretch from the Columbia and Okanogan rivers on the west to the Bitterroot Mountains on the east—with Lewiston as the capital. "The inhabitants of this section. . . know nothing about the Puget Sound portion," Scranton wrote. "We care not who is elected nor what laws they pass . . . They are all inoperative with us." Also: "During four months of last year no communication could be had with the place at all. Its distance is between seven and eight hundred miles, interspersed with huge forests, roaring rivers and rocky bound shores of ice with impassable barriers of snow."

The Territorial Legislature responded to Scranton's campaign in *The Golden Age* by giving its top legislative posts to two members from the mining area. A.J. Simms was named president of the Council, or upper chamber, and Thomas M. Reed became speaker of the House. The purpose, apparently, was to give two prominent eastern politicians an incentive to keep their region, and themselves, in Washington Territory. Olympia was fighting off efforts to set up a mining territory but the numbers of miners and their friends were multiplying rapidly, and Olympia soon realized that if it was to retain control of Washington Territory, it would have to eliminate the eastern voting bloc.

In April, 1862, Olympia proposed a division that would include the mining camps in the new territory and leave the West side in political control of the Walla Walla region and the potential farmlands of the Palouse. Some in the mining areas objected to this plan, saying that if Washington Territory could be left as it was for two or three more years, the eastern part might be able to achieve statehood without going through the usual territorial phase—as Nevada was soon to do. But the pressures for an early division of Washington Territory were simply too great. The territorial government was not equipped to

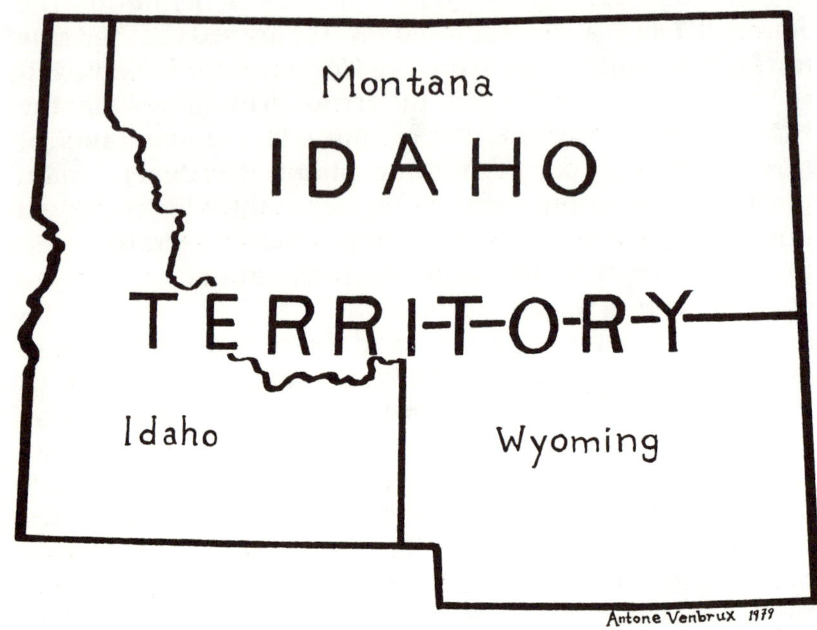

The boundaries of the new Idaho Territory in 1863.

cope with these vast distances and booming populations.

The surveyor-general of Washington Territory, A.G. Henry, selected a dividing line that followed the meandering eastern edge of Oregon and then shot due north from Lewiston to the Canadian border. East of the line were the mining camps and the populations that threatened to drain off the political power of the west side. It left everything west of Lewiston to Olympia, and became known as the Olympia plan.

When Congress took up the division of Washington Territory at the end of 1862, it had four choices:

1.   To draw the line at the Cascades;
2.   To draw it farther east at the Columbia River;
3.   To draw it north from Lewiston;
4.   Or to draw an east-west line at the 46th parallel, cutting off what is now southern Idaho—known as the Walla Walla plan.

One of the key players was James M. Ashley, chairman of the House Committee on Territories and the target of feverish lobbying by advocates of the four plans. One of the most influential of these seems to have been Captain John Mullan, the road builder, who was planning to run for Congress from the new territory. Mullan convinced Ashley that the new territory should include the Boise and Salmon River mines in what was then Dakota Territory and that Pierce, Elk City and Lewiston should remain part of Washington.

Ashley pushed this plan through the House on February 12, 1863. Meanwhile, Delegate William H. Wallace of Washington Territory, a personal friend of President Lincoln, was lobbying vigorously in the Senate for amendments that would radically alter the House bill. Wallace prevailed. The Senate approved a partition that vastly increased the size of the new territory while setting its western boundary at Lewiston, where A.G. Henry had drawn it.

The House bill referred to the new territory as Montana, but Wallace told senators that the residents of the region much preferred Idaho. Senator Henry Wilson of Massachusetts moved that the name be changed to Idaho, declaring that "Montana" was meaningless (not quite; it is Spanish for *mountain*). Added Senator B.F. Hardin of Oregon: "Montana, to my mind, signifies nothing at all. Idaho in English signifies 'the Gem of the Mountains.' This is mountainous country and the name Idaho is well understood." The Senate adopted that amendment along with the others.

Ashley was furious. He asked for a conference committee to iron out differences, but by now it was evening of the final day of the session and there was no time. The House accepted the Senate version and Lincoln signed it the following day.

Idaho Territory was born, but in their haste to adjourn the lawmakers had quite forgotten to make funds available for its administration—an oversight that doomed Idaho to years of financial tribulation.

President Lincoln signed the organic act on March 4, 1863, and the first unofficial report of the event reached Lewiston two weeks later. The details were vague and less than accurate, as it turned out, but Lewistonians celebrated anyway with a 100-gun salute. In his report to the *Portland Times*, Alonzo Leland felt it necessary to explain why the rejoicing was not more explosive: Lewiston had not yet been assured that it was a part of the new territory. Nearly a month later, when Lewiston's civic leaders began poring over the official report, they found that Lewiston was in fact part of the new territory but that the lands to the west of it were not; Lewiston had been left dangling on the very edge.

President Lincoln named William H. Wallace to be the first governor of the new territory and Wallace chose Lewiston as his capital, partly because it was the Idaho city nearest to his home at Steilacoom, Washington, and

This building at Third and C Streets in Lewiston was, for a brief time, the capitol of Idaho Territory.

partly because it already was a crossroads and trading center. When the governor arrived at Lewiston later that summer, however, nine out of ten former residents of the northern Idaho mining camps already had moved to the Boise Basin, shifting the population center far to the south of the new capital. Apparently unaware or unconcerned that his capital was bound to be temporary, Governor Wallace quickly arranged for a census and started planning the territory's first election.

That first election campaign may have been the shortest, as well as the most dificult, in Idaho's history. The governor could not apportion the Legislature until he had the census and the U.S. Marshal would not present the census until September 22, just 40 days before the election on October 31. Candidates had to campaign over an area larger than the state of Texas—an almost roadless, bridgeless wilderness without telegraph or telephone. Among the many candidates for territorial delegate to Congress, the prize plum in that election, were John Scranton of *The Golden Age*, Captain John Mullan, and, not surprisingly, Governor Wallace himself, who got the Republican nomination. Wallace had lobbied hard in Congress for the creation of the new territory. He could see political opportunities there that did not include the governorship.

Wallace won, by 3,910 votes to 3,543 for the Democrats' John M. Cannady. He swiftly completed his gubernatorial duties and prepared to return to the national capital, where he had served only the year before as the delegate from Washington. Lincoln then appointed William B. Daniels, the territorial secretary, to be the first of several acting governors.

It was not a particularly tidy election. U.S. Marshal Dolphus Payne brought in 479 votes for Wallace from Fort Laramie on the eastern border of the territory even though the census showed only 100 voters there. Since Payne had brought back no formal records of the election in that precinct, the canvassers had to take his word for the count. There were dark mutterings of a "Laramie fraud," but no charges were brought and Payne did not linger in Idaho.

There were further angry mutterings among the newly elected members of the first Territorial legislature when they met at Lewiston in December. Some of them had come from counties east of the Rockies in what is now Montana, traveling to Lewiston over several hundred miles of wilderness on horseback. Some others had ridden north across the central Idaho mountains from the southeastern part of the territory in what is now Wyoming. The population had shifted dramatically, leaving the capital isolated from the bulk of the voters, and as the Legislature went into session, its members shared an understanding that something would have to be done about that.

7

A Capital Clash

Lewiston's leading hotel, the Luna House, had been reserved for the inaugural ball in preparation for the first session of the Territorial Legislature, and it would serve as the legislative hostelry. By far the most imposing building in town, it had been built two years earlier of hewn logs—originally with a canvas roof, since Indian treaty restrictions made "permanent" buildings illegal. By December of 1863, however, innkeeper Hill Beachey had quietly managed to provide, for the comfort of his guests, a genuine roof of wood. The hotel had an air of elegance, with its well-furnished lobby and dining room on the ground floor. Upstairs there were twenty bedrooms, two of which served as the town jail.

Another of Lewiston's few wooden buildings was chosen as the Legislature's meeting place. It was of rough lumber, a one-story structure with an attic, on the west side of Third Street just north of C Street. A false front was added to give it an appearance worthy of its use.

To get the town ready for its important new visitors, workers had been moving boulders off the streets. They had torn down the abandoned frames of all-weather tents that had been emptied by the recent rush to the south. A reception committee was preparing to wine, dine and entertain elected guests from all parts of the territory.

By December 7, all the legislators were in town, many

having traveled over long distances in the raw winds of autumn. Those from the south came by two routes, over the central Idaho mountains pioneer style—riding one horse and leading another—or around the mountains by stage coach through Oregon and Washington. Getting back home in the dead of winter would be even more difficult.

So it was no surprise that one of the first bills, presented by R.P. Campbell of Boise City, called for moving the capital from Lewiston to that place. L.C. Miller of East Bannack, on the Montana side of the Bitter-roots, called for striking out Boise City and inserting Virginia City. Milton Kelly of Boise City argued for the bill as it stood. Alonzo Leland of Lewiston urged "indefinite postponement" of the capital question. If the Lewiston faction had deliberately fomented the cont-roversy, it worked: Because the issue was pulling lawmakers in so many directions, it became an unwelcome distraction. There were too many other details to attend to in setting up a functional government, and the Legislature let the capital issue languish until time ran out.

On the closing day of the session, February 4, 1864, Stanford Capps, a Pierce attorney, moved for indefinite postponement of the question but the Legislature adjourned without voting. The capital was still Lewiston's by default.

William A. Goulder, a lawyer-journalist and a future legislator, was present and described the final session in his memoirs:

"Alonzo Leland, of happy memory, got the floor and in spite of everything that could be done to stop him, talked bill and session and nearly everyone else to death . . . When everybody else had left the hall and the lights were all out, the voice of Leland could still be heard talking away to the darkness and silence, and he was found next morning seated in the middle of the floor of his office still talking, with the torn fragments of the dead bill scattered around him."

*Alonzo
Leland*

The Territorial Legislature would not meet again for another ten months, and in the meantime Lewiston's population continued to dwindle. The town could count 359 souls that summer while the number at Boise rose to 1,648. Scranton's dream of Lewiston as the capital of a big, new mining and agricultural center was fading. He and others remained embittered because those "slippery hypocrites" in Olympia, while seeming to set up a territory for Lewiston, had butchered the plan by a cutoff that left Lewiston hanging on the western boundary.

Legislators from far eastern Idaho—later Montana— had to become continental travelers just to get back home. To reach Virginia City, a crow's flight of some three hundred miles southeast, one first headed west to Portland, from there by boat to San Francisco and then to Virginia City by way of Salt Lake City—a journey of two thousand miles. Foreseeing such difficulties, the first Territorial Legislature had recommended that Congress authorize a territory for Virginia City and Upper Missouri miners. That area had been dependent on informal miners' meetings to enforce order, and there was little. Smooth-talking Henry Plummer, perhaps the most ruthless of all the frontier desperadoes, had been elected sheriff, indicating how bad things were.

Sidney B. Edgerton, the first chief justice of the Idaho Territorial Supreme Court, spoke out in favor of a new territory of Montana, persuaded Congress, and emerged as the new territory's first governor. The portion of Idaho Territory that is now Wyoming was cut off at the same time, in the summer of 1864, reducing Idaho to a more reasonable size.

Meanwhile, Idaho Territory had a new governor, Caleb Lyon of New York state, who had been appointed by President Lincoln to succeed William H. Wallace.

At Lewiston, the creation of Montana Territory was bad news for it lopped off all of Idaho east of the Bitterroots, reducing Scranton's vast east-west expanse to a pinched panhandle. As Lewiston prepared for the second session of the Territorial Legislature, its future as a capital city looked grim.

The Boise area delegates came determined that this time they would take control, and they had the forces. When the session opened on November 14, 1864, southern Idaho was able to send delegates from four counties instead of one. While the northern mining camps were steadily losing population, southern Idaho was acquiring new communities of impressive size. These included Idaho City, with 6,275; Placerville, 3,254; Pioneer, 2,743; and Centerville, 2,638. Northern Idaho, at the same time, had a total white population of 2,970.

Steven S. Fenn, a civic leader and organizer, was chosen to direct the effort to keep the capital at Lewiston and Alonzo Leland would be his spokesman. H.G. Riggs, one of the founders of Boise, headed the Boise group. Riggs' House bill, sometimes referred to as "the sure death dose," was in the hopper by November 23. "He (Riggs) would have made a useful member if he were not troubled with 'territorial capital' and 'Boise City' on the brain," according to Moscow historian Kenneth Holmes. Riggs sought not only the territorial capital but a branch mint, an assay office, a distributing post office, a division of Boise County and location of the county seat. Except for the mint, he managed to get them all for Boise.

After some skirmishing, the House voted to move the capital to Boise and the Council, the upper chamber, soon followed. Stanford Capps, Fenn and E.B. Waterbury of Lewiston all signed protests, but to no avail. The Lewiston people tried for a veto, even while remembering Governor Lyon's earlier comment that "Boise City knows how to see a governor." (And Lyon had reason to know; on his first visit to Boise the year before he had been lavishly entertained at the Overland House, the city's finest hotel, and the Boiseans in turn had been charmed by the governor's eloquence and wit.)

As a last resort, Fenn sought to make use of a comment President Lincoln had made to the effect that he was concerned about the infiltration of Confederate sympathizers into southern Idaho. According to Fenn, this indicated that Lincoln wished the capital to remain where it was. The effort was doomed. Governor Lyon signed Riggs' "death dose" bill on December 7, 1864.

There was yet one final straw, however, and Lewiston grasped it. Fenn and others claimed that the Riggs bill was invalid because it was enacted before some of the members of the lower house had officially taken office. They were elected for terms beginning January 1, 1865, the Lewiston group said, and therefore the Legislature could not legally enact any bills before that date. Thomas M. Pomeroy, the attorney for Idaho's First District, went to court, declaring that both the law to move the capital and a warrant to pay moving expenses were illegal. He called for a writ to restrain Governor Lyon and Silas D. Cochran, the acting secretary, from moving any territorial property out of Lewiston until this legal difficulty could be resolved.

The writ was obtained and served in late December as

the legislators were preparing to adjourn. First they made light of it. Then they talked of ignoring it and preparing the territorial seat and archives for quick shipment. Learning of this, Probate Judge John G. Berry issued a writ for the arrest of the governor and the secretary with instructions that it would be served only if necessary to prevent the removal of the seal and the records.

On the morning of December 27, Governor Lyon was standing on the Clearwater River bank gazing longingly at a flock of ducks. He was heard to remark that he would go for his gun. Shortly thereafter, the governor, accompanied by two southern Idaho legislators, Solomon Hasbrouck and Dr. Ephraim Smith, were seen carrying guns toward a skiff on the beach. They embarked, and the boat was soon caught in the current and carried out of the Clearwater into the Snake. Some distance downstream on the Snake, the three men landed the boat and walked to the lower Snake River ferry. There a government wagon, drawn by two mules, was waiting. Lyon and Hasbrouck crossed the river on the ferry and rode the wagon to Walla Walla.

With the governor gone, Deputy Sheriff Thomas Patterson served a writ on Secretary Silas Cochran, forbidding him to leave the territory. When the secretary protested, Patterson put a six-man armed guard on him. Meanwhile, from his temporary post in Walla Walla, Lyon delegated his authority to Major Sewell Truax, who had recently been posted to Fort Lapwai. Then he instructed Cochran to box Idaho's territorial seal and archives and deliver them to Truax for removal to Boise. With a guard at his elbow, Cochran refused, saying that Lyon had no authority outside the territory. The governor sent back word by Truax that Cochran was fired and that Major Truax was now the territorial secretary. Cochran refused to vacate his post, saying he had asked the national capital for instruction and was awaiting a reply.

Infuriated by Lyon's trickery, Lewistonians gathered on January 4 for an indignation meeting. In resolutions forwarded to Congress, they pleaded for "relief from the evils and embarrassments'' to which they had been subjected. They demanded the removal of Governor Lyon for deserting his post and leaving the territory in violation of a court injunction. They asked that the counties whose legislators had voted to remove the capital be expelled from the territory and that Washington Territory east of the Columbia and Okanogan rivers replace southern Idaho as parts of Idaho Territory. (It would not be the last time northern Idaho sought to separate itself from the south.)

Congress ignored the resolutions.

When it became apparent that the governor had no intention of returning to Lewiston, Acting Secretary Cochran was dispatched to Walla Walla to seek a conference with Lyon. But Lyon was not there. The governor had gone to Portland, where he was delivering lectures on his travels in the Holy Land. The acting secretary returned to Lewiston and there proclaimed himself acting governor.

The Territorial Supreme Court would have to sort this out, but it was having problems of its own. The court could not rule on the capital location until it had organized itself; and it could not establish itself as the capital without knowing where the capital was. The territorial government was in helpless disarray, sans governor, sans secretary, sans marshal, supreme court or capital.

*   *   *

The man who would eventually play the key role in all this was then on his way to Lewiston. Clinton Dewitt Smith of Maryland had been appointed the previous July 4 as the new territorial secretary, succeeding William B. Daniels—who had become acting governor when William H. Wallace became a territorial delegate to Congress.

Smith had spent nearly eight months and most of his personal funds in trying to reach Idaho. He first started over a much-used route across the plains. After weeks of maddening delays, he became convinced the Indians were no longer permitting emigrants to pass through that way. Smith returned east and started again. This time he chose to go by way of the Isthmus of Panama and finally arrived at Portland in February, 1865. There, in a meeting with the missing Governor Lyon, Smith learned of the chaotic state of affairs at Lewiston in Idaho Territory.

Smith tried to persuade the governor to return to Idaho with him but Lyon refused, saying he had been threatened with death at Lewiston. Leaving Portland, Smith traveled to Oregon City where he obtained funds to pay off the federal debt in the Lewiston area. He also asked, and was promised, military aid if necessary when carrying off the territorial seal and archives.

Lewiston welcomed Smith warmly when he reached the city on March 2, 1865. Smith brought with him a genial personality and—more importantly—a promise to pay the Lewiston portion of the federal debt in the territory. The territorial government had been operating for two years on IOUs, and its warrants had fallen to less than fifty percent of face value. It had become an embarrassment. But the new secretary proved not to be as much help as he promised. He paid only part of the Lewiston area debt and he gave Lewistonians some other indications that he was not to be the answer to their prayers.

On March 29, the secretary started off on one of his frequent horseback rides, this time accompanied by two friends, Frank Kenyon, a former editor of *The Golden Age*, and Horace C. Gilson. Smith had left Solomon R. Howlett in charge of the office, telling him he would return in an hour. Five hours later, Smith had not returned, nor had he returned the next morning. At 10 a.m. on the 30th, word came that Smith had left Fort Lapwai for Lewiston, accompanied by a band of soldiers, and the town was in an uproar. The place was buzzing with rumors, including a report that the soldiers had instructions to burn the town and arrest some of its leaders. (The latter rumor was prompted by a jest of Smith's that if he were killed in the "invasion" of

Lewiston, the soldiers should burn the town.) The town marshal, along with some other civic leaders, calmed the angry crowds and the marshal cautioned against any show of resistance in the face of the soldiers.

A small detachment of troops rode at once to the Clearwater ferry and waited there while Smith eluded the tumult by slipping in at the city's back door through a dry slough. Other soldiers brushed aside the sheriff's guard, broke the lock, and carried off the territorial seal and as many of the records as they could conveniently handle. Smith and the detachment of U.S. troops then crossed by the ferry into Washington Territory and out of the jurisdiction of the city of Lewiston.

The territorial capital finally was enroute to Boise.

At Lewiston, it was considered—and to some degree still is—as outright theft, and as an intolerable use of military force to achieve what could not be achieved by legal means. To the south, it was viewed differently. Writing in the *Idaho Statesman* at Boise, J.S. Reynolds reported: "The mob at lewiston (deliberate lower case?), after finding they could no longer keep the officers and archives there by force, turned upon those citizens . . . who had favored the execution of the law. Several of the most prominent citizens were ordered to leave within twenty-four hours. Their wrath knew no bounds. The whole town was under arms seeking whom to devour . . . They had not the courage to kill anybody—at last accounts. S.D. Cochran, who has figured as Secretary pro tem, probably without any authority, charges Secretary Smith with being intoxicated at lewiston. That is too bare-faced a lie to need refutation. If the cowardly curs were not entirely irresponsible they would be compelled to defend prosecution for libel."

Clinton Dewitt Smith, both secretary and acting governor of Idaho Territory, was received with rejoicing at Boise on April 14, 1865—the same day that saw the assassination in faraway Washington of Abraham Lincoln. Smith was honored at a reception at the Overland

House on the day after his arrival and at a meeting of businessmen three days later. While southern Idaho was lavishly praising Smith for his prompt and energetic action and "his determination to execute the law," northerners were fiercely attacking him. Said the *North Idaho Radiator*: "Smith fleeing in violation of the court order and his pledged word . . . has proved himself a thief and should be removed from office as such . . . too dishonorable for an officer and too great a drunkard and liar to command respect as a man."

Lewiston sent resolutions to the national capital appealing "for a governor and Secretary of this Territory who will show a small degree of manhood as officials . . . If there was ever a territory ridden by a set of inefficient appointees, this is that territory. Most of them entirely remain away from their posts of duty." The town's civic leaders inquired at Fort Lapwai as to whether Lewiston was now under "military or civil authority." They accused Lieutenant S.A. Hammer, the officer in charge of the escort, of non-military conduct. They also claimed he had interfered with the duties of a civil officer, U.S. Deputy Marshal J.K. Vincent, who had been deputized to serve the last court injunction on Secretary Smith. Lieutenant Hammer not only refused to help the officer serve the paper, according to this charge, but ordered the deputy marshal off the ferry.

They openly accused Smith of failing to pay the federal debts at Lewiston, as he had promised to do; and accused him, further, of taking some of Lewiston's federal money with him to Boise. Lewiston's list of grievances did not end there. It claimed that Boise had asked an exorbitant sum to pay expenses of moving the capital; that Boise was the slowest city in the territory to send regular contributions to the territorial treasurer, being always in arrears; that several important Boise city and county officers had helped themselves to public funds.

Reporting an indignation meeting at Lewiston on April 8 or thereabouts, Reynolds of the *Statesman* said it was a call for money to continue the fight against Boise City, "but they couldn't raise a dollar." According to Leland's paper, *The Golden Age*, the assembly responded with a "rousing" and unanimous "aye" when asked whether it wished to continue the fight, and arrangements then were made to collect the necessary funds.

There was even less resemblance between the accounts in Boise and Lewiston papers when the last of the territorial property was taken from Lewiston on October 9, 1865. *The Radiator*, of Lewiston, said that the town had recognized the federal authority of Marshal J.H. Alvord and surrendered without a murmur. At Boise, the *Statesman* described a drunken judge, Alexander C. Smith, raving and cursing in "the most vulgar and profane manner," until all the attorneys "left the courtroom in shame." It said a team of oxen had been "secreted" near the government wagons, indicating an attempt to destroy territorial property before it could be taken.

Judge Smith, a federally appointed justice of the Territorial Supreme Court, was one of Reynolds' favorite targets. When the *Statesman* published Smith's opinion that "the capital is still at Lewiston," Reynolds called him "incompetent to have an opinion on any subject, much less to write one."

At least one southern Idaho paper disapproved of Secretary Smith's "theft" of the territorial seal and archives. The editor of the *Idaho World*, of Idaho City, wrote: "I think to use the mildest terms, it was a misconception of his duty. Smith should have waited until the case was legally decided in favor of Boise City, which it ultimately would have been. Who made the secretary a judge of the acts of the last Legislature?"

William A. Goulder, in his *Reminiscenses*, wrote in 1909: "I yet believe with my good friend (Justice Smith) that the capital of Idaho is still at Lewiston. I think that decision still stands, clothed with the legal force that a court of justice could give it." Many Lewiston people believed, with Goulder, that Justice Smith's opinion had legal force and for many years cited it as proof that the capital belonged at Lewiston. But Smith had given his opinion as a district judge. When he and the other two district judges, acting as the Territorial Supreme Court, ruled later, the court held that the second legislative session had been lawfully assembled and therefore competent to act. In its first regular session, on June 14, 1866, the Supreme Court had decided in favor of Boise City, two to one.

*　　*　　*

Clinton Dewitt Smith, reviled as a villain in the north and hailed as a hero in the south, died on August 19, 1865, at Rocky Bar in southern Idaho. His friend and riding companion, Horace C. Gilson, succeeded Smith as territorial secretary. Gilson dropped from sight shortly thereafter while carrying some $14,000 in territorial funds and was not seen in Idaho again.

Caleb Lyon, after his unexpected exit from Lewiston, traveled leisurely around the West, stopping at the best hotels in Portland, San Francisco and elsewhere. He would explain that he was enroute to the national capital and incidentally doing great things for Idaho. The second territorial governor was a man of sophistication and some pretension who referred to himself always as "Caleb Lyon of Lyonsdale," a reference to his home town in New York state. He had been a soldier, a member of Congress, a traveler and art collector, and made a hobby of giving illustrated lectures about his trips abroad. After an absence of ten months, he returned to Idaho. He resumed the governorship and planned to become a senator from Idaho once it became a state. His Indian policies antagonized many in southern Idaho, however, and in 1866 he decided not to seek reappointment.

On his departure, the *Idaho World* of Idaho City wrote: "Governor Lyon leaves Idaho Territory with an unsullied reputation as a man and as a politician." But according to the *Statesman* of Boise, "Governor Lyon leaves Idaho the most thoroughly despised by all parties of

50

any man who ever came here . . . For the last two months he kept to his room as though he was ashamed to be seen here, and left as though he was ashamed to be seen leaving.''

Later, while traveling by train in New York state, Lyon reported the theft of $46,000 from his money belt. Perhaps coincidentally, $46,418.40 was found to be missing from Indian funds. In March, 1867, the federal government announced that it would recover the money from the bonding agent, but no action was ever taken against Lyon. He died at Rossville, N.Y., on September 7, 1875.

8

The Vigilantes

The law was not much honored when Lewiston was settled—illegally, on Indian land—and for a time thereafter when vigilante committees made their own "justice." Idaho Territory, founded March 3, 1863, had no law code of its own until February 4, 1864. Crimes committed before that date, the Territorial Supreme Court ruled later, could not be punished since the offenders had violated no law. Crimes real or alleged were punished, just the same, by men who felt they had no choice but to take the law into their own hands.

The waves of people who flowed into the towns and mining camps of the Lewiston region were typical of a western pattern: First came the prospectors, a generally honest, hard-working bunch; then came the merchants and others hoping to mine the miners, usually in legitimate ways; then came the gamblers, the individual sharks and desperadoes; and finally the most dangerous of all, the organized gangs of highway robbers and cutthroats. With the arrival of the last came reports from every direction of murders and holdups, of people disappearing without a trace.

During the early 1860s, while the region was still a part of Washington Territory, the law-abiding were expected to look to far off Olympia for their protection. There was none there. So the Vigilance committees—the vigilantes—were born.

Most of them were not committees at all but hastily organized groups of men who meted out whatever punishment they saw fit and then disbanded. The punishment was not always death. When a Chinese miner blew up a stove in a white men's meeting hall at Pierce with a piece of dynamite hidden in a stick of wood, he was first condemned to death. After some debate, however, his captors decided instead to give him 100 lashes laid on by the strongest man in camp. Somebody pointed out that since the defendant probably would not survive the 100 lashes, it amounted to a death sentence. After further discussion the group settled on 25 lashes. These were delivered and the defendent left Pierce, badly bruised but whole.

On another occasion, a group of citizens met the steamer that was carrying three accused murderers from Portland to Lewiston to stand trial, took them off the boat and hanged all three without mercy or ceremony. Episodes like this gave the vigilantes a bad name that lingers today. When we think of vigilantes and posses, we think of lynch mobs. But the vigilantes, operating as such, were not mobs but purposeful men doing a nasty and necessary job. It was a Lewiston lynch mob, not vigilantes, that took James W. Wood out of jail in 1870 and hanged him for the murder of Thomas Duffy after the governor had commuted Wood's death sentence to life in prison. Vigilantes operated in the absence of law, lynch mobs in spite of it.

Murder was common in the mining camps and frontier towns, where people were prone to settling arguments with guns and knives, but the vigilantes' main concern was the people who disappeared on the trails along with their gold and their horses. Gangs of road agents ran wild, unfettered by the law and formal justice. Indeed, two of the most notorious outlaws in Idaho history, David Updyke and Henry Plummer, got themselves elected as sheriffs—Updyke in Ada County and Plummer in the Bannack district east of the Bitter-roots in what is now Montana. With the law on the side of the road gangs, there was no place to turn but to the vigilantes.

*　　*　　*

A woman who became acquainted with Henry Plummer when she was 13 years old said many years later that "He looked more like a gentleman than any man in Bannack." She was Martha Edgerton, daughter of Sidney Edgerton, the first governor of Montana. "He had the reputation of being the best dancer in Bannack," she said. Plummer had come to Bannack from Nevada City, California, by way of Lewiston and the Oro Fino mines. While serving as town marshal of Nevada City he had shot and killed the husband who surprised him with his lady love. He was given a ten-year sentence, then pardoned when he declared that he was dying of tuberculosis. He later killed another man, in a quarrel over a prostitute, and again went to jail. This time he held up a guard with a smuggled gun and walked out.

Plummer fled Nevada City and went to Walla Walla where he teamed up with Bill Mayfield, a thief and murderer who was later killed over a card game in Boise. Plummer arrived in Lewiston in 1861 and, operating between Lewiston and the Oro Fino mines, organized the area's first road gang. By early summer of 1862, Plummer's gang included almost every thief and cutthroat in the region between Lewiston and Virginia City. He maintained several retreats, or "shebangs," as they were called, where gang members on the run could find refuge. One of these was between Alpowa and Pataha creeks west of Lewiston on the road to Walla Walla. Others were scattered among the mining camps to the east.

Some members of Plummer's gang came close to disaster one night in the winter of 1861-'62 when they killed a Lewiston saloon keeper, a man named Hillebrant or Hildebrand, as he lay in bed in his cabin. There was much loud talk of arranging a hanging but Plummer himself argued eloquently against it, claiming it would make Lewiston look bad. The townsmen, unaware of Plummer's connection to the gang, allowed themselves to be talked out of it and the episode ended quietly.

The Plummer gang found rich pickings in the Lewiston-Oro Fino country but was forced to disband and move on after a brawl in an Oro Fino saloon that resulted in the shooting death of the proprieter, Patrick Ford. Plummer went to Elk City but left there after running into some men who had known him in California. He and Jack Cleveland arrived in Bannack around Christmas of 1862 and before long other members of the gang drifted in, attracted by the rich mines nearby. Here the Plummer gang resumed operations, always protecting Plummer himself from any taint of illegality. Here also, Plummer and Cleveland, who had quarreled over a woman, had a falling out and each developed a fear that the other was planning to kill him. Plummer got the drop on Cleveland first and shot him as he leaned against the bar of a Bannack saloon. Plummer pleaded self-defense, produced a witness, and was acquitted.

Shortly thereafter, Sheriff Henry Crawford, thinking Plummer might be after *him*, shot Plummer with a rifle ball but missed a vital spot and fled. When Plummer recovered, he was elected sheriff in Crawford's place. As sheriff, Plummer continued to direct his outlaws in their bloody business while charming the women and impressing the men with his grand talk and his wit. According to Hoffman Birney, author of the book *Vigilantes* (1929), it was Plummer who masterminded the murder of the Lloyd Magruder party in the autumn of 1863, and the supporting evidence is strong.

Henry Plummer's string ran out in January, 1864, when some of his men botched a robbery and inadvertently implicated the sheriff. A vigilance committee was formed to look into Plummer's activities. It soon found out that the sheriff had been leading a double life and decided that the scaffold he had recently built for another prisoner would be used instead for him. A small group went to the house where Plummer was staying on a Sunday evening, escorted him quietly to the gallows and hanged him along with two of his men.

According to vigilante records, the Plummer gang had killed at least a hundred men since Plummer's arrival at Lewiston in 1861.

*   *   *

Vigilante justice ended in northern Idaho with the trial, conviction and execution of James Romain, Christopher Lower and David Renton, also known as Doc Howard, for the murder of Lloyd Magruder. Magruder was a well-known, well-liked Lewiston miner, packer and legislator who had been a candidate for Congress in the first territorial election. He was a lawyer and justice of the peace and a leader in the Democratic Party. Magruder had left Lewiston early in August, 1863, with a pack string of some 50 mules laden with miners' supplies—everything from flour to rubber boots to axle grease. He and a crew of helpers were headed for Bannack, now in Montana, some 300 miles away.

At about the same time, three young men also left Lewiston, passing word that they were going to Portland. After traveling west for a day or so they turned around and headed east toward the Bitterroots. They were Romain, Lower and Renton. Romain and Renton overtook Magruder in about a week. Lower joined them a day or two later. The three told Magruder they would like to travel with him and would be glad to help along the way with the animals and the night watches, and Magruder took them on.

Bannack was a disappointment. Most of the miners had abandoned the place in favor of newly discovered diggings at Alder Gulch, near Virginia City. Thither Magruder went and found eager buyers for his supplies. As his store of goods evaporated, his bag of gold dust fattened. He sold out and prepared to return to Lewiston only to find that his hired hands had decided to stay on and do some mining. He began looking about for help and found William Page, who had worked as a livestock man and guide. He hired Page. The three who had been tagging along told Magruder they had lost interest in the mines and would just as soon hire on with him for the return to Lewiston. As he prepared to start home, Magruder wrote a letter to his wife, Caroline, advising her that he would remain where he was for another 12 days. For the trail-wise packer, that letter was a bit of insurance intended to confuse anyone who might intercept it.

After he had stopped briefly at Bannack to buy mules, Magruder's crew included Page, Romain, Renton and two brothers, Horace and Robert Chalmers. At Beaverhead, Magruder hired Charley Allen and at a place called Rattlesnake, Lower showed up and was added to the crew along with a man named Phillips.

What follows is Page's version of the events that ensued, as he recounted them later in court.

After several uneventful days on the trail, Lower approached Page and asked him to drop to the back of the train where Renton and Romain wished to talk to him privately. During the conversation with these two, Renton told Page that Magruder had a lot of money and the boys meant to have it. Renton said that Page, who had been sleeping alone, should sleep that night with Phillips and that if he heard any noise in the night he should take no notice of it. He told him not to be frightened; the others would do all the dirty work. Renton told Page that if Phillips woke up, Page should shoot him in the head. Romain disagreed; he said that Page wasn't a good enough shot and should aim instead for the gut. Several times during the rest of that day, Renton and Romain rode up to Page and urged him not to be frightened.

That night Page lay awake, listening and trembling, but nothing happened. The next day, toward evening, Renton and Romain told Page that they would have the money that night, and they cautioned Page again not to be frightened. Lower and Magruder had the first watch.

Lower walked up the hill to see if the animals were all right. He returned shortly and said he would take an axe up to do some fencing and build a fire. As Page watched, Lower started up the hill with Magruder following. Magruder paused and looked back into the camp, then continued after Lower until both were out of sight. Page turned in but awoke at midnight and heard someone coming down the hill. He supposed it was the watch coming back and that it must be his turn. As he prepared to rise, he looked up and saw it was Renton and Lower and that they were lying down on the blankets next to Romain. Then Renton and Romain got up and walked past Page, each with an axe in his hand, to where the Chalmers brothers were sleeping. Page heard several long groans from that direction, and after the groaning stopped Renton and Romain returned and lay down again with Lower.

A few minutes later Renton got up, with a shotgun, and went to the tent where Allen was sleeping. Romain also passed by with an axe in his hand. Page started to rise up but Romain told him twice, quietly, to lie still. Page heard the gun go off in Allen's tent and he saw Romain at the same time strike Phillips a hard blow to the head with the axe. Phillips screamed, and Romain hit him again, and again. Romain turned to Page, pointed a finger at him and accused him of trembling. He told Page not to be frightened. Renton arrived and addressed Page by a nickname: "Uncle Billy, don't be frightened. All the dirty work is done."

They assigned Page to sort out the kitchen things and keep only what was needed. And they asked him to go up the hill to check on the animals and tend to the fire. He did so, and on his return they asked him if he had fixed the fire. He said it had got to burning in the grass and dry leaves and that he had put it out. He shouldn't have done that, Lower said; Lower told Page he had deliberately kicked the fire about in order to burn the blood. Meanwhile, the men had found less money than they expected.

They had searched the bodies and had tied Phillips and Allen up with a picket rope. Page helped to tie the brothers up and finished packing the kitchen as the others built a big fire and began burning pack saddles, blankets, bridles and anything else they didn't need. After the fire burned down, they picked out the buckles and rings from the bridles, put them in a gunny sack along with unwanted tin ware and frying pans and hid them behind a log. While Renton and Lower went to tie up Magruder's body, Page and Romain rolled the other bodies into a deep ravine— wearing moccasins so the tracks would appear to be Indian. Then they caught and saddled some animals, killed the rest, and moved out.

At the next camp, they checked to make sure there were no names on any of the purses and they emptied the money—eleven or twelve thousand dollars, according to Page—into five bags. Lower stuck the handle of his axe in the ashes of the fire and dried the blood, then scraped it off. He got the old handle out and put in another. Romain threw away Magruder's watch and compass. Back on the trail, they bypassed Elk City and at one point rode well off to one side to avoid a pack train that was passing through.

They knew they would have to cross the Clearwater River somewhere in order to get past Lewiston without being seen. Page, who knew the country well, led them to a place where the river could be forded easily on horseback in most seasons. But heavy fall rains had turned the stream into a torrent of white water. The men debated whether to risk a hazardous crossing here and decided it would be less dangerous to pass through Lewiston. It proved to be a fateful decision.

They rode into Lewiston on October 19, and Renton and Romain went looking for a boat while Page tried to find care for the animals. They spent that night in town, unavoidably, and early the next morning took the stage to Walla Walla.

Meanwhile, Hill Beachey, the owner of the Luna House hotel and of the Walla Walla stage line, was in deep distress. He had suffered a nasty nightmare in which he clearly saw his friend Magruder falling to the ground with an axe in his skull. Beachey could not get the specter out of his mind. And when another packer, just back over the same Bitterroot trail, told him that Magruder had started for Lewiston two days ahead of him, Beachey sounded the alarm. Some residents recalled seeing four rough-looking men in town, wearing heavy shawls that covered their heads. They had signed strangely short names on the register of the Hotel De France. One of them had appeared about town late at night and another had asked about hiring a boat to cross the river. Beachey remembered that a man matching the description had come into the lobby of the Luna House to buy tickets for Walla Walla.

Reasoning that the suspects must have come in by horse or mule over one of the mountain trails, Beachey visited every livery stable and corral in town without any luck. Then he remembered another livestock man, one Bishop Goodrich, who operated a ranch in the Tammany area south of Lewiston. Goodrich showed him a horse and five mules, also bridles, saddles, leggings and spurs—and a shotgun. He told Beachey he had promised to care for the animals and equipment until spring. Beachey quickly recognized two of the animals, and a saddle, as Magruder's property.

Now Beachey asked himself: Would they flee into British Columbia or California? Whatever, he would go after them. But first he must get two sets of arrest papers, each signed by William B. Daniels, acting governor of Idaho Territory. Daniels must state that Beachey and his traveling companion had been designated to receive and return the fugitives for trial. Daniels, new to the job and the area, had to be persuaded to sign papers naming Beachey a deputy sheriff of Nez Perce County and directing arrest warrants to both the governor of British

Columbia and the governor of California.

Armed finally with these papers, Beachey and a companion, Thomas Pike of Lewiston, took a private passage to Walla Walla in order to beat Beachey's own stage line, but the trail was getting cold. At Walla Walla, they learned that four men answering their descriptions had passed through but with names different from the ones given at the Hotel De France. At Wallula and The Dalles, Beachey and Pike found promising clues indicating they were closing in on their quarry. The four men had stopped at The Dalles and stayed overnight there with friends—to whom they had hinted of a fatal fight over a mine. But Beachey and Pike just missed the sternwheeler for Portland. On arriving there, they learned that the four fugitives, after talking about going to British Columbia, had shipped out on the Sierra Nevada for San Francisco two hours ahead of them.

In Portland, Beachey encountered a Lewiston friend, A.P. Ankeny, a packer who had got word of Beachey's mission and hurried to Portland. Ankeny was certain Magruder had met foul play because he could not possibly have strayed from the well-marked and well-traveled Bitterroot trail. He agreed to join in the pursuit, as did another Lewiston man, Thomas Farrell.

The next ship for San Francisco would not leave Portland for another ten days, so the pursuers took a gambler's chance. Adverse winds could have delayed the Sierra Nevada on the Columbia River bar, and Ankeny hired a tug in hopes of intercepting it. But the ship was across the bar and on its way.

For Beachey and his party it was the beginning of a long period of endless stage coach rides and sleepless nights. They started to San Francisco by land, heading first for Yreka, California, the nearest telegraph connection with San Francisco. Beachey hoped to get a telegram to Captain J. W. Lees of the San Francisco police before the ship docked there. At Shasta, Beachey got word by wire from Captain Lees that the ship had made port and discharged its passengers before Beachey's telegram reached him. But there was good news, too: Somehow Captain Lees and his men had managed to track down the four fugitives and had them already behind bars.

It had taken good police work, for the fugitives had played their game well. Once ashore, the four had separated and thereafter were never seen together. Two of them had invested in expensive clothes and were brushing elegant elbows at a first-class hotel. Two others had posed as Oregon prospectors in town to recuperate from the rigors of the mining camps. Renton and Lower, both escaped convicts from a California prison, assumed when they were arrested that they had been recognized as such. They had retained a criminal lawyer who was attempting to free them on a writ of habeas corpus.

The requisition for the arrest of the fugitives that the acting governor of Idaho had signed did not impress the California authorities. They insisted on a long and complicated study of the laws governing the handling of fugitives from justice. For one thing, there was an argument as to whether a fugitive from a territory would meet the same qualifications as one from a state. And the lawyer representing Renton and Lower objected that the suspects were merely "presumed" to have fled from justice and were not yet known to be in California.

Meanwhile, Beachey paced and fumed and insisted that there would be a fair trial of all four at Lewiston. It didn't help that in the year before, three men taken from Portland to Lewiston to face trial had been hustled off the boat at Lewiston and hanged by a lynch mob. Or that the Portland Oregonian kept hinting that Beachey's four might expect a "necktie party" in Idaho. But Beachey persisted and Governor Leland Stanford of California at length agreed to Beachey's claim for custody of the prisoners. That was November 2, 1863. The California Supreme Court still had to act, and it took the justices nine more days to rule in Beachey's favor.

At Lewiston it was now assumed by all that Magruder

had indeed been murdered and there was talk there and in the mining camps of seeing justice done the quick and easy way. General George Wright therefore arranged for a military escort to meet the Beachey party at Vancouver and see the prisoners safely into Lewiston. Waiting at Vancouver, when Beachey arrived there, was the stern-wheel steamer Julia, its steam up and the military escort on board, waiting for its passengers. Except for the usual portage stops at Cascade and The Dalles, the trip up the river was uneventful and Beachey arrived at Lewiston with his prisoners on December 4.

What happened then is not clear. According to one account published in 1903, "The party reached Lewiston . . . and was met by the vigilantes of that town; but Beachey stoutly defended his prisoners, telling the people he had promised the men a regular trial." According to the *Portland Oregonian* of December 10, 1863: "When the stage halted before the Luna House where a dense crowd had gathered to see the prisoners and to greet the proprietor, Mr. Hill Beachey, perfect order prevailed. As the prisoners emerged from the stage the crowd instantly and quietly parted an alleyway through which they passed into the bar room and thence upstairs into a chamber. As Mr. Beachey alighted from the stage three deafening cheers were sent up for him."

Beachey knew he had his murderers, but how was he to prove it? He had studied the men intently and was sure that the weak link was William Page. Therefore Page was held in a room by himself and Renton, Lower and Romain were held together in another room. According to one account, Page broke down after he was led past the open door of a large room containing nothing but four nooses hanging from ceiling beams. Another story has it that the prosecution posted three citizens under his window with instructions to let Page overhear their plans to lynch him. At any rate, Page did talk, revealing a sharp memory for detail and no trace of sympathy for his companions.

The trial—the first legal criminal trial in Idaho

history—was set for January 4, 1864, with Judge Alexander (Aleck) Smith, the District 1 justice of the Territorial Supreme Court, presiding. But after waiting in vain through the 4th, 5th and 6th for Judge Smith to appear, Judge Samuel C. Parks, the 2nd District justice, offered to hear the case. E.F. Grey was the prosecuting attorney, assisted by William C. Rheams and Milton Kelly. The defense attorneys were J.W. Anderson and W.W. Thayer. The jury that was impaneled January 19 included George H. Sandy, a Lewiston merchant, as foreman, and Henry Marshall, Joseph Wagner, Erphiel Beam, Samuel Ramsey, N.B. Holbrook, Richard Leitch, Nathan W. Earl, John Mooney, Henry Myers, Francis Cabe and J.P. Shockley.

In almost three days of testimony and cross-examination, Page told the jury what he had seen and heard during his sojourn on the Bitterroot trail with Renton, Lower and Romain. The trial ended on the 22nd and the jury returned its verdict the next morning. It found the three others "guilty of murder in the first degree and the punishment shall be death." The three were sentenced on January 26 to be hanged on March 4.

The day of execution was dark, windy and dusty. A company of infantry arrived from Fort Lapwai in the morning to act as escort and guard. At half past eleven, a citizens guard conducted the three prisoners from the Luna House, which then served as the town jail, in a wagon. The execution grounds were about three quarters of a mile from town in a small, secluded valley, now the foot of Poe Grade in Fenton Park. The troops arranged themselves in a square about the scaffold and a large crowd of several hundred men stood outside the square. On the scaffold stood the sheriff, James H. Fisk, two deputies, Hill Beachey, the citizens guard, newspaper reporters, and the Catholic chaplain, the Rev. J.B.A. Brouilette, who had come for the occasion from Walla Walla.

After the chaplain's prayer, each prisoner spoke,

protesting his innocence and calling for a fairer trial in the life to come. At 28 minutes past noon, the drop fell, the ropes snapped taut, and it was done.

*   *   *

In return for his testimony, Page got his freedom, but he was shot to death on Christmas day in 1866 by a gambler named Albert Igo. Igo was acquitted on a plea of self-defense. Caroline Magruder received a payment of $17,000 from the San Francisco Mint, where Renton, Romain and Lower had taken their gold for coining. The Territorial Legislature reimbursed Hill Beachey for his expenses in bringing the fugitives to justice—a total of $6,244.

In May of that year a party was organized to visit the scene of the murders. Page led the way to a remote spot between a black cliff on one side and a steep precipice on the other. Everything was as Page had described it: the gunny sack containing the buckles and rings and the cooking pans, hidden under a log; the wolf-mangled remains of the bodies; and the ashes of the fires. A marker was later nailed to a nearby tree trunk. Some years later the tree blew down in a mountain storm and the marker, together with part of the tree to which it was still attached, was carried to Lewiston and claimed there by Dr. H.L. Talkington for the museum of the Lewiston State Normal School, later to become Lewis-Clark State College. The college still has the relic.

As for the murder site itself, the woodsy growth of many years has hidden it completely. History buffs have tried to find it, following old and vague directions, but none has succeeded.

In the grassy vale where the executions took place there is a marker honoring Hill Beachey, whose determination to see legal justice done brought an end to the vigilante period in northern Idaho.

9

Getting There

On June 30, 1873, the stage from Walla Walla set a record by covering the 100 miles to Lewiston in a single day. Driver Vane Favor and his passengers began the journey at Walla Walla at 2 a.m., stopped for fresh horses at Pataha, and clattered into Lewiston at 6 o'clock that evening. Three years later, Lewiston Merchant John P. Vollmer installed, between his home and his office, the first telephone in the Pacific Northwest. The people of the town greeted the first achievement with cheers and wild partying; the second with polite interest. The telephone was a beguiling curiosity, but to carry a stage full of people over a hundred miles in a single day—now that was something.

The townsfolk of Lewiston had their priorities right. Getting there was the important thing in a land of big mountains, swift rivers and long distances.

The first white men to enter the region traveled on horses, like the Indians who had been there before them. But when the snows were deep, horses were useless and there was no way to move but on foot. In the bitter winter of 1861-'62, when the snow in the mountains came up to a horse's belly and higher, men packed freight from Walla Walla to Lewiston, about a hundred miles, and from Lewiston to the mining camps, another eighty miles, on their backs. Food, tools, letters, newspapers—everything moved one step at a time over trails trampled in the snow.

Perhaps the most remarkable of these packers was Israel B. Cowan, a small, wiry man who carried the express from Lewiston to Pierce City in the winters of 1863 and '64 on his back. Cowan made the trip of eighty miles in ten days on a club foot, leaving his unique signature in the snow. At the end of each trek, as he approached Pierce City, the merchants and miners would walk down the trail to meet him and help carry the letters, newspapers and freight in his pack. His stamina and reliability were legendary. One miner wrote to a friend, "With Cowan bringing the mail, even tho crippled, your letters will reach me."

On the trail to Florence, above the Salmon River to the south, the poet Joaquin Miller carried freight in the winter of 1861-'62 through snow as much as ten feet deep and suffered snow blindness that bothered him for the rest of his life. Some of the packers traveled alone, some in groups walking single file. Sometimes the leader would be the only one who could see clearly, the rest having been blinded by the reflected light.

People thought nothing of trekking long distances on foot in winter, and the perils of the trail were taken for granted. *The Golden Age* of February 5, 1863, reported that "Mr. Dennee of Haggard, Dennee and Co. Express, came in with Mr. Glascock from Elk City on Sunday in five days across the mountains on snowshoes." On January 28, 1864, the *North Idaho Radiator* carried this item: "Conrad Linch, a German, became so much frozen enroute from Oro Fino to Lewiston that both legs required amputation below the knee in order to save his life. Dr. M.A. Kelly performed the operation with entire success, and Linch is now doing well." The *Idaho Free Press* at Grangeville reported in February, 1888, that Russ Hogan had left for Shearer's Ferry on the Salmon and noted that "He will carry mail on snowshoes from that place to Warren this winter." Hogan apparently did not carry the mail for long, because on the following March 1, the *Free Press* had this to report: "W.D. Yandall, the mail carrier who was supposed for a time to have perished in the snow between Shearer's Ferry and Warren, was in town this week. He reports that he was buried in a snowslide about 14 feet deep, which he succeeded in getting out of by crawling to a cabin where he lay for about 10 days before he was able to travel."

When there was a thaw followed by a hard freeze, the snow might crust sufficiently to carry the weight of a loaded man—as much as 350 pounds—and the walking would be relatively easy. It might then even be possible to carry the freight on mules. Many a packer did, gambling that the crust would hold. If it didn't, and the mules broke through, the packer would be stranded with his freight and a string of helpless, bloodied animals thrashing about in the brittle snow.

On fresh, soft snow, the traveler had no better friend than the long Norwegian snowshoe, used widely in the Clearwater country. Another kind of snowshoe, almost a ski, has been described by Thomas C. Donaldson, an early-day miner, lawyer and judge. "All through the Idaho mountains," he wrote later, "one could see, lying on the ground near the roads or trails, rough snowshoes made of split tamarack or pine logs. These shoes were about six feet long, half an inch thick, five or six inches wide and bent at one end and were split and tied on the end with strings or thongs. A man could make a pair in a very short time and invariably dropped them at the spot on the road where he had no further need of them. The next man who came along was entitled to their use as well."

When the snow melted off, pack trains could move in safety again and for most of the year people got where they were going on horseback.

For ten years in the Sixties and early Seventies, Warren P. Hunt carried mail to the mines, riding a horse and leading a single pack animal. His route took him from Lewiston to Florence with stops at Mount Idaho, White

Bird, Slate Creek and Warren. The postal contract merely paid his expenses, he said later; he made his profit carrying gold dust at 4 percent of its value and in other specialized services. He took a miner's watch in for repair for $1.50 (not including the repair charge), and to carry a 12-yard calico dress to a woman at Florence he would charge $5, almost doubling the price of the dress. The carrier provided his own stopping points and two fresh horses every 20 to 25 miles. He made his rounds weekly during good weather and every other week in winter.

It was Hunt's great pride that in all of those ten years of traveling alone over rough country among rough men he never lost a letter or an ounce of gold. But he came close. Once, when he got wind of a holdup in the making, Hunt placed his mail pouch in a burlap bag, strapped it to a mule and sent it on ahead. The highwaymen missed again; it never occurred to them to look for valuables in an unguarded burlap bag. On another occasion when Hunt had reason to think he was being followed, he set out a day early. Arriving unexpectedly at his Salmon River ferry crossing, he found the ferry tied to the opposite bank and the ferryman gone. He dared not retrace his tracks. He considered swimming the animals across the river but abandoned the idea as too risky. Instead, he climbed the high ferry pole, wrapped his arms and legs around the cable and worked his way across the river on the wire. On the other side, he shinnied down the pole, brought back the ferry, picked up the mail and the horses, and continued on to Lewiston.

Pack trains were the only means of carrying large amounts of freight to the mines. Strings of as many as 50 animals, heavily laden, were guided by trained packers accustomed to spending many days on the trail. The animals usually were tied head to tail to prevent bolting from the line and perhaps to prevent their falling from steep slopes.

Packers earned $100 to $125 a month and board, excellent wages for that period. The packing companies charged 40 to 80 cents a pound depending on distance and weather conditions. The weights carried by their mules were almost unbelievable. Sister M. Alfreda Elsensohn, in her book *Pioneer Days in Idaho County*, recounts loads of heavy machinery including anvils, and in at least one case, a piano. Mrs. Sarah Rowley, a Lewiston pioneer of 1873, recalled that on one trip a woman rode on one side of the mule with her cook stove strapped to the other. The pack trains also provided the first mail service, carrying letters for 50 cents to $1.50 each. Newspapers with accounts of civil war battles, some fought only weeks earlier, were snatched up in the mining camps at a dollar a copy.

Chief among the pack train operators at Lewiston were the firms of Grostein & Binnard and A. Benson. They prospered mightily, and for a time, Grostein & Binnard was rated the largest business firm in Idaho. It operated branch stores at Mount Idaho, Colfax and Genesee, and branch pack stations at Warren, Elk City and Newsome among the mining districts.

The first packing shed area at Lewiston was near the waterfront or boat landing on the Clearwater River. But for many years the packing sheds were near the sheltered gully which later was dug out to form Fifth Street Grade. There hundreds of mules and some horses were fed, harnessed and loaded for the trails. And there they found shelter during hard winter storms. This site became Lewiston's business center and remained so for more than fifty years.

*   *   *

It didn't take long for the wise to find ways to separate the miners from their gold. To own a pack string was one way; to own a ferry usually was better than to own a claim. Lewiston was inaccessible from the west and north except by water too deep for fording, and John Silcott turned that fact into a small fortune.

At first most river crossings were made in Indian canoes, usually paddled by women, but they were small and bouncy and frequently unavailable. At Lewiston,

D.M. White built a rowboat. It worked so much better that he and John Silcott decided to go a big step further and build a ferry. They worked on it for three months, whipsawing the lumber and spiking it together. They needed a cable to guide the craft back and forth across the Clearwater, but there was none available in the West that was long enough; they had to bring one in from the East, around the Horn. When completed, the ferry was 12 feet wide and 24 feet long. Along both sides were railings and at each end the builders had put a hinged landing board that remained up during the crossing and could be put down on shore to serve as a gangplank. They raised their cable on poles 60 feet over the water, only to learn that Congress demanded a height of 70 feet. Silcott and White left it at 60 feet and made each passenger agree not to make demands in case of an accident. Business was good. The ferry ran continuously from daylight to dark and at any time there might be thirty or more people waiting on the shore to cross. Silcott and White often took in $250 a day, much more than most miners ever saw.

Like most ferries of its time, this one used the river's current to power it back and forth. It was attached to the overhead cable by ropes and pulleys that could be adjusted to turn the boat at an angle to the current. The current pushing against it drove the ferry along the cable from one shore to the other and—after some manipulation of the lines—back again.

The Silcott Ferry, as it came to be known, crossed the Clearwater from the foot of Fifth Street on the Lewiston side to a spot on the north shore where Silcott had his home. The house burned in 1971 and the site is now occupied by a log chipping plant.

Silcott also operated a ferry six miles downstream from Lewiston on the Snake near the Nez Perce camp of Chief Timothy (Silcott's father-in-law). Travelers from Walla Walla to Lewiston crossed from the south side of the Snake to the north at that point, then recrossed from north to south over the Clearwater on Silcott's Lewiston

John Silcott's ferry, crossing the Clearwater from its north side landing toward the Lewiston landing at the foot of Fifth Street.

ferry; the ferryman levied a single charge for both crossings.

Silcott's ferries soon were followed by others on the Snake, the Clearwater, the Salmon and their tributaries. Alvin Viles established one on the Clearwater above Lewiston near the present Potlatch Corp. lumber and paper mill. Viles called it the Central Ferry, but it became the Armstrong ferry a few years later when Viles sold it to J.L. Armstrong. A Kentuckian with an Indian wife (he is referred to in the records as a "squaw man") operated a ferry in the same general area called the Kentuck.

A map made by George Woodman, compiled from his travels and surveys in 1864, shows a small ferry crossing the South Fork of the Clearwater on the trail between Florence and Elk City. A ferry established on the Clearwater in 1861 by Col. William Craig and Jacob Schultz to serve the Oro Fino mines was a canoe. Some believe it may have been one of the wooden canoes built by the explorers Lewis and Clark 56 years before. For some years, the ferry consisted simply of this one canoe. John Greer and John Molloy acquired the ferry in 1877. When the railroad arrived in 1899, Greer formed a partnership with John Dunn, and the two platted a township that became the present town of Greer.

Tom Beall, a Lewiston pioneer, saw a chance to make some money ferrying people across Potlatch Creek at a place now called Arrow Junction. He borrowed a flat-bottom boat from the Indian agent at Lapwai and got three Indians to help him get the boat up the creek. There he went into business, charging $1.50 for a man and a horse, with the horse swimming, and 50 cents for a man on foot. Beall and the Indians were aware that the creek could be easily forded only a few yards downstream, but the average traveler would have no way of knowing that as long as the river remained high.

Beall and his crew made good money with their little boat. Then the river began to drop and Beall began to worry. As Beall told the story years later to the *Lewiston*

Tribune:

"One morning a party came along and the older man of the party I knew, but he had forgotten me. His name was Lige Bunton. He asked me the rates; I told him. He said he would not pay it. I told him there was the creek; help himself. He went up the creek to a place that looked as if it was fordable and he had a young man try it. Now the boulders were as big as barrels at that place, so when the young man got among those boulders his horse fell and got his leg tangled up in the bridle rein, and he would have drowned but the reins broke and saved the horse. I told the old man I did not want any corpses on my hands. His ferriage amounted to $17 but I would cross him for $15. So the bargain was closed at that figure. I had crossed all their stuff and was just on the eve of swimming their horses when a couple of Indians came along and went below the boat about 50 yards. Bunton was watching them and so was I. Well, where the Indians crossed the creek the water was about knee deep.

"Bunton looked at me and I looked at Bunton. He says, 'What do you call this creek?' I said, 'They call it Potlatch Creek.' He says, 'I know better, it is Robbers Creek.' I told him I had the $15 and he could call it what he damn well pleased."

By 1865 when horses were pulling wagons and stages in much of the region, the ferries became larger and so did the profits. Eventually, government had to step in. In January, 1866, the Territorial Legislature granted a franchise to Daniel Inman and Amasa Mann to operate a ferry on the Clearwater six miles below the mouth of the North Fork. Later, when the counties became well enough organized to do so, they took on the business of licensing and regulating the ferries.

Typical charges to cross a river in north central Idaho in those days:

A team and wagon, $3.50.

A pack animal, loaded, $1.50.

A pack animal, empty, 75 cents.

Loose animals, 50 cents each.
Sheep and hogs, 20 cents each.
A man on foot, 50 cents.
A man and horse, $1.50.

Edward Pearcy, who operated a ferry on the Snake River about a mile south of the confluence of the Snake and Clearwater, was still charging high rates in 1872: $8 for a wagon and team of horses, mules or oxen, plus $4 more if the wagon was heavily loaded—that is, carrying 400 pounds or more. Thus a family could be charged $12 just to get into town once. The Nez Perce County Commissioners, wishing to encourage immigration, not prevent it, forced Pearcy to reduce the charges to $3 for a rig and team but allowed him to collect the $4 for a heavy load. The county also approved charges of $1 for a horse and rider, 50 cents per man on foot, 50 cents per pack animal, 25 cents for each loose horse or cow and 10 cents per sheep or hog. For a one-horse vehicle, Pearcy was allowed to charge $1.50.

The Territorial Legislature authorized James Hunt to maintain a ferry across the Salmon River near Meadow Creek in Idaho County in 1865. Shearer's Ferry was established at about the same time on the Salmon between Riggins and French Creek. It was much used by miners and pack trains headed for the mines of Florence, Burgdorf and Warren and it must have been a busy place. The Idaho County Commissioners granted the request of F.A. Shearer that the trail running from the ferry to Florence be declared a county trail—a sign of its extensive use. And Shearer's operation included a hotel that also served as post office and saloon.

The ferryman's life wasn't always an easy one. In 1889, the *Free Press* reported trouble at Cleary's Ferry, which crossed the Salmon at John Day Creek: "The ferry at John Day's broke its cable last week while the boat was in mid-stream and drifted down the river about one-half mile before the landing was effected. Several horsemen were on board when the cable parted and the boys thought their time had come." And this from the *Free Press* a few months later: "The ferry boat at John Day capsized Saturday, 25 cattle drowned and the attendant had a narrow escape."

William A. Goulder gave up mining at Pierce for a season in the early Sixties to help a friend, a fellow named Reed, operate Reed's Ferry on the Clearwater where travelers crossed on the way to the Pierce and Oro Fino mining camps. "It was a cable ferry," Goulder wrote later, "rigged with ropes and pulleys and moved by the force of the current. In low water there was but little current, making the crossing slow and tedious. When the mush ice came and nearly filled the river, the current ceased to be effective. Then we had to cut the mush ice along the upper side of the boat and wait for the weak current to float it out of the way. Then we had to push the boat with poles into another mass of ice and thus repeat the process until the opposite shore was gained, by which time another mass of the enemy had crept down, filling the river." In spring, the swollen river filled with driftwood that made every crossing risky. During one such passage, a huge cedar tree came racing down, roots first, and struck the ferry amidships. The cable broke and the ferry, carrying loaded pack mules, was swept two miles down the river while Mrs. Reed stood screaming on the bank. The boat finally floated into an eddy and Goulder was able to get a line snagged around a tree on shore.

Such accidents were not uncommon. According to the June 24, 1898, edition of the *Lewiston Times*: "The government ferry at Spalding broke loose from its wire cable Saturday and floated down the river, narrowly averting a collision with the Lewiston ferry, which was in the process of crossing the river. Two drunk Indians were operating the ferry at the time it broke loose. The Spalding ferry boat is lodged on the beach near Alpowa, 12 miles below Lewiston." On August 4, 1915, the *Lewiston Tribune* noted that Corbett's Ferry, on the Clearwater above Greer, was out of operation. "Owing to the ferry boat being damaged, Corbett's Ferry was laid up for repairs Sunday. One of the pontoons sprang a leak and sank.''

In swift waters, the pontoon boats worked better than barges like Silcott's. Such boats typically rode on two pontoons, one at each end set at right angles to the deck. The pontoons presented enough mass to the current to move the boat across while allowing excess water to pass under. A barge in swift water would put too much pull on the cable for safety. Where there was too little current to move a ferry, as in some places on the Salmon, the ferryman hired strong men to row the craft across.

The cable ferry, current-driven, was simple and efficient, burned no fuel, and was both serviceable and reliable most of the year in the Lewiston region—and year around in some parts of the world where it is still used. Silcott continued to operate his Lewiston ferry, after replacing the original boat, until the 18th Street Bridge was built over the Clearwater at Lewiston in 1913. A few plain wooden cable ferries—identical to those early craft—were still doing useful work in eastern Washington as late as the 1970s.

* * *

The first hint of a stage line to Lewiston appeared in *The Golden Age*, Lewiston's first newspaper, in January 1863. *The Golden Age* said that ''Thatcher, Rickey & Co.'' were planning to inaugurate the service. *The Golden Age* carried no further mention of Thatcher, Rickey & Co., but in its issue of February 5, 1863, there is a news item noting that Capt. James W. Porter had been appointed provost marshal of Washington Territory, and ''left for Vancouver on the Friday morning stage.''

Hill Beachey, the proprietor of the Luna House, then Lewiston's finest hotel, had become the owner-agent of the stage line by that fall. In September of 1863, Durkee & Crampton were advertising a ''new stage line from Lewiston to the Mountain on the road to Florence.'' Durkee and Crampton may have meant the Mountain

House, a trading and gathering spot some 15 miles from Florence. By 1870, when wagon roads were rapidly replacing Indian trails, people were able to travel by stage between many of the towns of the Lewiston region. By this time freight and stage lines were fanning out from Lewiston in every direction, enhancing the town's position as a trading center.

By far the best known and best remembered of the stage coach drivers of the Lewiston country was Felix Warren, who was said to be so skillful with a whip that he could flip a flea off a dog's tail. At one time in his career, Warren owned 200 horses and 30 stages and operated more than 500 miles of stage lines out of Lewiston. He organized his first stage line, between Almota and Colfax, in 1875, and retired at Lewiston in 1915. He drove a coach and eight in the Cherry Blossom Festival at Lewiston in 1935, at the age of 83, and died two years later. Warren was a big, robust, friendly man, a fancy dresser who had a way with horses, women and little children. He insisted that his stages run on schedule, but he was willing to abandon the schedule when necessary. The historian Kenneth Holmes tells about the time Warren was driving a coach from Lewiston to Genesee with two female passengers, a young wife and an older woman. Just as the coach reached the summit of the Lewiston Hill, the older woman cried out, "Mr. Warren, we'll have to stop! We've got a baby on our hands." Unperturbed, Warren pulled to a stop, got down from the coach, unhitched the horses and let them graze. He walked to the edge of the canyon and stood looking over the valley for about half an hour. Then he heard the cry of the baby that had been born in his coach and soon the older woman called to him that they could go on. Warren hitched the horses and drove carefully to Genesee.

On another occasion, in the middle of winter as he was rocking along on his windy perch, Warren heard a baby cry inside the coach in a tone that told him something was wrong. He stopped the stage, went back to the baby's

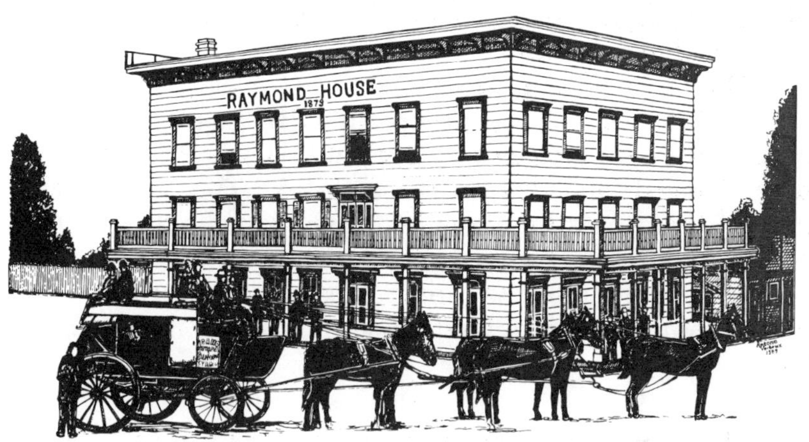

Felix Warren, driving a coach and five, pauses in front of the Raymond House at Fifth and Main Streets in downtown Lewiston.

mother and said, "You change that baby's diaper. He's cold." The mother tried, but her fingers were so numb she couldn't get the diaper off. Warren climbed into the coach, took the baby, and changed the diaper himself.

On the good roads, Warren's passengers rode in Concord coaches—big and roomy enough to carry 16 to 18 people inside and on top and pulled by six horses. On smaller and rougher roads and trails, people made do with little two-horse rigs called mud wagons or jerkies.

The comfort of the Concord coach was only relative; the stage coach may look romantic, viewed through the haze of time, but it made for hard traveling. Thomas C. Donaldson, who rode many an Idaho mile in the stage coaches of those days, recalled in later years what it was like: "The amount of physical suffering consequent upon a long trip on a stage coach can never be adequately described. I have ridden continually for days and nights sitting upright with my knees jammed against the knees of another unfortunate and both of us suffering the agonies of the damned." The Rev. Daniel Tuttle, a missionary bishop of the Episcopal Church who traveled often by stage coach to

Lewiston, once wrote that "most times I enjoyed that mode of traveling, many times I grimly endured it, and a few times I was rendered miserable by it."

On the other hand, at least for the travelers in northern Idaho, there were almost no holdups. By the time the stage coaches were running east of Lewiston, Henry Plummer had been hanged and his gang scattered. The newspapers published at Lewiston in the 1870s mentioned only one robbery, "the first in several years." When that stage arrived at its destination minus the money box, the law went looking for the gunmen, found them quickly, and put them behind bars.

*   *   *

Had it not been for the first interstate bridge, opened between Lewiston and Clarkston in 1899, local history would have been deprived of one of its most colorful characters. He was J.L. Kerns, a tall, rangy, usually friendly gentleman, who was hired to collect the tolls. Kerns was a man of stout purpose and remarkable loyalty to his employer, the Lewiston-Concord Bridge Co. (Clarkston was called Concord at one time). It was said by Kerns' admirers that he almost never let a fare go uncollected. When the bridge was opened on June 24, 1899, the first dignitary to cross ceremonially was E.H. Libby, one of the organizers of the company, riding on his horse, Judge. Waiting on the Lewiston end of the bridge was Kerns, and Kerns collected the fare—probably 10 cents.

As the toll collector, he worked alone and with only occasional relief. He opened the bridge for business every morning at 6 and closed the gate every night at midnight, seven days a week, for fourteen years. He slept in a little house beside the bridge on the Lewiston side. Sometimes Clarkston young people, returning on foot from an evening in Lewiston, would arrive at the bridge after midnight and climb over the gate. And as often as not, the light-sleeping Kerns would leap from his bed, throw on his robe, and run out demanding the tolls. A foot race would ensue, the youngsters hooting and giggling and Kerns pounding after them, his robe flying out behind.

It was sometimes possible for one member of a crossing family to escape the toll by riding in the back of the wagon, hidden under a blanket. And it was well known in the community that on those occasions when Kerns' son was collecting in his father's place, the chances were good that the boy would be asleep.

The company had a rule against running horses on the bridge. The story is told about the time Bill Jones galloped his horse over, and Kerns shouted to him that it would be a $10 fine. Jones threw Kerns a $20 bill, declaring he planned to go back as fast as he came.

Like the ferries of those days, most of the bridges were privately built by entrepreneurs such as E.H. Libby, Charles Francis Adams and other organizers of the Lewiston-Concord Bridge Co. Territorial governments lacked the means to build wagon roads, much less big bridges. The interstate bridge was a steel cantilevered span with a high center arch to accommodate the large steamers going to and coming from the Snake River Avenue docks. The steel had been fabricated on the East Coast, and was originally intended for a river in Argentina. The Argentine firm collapsed, and the Lewiston-Concord Bridge Co. found that the bridge would fit the Snake River with only minor adjustments. It took the company four years to put it up and its opening meant the end of Pearcy's ferry, which plied between Clarkston and Lewiston near what is now the east end of Elm Street in Clarkston. Silcott's ferry across the Clearwater at Lewiston continued to operate, however, until 1913, when the 18th Street Bridge—not a toll bridge—put *it* out of business.

Also in 1913, the states of Washington and Idaho bought out the owners of the interstate bridge and eliminated the tolls. It was a great day, that December 4, in Asotin and Nez Perce counties. People came from both sides of the river to enjoy the novel experience of walking across the bridge free—though some said they would miss the smiling face and outstretched hand of J.L. Kerns.

10

Steamboat Days

Meanwhile the steamboats continued to ply the Snake between Riparia and Lewiston and from Lewiston as far south and east as the waters would permit. Lewiston had been founded, in a sense, by the Colonel Wright and it continued to depend on the sternwheelers long after they had been replaced on the Columbia by railroads. Indeed, the last one didn't make its final departure from the Snake River Avenue docks until one raw February day in 1940, 34 years after the rails reached Lewiston from the west.

Throughout the Sixties and Seventies, the Oregon Steam Navigation Co. maintained a monopoly on the Snake and Columbia rivers that was only occasionally interrupted. Ephraim Baughman and his partner, A.P. Ankeny, competed for a while with their small steamboat, the Spray, which had been built in 1862 especially for swift, shallow waters, and W.P. Gray operated the Cascadillia on the Snake and Clearwater at about the same time. The OSN bought the Spray from Baughman and Ankeny for twice what they had paid to build it, and before long had regained its monopoly.

Without competition, the OSN was able to charge what it wished for carrying passengers and freight, and its rates were high. It was not unusual for the OSN to pay for a new sternwheeler in a single season; one OSN steamer paid for itself on its first trip. The company charged $90 a ton and up to haul freight from Portland to Lewiston, a passage of seven days. Baughman, who piloted the OSN steamer Colonel Wright, once recalled that on one trip the company took in $21,000 including $11,000 in passenger fares and the rest in freight charges. The company's rates shocked both passengers and shippers. Before long, chagrin became anger and grew into a movement to sink the greedy company if a way could be found to do it. That feeling persisted throughout the region for as long as the steamboat dominated the long-haul passenger and freight business.

The first powered boat on the Columbia was the Beaver, in 1836, whose "engine" consisted of six horses on a treadmill. The Columbia's first genuine steamboat was the Lot Whitcomb, a sidewheeler 160 feet long with engines generating 14 horsepower. It was on the Lot Whitcomb in 1851 that Ephraim Baughman, later to become a giant in the annals of river transport, apprenticed as a fireman at the age of 16. Ten years later the OSN, recognizing Baughman's uncanny affinity for river currents, asked him to pilot the first sternwheeler to brave the uncharted waters of the interior. Captain Len White's instructions were to take the Colonel Wright "as near as possible" to the new mines at Pierce. The year was 1861. As the pilot, Baughman could get the boat no more than thirty miles upstream on the Clearwater. There White unloaded the freight and passengers headed for the mines and brought the Colonel Wright back downstream to the confluence where the rest of the passengers debarked and, in effect, established the town of Lewiston.

As the head of navigation, Lewiston became an important trading center. But getting there, even by boat, wasn't easy. To travel from Portland to Lewiston by steamer in those days, the passenger had to climb on and off three sternwheelers, cross three long waterways, and at each of the two portages he either rode a mule-drawn rail car or stage coach between steamer landings. Navigation on the Columbia was then blocked by two impassable stretches of falls and white water—the Cascade Falls east of Portland and the Celilo Falls near The Dalles. They divided the river into three relatively calm sections called the "lower," the "middle," and the "upper" rivers.

In its heyday, the Oregon Steam Navigation Co. operated six sternwheelers on the lower river and four on the middle while navigation on the upper river was just beginning. Eventually the OSN bought out the portage owners and replaced the mule-drawn cars and stage coaches with narrow-gauge railroads to carry travelers around the rough-water stretches.

During the height of mining activity on the Clearwater, the OSN provided fairly regular steamboat service from Portland to Lewiston. But after new gold strikes in the Boise Basin had lured miners south, and drained the region of much of its population, the steamers stopped coming. At Lewiston, already having problems enough, that caused a minor panic.

In the fall of 1862, Lewiston's population of several thousand had shrunk to around four hundred. The steamboat whistle no longer echoed off the northern hills, and the Snake River Avenue docks were empty. The OSN now was terminating its river runs at Umatilla, Oregon. From there prospectors could get to the mines of the Boise Basin by fast stage in six days. John Scranton, then the editor of *The Golden Age*, issued a call to arms. He demanded that Lewiston save itself from extinction by opening its own boat service to Boise. Boats would always be cheaper and better than stages, Scranton declared, and he had some experience in the matter: Before coming to Lewiston, he had operated a successful boat line on Puget Sound.

But old time rivermen had their doubts. Most of them had helped line sternwheelers through Snake River rapids and all had heard of even swifter water upstream. Puget Sound was not the Snake, and Scranton was a fool.

Or was he? A scouting party of three men—Charles Clifford, Washington Murray and Joseph Denver— reported the river was navigable from Lewiston to Fort

By 1862, when this picture was taken from the bluff south of Lewiston, wooden buildings were rapidly replacing the tents that had sprung up the year before. The Luna House, the city's first hotel, at center right, still had a canvas roof, however. (*Nez Perce County Historical Society.*)

Two freight wagon drivers pause for the photographer on the muddy main street of Pierce near the turn of the century. (*Lewiston Morning Tribune.*)

Hill Beachey, operator of the Luna House hotel, who pursued and apprehended the murderers of Lloyd Magruder. (*Nez Perce County Historical Society, R.G. Baily collection.*)

Thomas J. Beall (pronounced BELL), an early Lewiston civic leader and stockman. A farming area east of Lapwai Creek, the Tom Beall, was named for him. (*Lewiston Morning Tribune*.)

Dr. Henry Stainton, an early Lewiston mayor, poses for the photographer in front of his office. (*Lewiston Morning Tribune*.)

The Weisgerber brothers' California Brewery and home, on the west side of First Street, about 1870. The drawing is from Elliot's *History of Idaho Territory*. (*Lewiston Morning Tribune*.)

A winter view across Snake River Avenue toward the original interstate bridge, shortly after the turn of the century. (*Lewiston Morning Tribune*.)

The Mountain Gem at Eureka Bar, some 50 miles south of Lewiston on the Snake River. She was built to replace the Imnaha, which was destroyed in 1903 after losing power in swift water. (*Nez Perce County Historical Society.*)

Ed Pearcy's ferry crossing the Snake River from Clarkston to Lewiston, probably in the Nineties. The ferry went out of business when the original interstate bridge went into service in 1899. (*Nez Perce County Historical Society.*)

The Almota arrives at Spalding on a Sunday excursion in about 1880. (*Nez Perce County Historical Society*.)

The Snake River Avenue docks in 1907, from the Clarkston side of the river. (*Nez Perce County Historical Society*.)

The steamboat Lewiston, the last sternwheeler to serve the Lewiston region, passes under the Interstate Bridge on its final trip downriver. The date was February 29, 1940. (*Nez Perce County Historical Society*.)

Felix Warren, left, accompanied by other old-timers, drives a stage coach down Main Street during a celebration in his honor. The year was about 1924. (*Nez Perce County Historical Society, Betty Rudfelt collection*.)

This was Fifth and D Streets in about 1900, looking northwest. The brick building, now Erb Hardware Co., then was occupied by the Cash Hardware Store, John P. Vollmer's wholesale business and—on the upper floor left—the *Lewiston Tribune*. (*Lewiston Morning Tribune*.)

An 1880s view of downtown Lewiston in winter. The brick building is J.P. Vollmer's Great Bargain Store, later the First National Bank and later still a branch of the First Security Bank of Idaho. (*Lewiston Morning Tribune*.)

Boise, and that there was "nothing in the river to impede navigation whatever."

Wrote Scranton: "A new route will now be opened for steam, the results of which cannot now be foretold. We shall penetrate Nevada and Utah territories by steam, as it is well known that it is only ninety miles from Salt Lake City . . . But a few more suns will rise and set before the shrill whistle of the steamer will reverberate along the

The sternwheeler Twin Cities at the Snake River Avenue dock, about 1910. The old interstate bridge is in the background.

banks of the noble river, and its echo will be heard for ages yet to come through the ravines, gorges and canyons and the mountain tops of our golden land as a symbol of ambition, perseverence and 'goaheadativeness.' ''

In the fall of 1862 the Spray, a small sternwheeler built for shallow waters, made a try at climbing the rapids in the Snake upstream from Lewiston. The pilot gave up after fifteen miles. Another vessel, the Swamp Angel, was driven somewhat farther, after which its owners advertised passage for "up to twenty miners and their outfits to the mouth of the Salmon River." The Swamp Angel reportedly did a brisk business on that stretch of the Snake.

Scranton and others continued to promote a steamboat route to Boise, and their hopes continued to bloom until 1865, when Thomas J. Stump, a skilled river pilot, made a final attempt aboard the Colonel Wright. Stump pushed the steamer through white water for eight days in gaining the first hundred miles. Then, attempting to pass a bad eddy, Stump drove the boat so hard he damaged both her engine and her hull. Realizing he could take the vessel no farther, he turned her about and made it back to Lewiston in five hours.

The Colonel Wright's engine was repaired and installed in a new boat called the Mary Woody, which plied Lake Pend Oreille. It made no money but it established a monopoly there for the Oregon Steam Navigation Co. As for the Colonel Wright, its hull was so badly strained that the boat was considered unsalvageable, and it was abandoned.

The OSN, meanwhile, was attempting to start a line on the southern Idaho portion of the Snake with a steamer named the Shoshone. The company had built the boat in the wilderness at a cost, staggering in those days, of $80,000. An old-time Lewiston river captain, J.E. Akins, recalled later that the Shoshone "was a real steamboat . . . built hundreds of miles from a foundry or machine shop and nearly as far from a sawmill . . . . All the lumber was whipsawed or hewn on the spot, and iron was transported from long distances on pack animals and worked into shape after its arrival on the grounds . . . The money spent would have built several fine steamers lower down on the river.''

The Shoshone passed its river trials handily in 1866, but the venture proved a costly failure for the OSN. Its competitor, the California Steam Navigation Co., found a shorter land route to southern Idaho and won the race. The OSN, unwilling to accept the loss, decided to bring the Shoshone down the Snake River to the Columbia. It dispatched a prominent river captain, Cy Smith, to southern Idaho with instructions to ''bring her down the river or wreck her in the attempt.''

Smith made a good start, but at Lime Point, with the dreaded Copper Ledge Falls looming ahead, he lost his nerve. Deserted by his crew, Smith sent word that the falls ''could not be run by man nor devil.'' For another season, the Shoshone lay idle in the wilderness, with two watchmen aboard. Then the company sent two of its best men, Captain Sebastian Miller and Engineer Dan Buchanan, to finish the job. It took Miller and Buchanan twenty days just to find the Shoshone in her wilderness berth. They traveled by boat to Umatilla, then took a buckboard to the Blue Mountains. When the road gave out and the snow came on, they discarded the wagon, made a sled and went on until the snow gave out. They rode horseback for fifty miles and when the horses gave out they continued the rest of the way on foot. The Shoshone had been built of mountain pine, which is brittle when seasoned, Captain Akin recalled. With no lumber to rebuild and no time to caulk, the two men started the deck pump and wet down the hull until the planking swelled enough to close the leaks.

Miller's plan was to drift with the engines backing, steering the boat by the pressure of the water against the rudder. For a while, all went well. Then, approaching a rapids, he made a slight miscalculation and drove the boat into an eddy that whipped it around three times. The

Shoshone emerged from the whirlpool like a dancer off balance, hit the rapids at a bad angle and banged into the rocks. The collision carried away eight feet of her bow. After emergency repairs, Miller and Buchanan got the boat headed downstream again, and so the voyage went—through the full length of what is now known as Hells Canyon— until the Shoshone floated into Lewiston at 9 a.m. on April 17, 1870. As he nudged the boat up to the Snake River Avenue dock, Miller called through the speaking tube to his engineer, "I say, Buck, if the company wanted a couple of men to take a boat through hell, they would send for you and me."

Miller had the vessel repaired at Lewiston, then took her over Celilo Falls to the Middle Columbia, where she served as a cattle boat until 1873. The company used her after that on the lower river and presumably recouped its investment.

Twenty years later, another frustrated owner tried to salvage his loss by ramming another boat, the Norma, through Hells Canyon from Huntington, Oregon, to Lewiston. Jacob Kamm had built a large steamer, thinking he could profit by carrying ore from the Seven Devils mines up the Snake River to a Union Pacific Railway station at Huntington. But the Seven Devils did not produce, and the vessel lay idle.

Built to carry three hundred tons, the Norma stretched out to 165 feet compared to the Shoshone's 136. Kamm assigned the piloting to Captain W.P. Gray, a skilled river man. Remembering the Shoshone, Gray decided to wait for high water. While the spring rains raised the Snake River, Gray strengthened his vessel with extra lumber wherever possible. Preparing to pass through nude mountains, he laid on more lumber for repairs.

On April 16, 1891, he took his first sweep, toward Copper Creek Falls. Almost immediately, a submerged rock tore a hole in the hull three feet wide and thirty feet long. The repairs took three days. Ready to resume the voyage, Gray eyed the falls some three thousand feet away and then informed his crew that the boat was too long to make the turn in the narrow canyon and would have to be bounced off the rock wall. The crew voted to install an extra bulkhead. That done, Gray launched the vessel into the stream. It hit the wall like a battering ram, rolled with the shock, and shot into Hells Canyon. Thanks to high water, the rest of the passage was uneventful and the Norma reached Lewiston almost whole.

By this time, the region had recovered from the doldrums of the late Sixties and steamboats were coming and going regularly from the Snake River Avenue docks. They carried ore from the mines and sacked wheat from river landings that served the farming areas. They carried deckloads of happy passengers on weekend outings up and down the rivers. From Portland, they brought the fancy furniture, marble fireplaces and expensive carpets that graced the Prospect Avenue homes of Lewiston's merchant princes.

Altogether some thirty-five river craft, almost all of them sternwheelers, worked Lewiston area waters during the eighty years of the steamboat era. Some were small, owned by mining companies and other private firms. The larger ones were operated by river transportation companies, usually on a schedule. Most prominent among the latter was the Lewiston—no matter what boat happened to be carrying that name, since several did at various times. The first Lewiston was built at Umatilla in 1867 but never saw the town she was named for; she was hustled off to the lower Columbia where she was renamed the Ann and later the Cowlitz. Lewiston number two was built of lumber and engine parts taken from another vessel, the John Gates. The third Lewiston was built at Riparia in 1905 and was able to haul 1,800 sacks of wheat upstream and 3,000 sacks down—more than either of her predecessors. After seventeen years of service, Lewiston number three was destroyed by fire, thought to be arson, while docked at Lewiston with another boat, the Spokane. Both vessels burned to the waterline. The roar of the fire, together with the hiss of the flames against the water, woke many residents of Lewiston and Clarkston in the early morning hours of July 13, 1922.

The fourth and final Lewiston was 160 feet long with a beam of thirty-six feet and a draft of sixteen. This was the boat that steamed under the Interstate Bridge, into the confluence and westward on February 29, 1940, to bring the steamboat days to a close. It was an historic moment. Cars lined Snake River Avenue and hundreds of people stood in a cold morning drizzle to witness the end of an era. At 8:55, the steamer gave a great whistle, to signal the raising of the Interstate Bridge. Nothing happened. The Lewiston whistled again. This time the bridge began to rise and Capt. E.C. Davis cast off as the crowd cheered. In midstream, a valve stuck, the engine stopped and the Lewiston drifted helplessly toward the bridge. Captain Davis was able to maneuver between the piers, and beached the vessel on the north bank of the Snake. The crew made repairs, Captain Davis cast off again, and again the valve stuck. He beached the boat, the crew made new repairs, and Captain Davis cast off once more. This time he steamed seven miles downriver before the engine quit and he had to put the boat ashore just below the W.J. Houser fruit packing plant at Alpowa. The crew finally solved all the problems and Captain Davis, frustrated but remarkably calm, made yet another start and got the Lewiston all the way down to Portland, where she went to work as a tug.

Among the other vessels serving the area during the steamboat period were the Cayuse Chief, the Okanagon, the Tenino, the J.M. Hannaford, the John Gates, the Harvest Queen, the Nez Perce Chief, the Twin Cities, the Inland Empire, the J.N. Teal and the Almota (which carried the heaviest load into Lewiston in all of stern-wheeler history: freight plus 508 passengers including a Georgia regiment sent to fight in the Nez Perce War of 1877).

The Imnaha, built at a cost of $35,000 to serve the

mines south of Lewiston, went into service there on June 30, 1903. She made several trips, fighting difficult currents, and was destroyed on the following November 9. A cable got caught in one of the eccentric rods, which carried power to the paddle wheel, and stopped the engine. The current carried the Imnaha, now floating helplessly, into Mountain Sheep Rapids and both Captain Harry Baughman and Engineer L.H. Campbell realized she was doomed. The vessel flew through the rapids, turned broadside and wedged herself momentarily against the bank. She remained poised there for only a few seconds, but time enough for every man to leap ashore, then floated free and smashed into a series of boulders. The wreckage was strewn for miles, but not a life was lost.

The Imnaha was replaced by the Mountain Gem, which worked on the river above Lewiston until 1905.

And there was the Annie Faxon, of mournful memory, a fast and pretty vessel thought by many to be the best of the fleet. Most steamboat crews considered two trips a week to Riparia, some 60 miles downriver from Lewiston, to be full duty. The men of the Annie Faxon drove their ship hard enough to make three. She blew up in the Snake River a few miles west of Lewiston on August 14, 1893, killing eight people. Among the debris that floated ashore was a box containing a dictionary of the Nez Perce language compiled by Susan McBeth, a Presbyterian missionary at Kamiah. Although water-soaked and damaged it was still readable, and it eventually found its way back to the writer's sister, Kate McBeth, and to the Smithsonian Institution.

11

The Somber Seventies

For Lewiston, the 1870s were not the best of times. Pack trains continued to leave for the mountains, but the sixty-mule strings were gone and twenty mules were now considered a large train. The mules themselves, once in great demand, were selling for a song. Every packmaster who left Lewiston for one of the mining camps with goods to sell knew he might find only cold ashes when he got there, so rapidly were the miners leaving for the south.

The bunch grass that grew everywhere around Lewiston produced fat cattle, as the Nez Perce Indians had learned, but the homesteaders needed a market. The rich soil produced abundant crops but there was never enough room on the steamboats to carry the wheat down the Columbia to where the markets were; accidents, repairs and low water made river transportation chancy and the freight rates imposed by the Oregon Steam Navigation Co., which ruled the waters by virtue of a long-standing monopoly, were outrageously high. Newspapers carried tantalizing reports of railroad building but the farmers saw no rails. Season after season they raised, harvested and threshed large quantities of wheat, then hauled it to river warehouses only to find there wasn't enough room.

Downtown Lewiston reflected the spirit of the times. Its buildings were a grand mismatch, some scarcely stable enough to stand, some apparently thrown together by slipshod workmen. Most of the false fronts, those rather pathetic efforts at distinction, were teetering. According to the season, the streets were ankle-deep in mud or dust, strewn with miscellaneous garbage and spotted with large rocks. A dead animal might lie in the street for a week or more, to be walked around.

The merchants of Lewiston by this time had already offered their stock at bargain prices and found few buyers. Their heady dreams of yesteryear, when the town seemed destined to blossom into a great trading center, had soured. The town fathers once had thought that Lewiston might become a terminal for river transportation on the upper Snake but those hopes died when the Colonel Wright returned to Lewiston battered and beaten after an unsuccessful attempt to penetrate Hells Canyon. The merchants' goal now was simply to hang on for one more day at a time. And so they all did, staring gloomily out their front windows at the miserable street they had renamed Montgomery to reflect the importance of what should have been the main thoroughfare of a thriving city.

All but publisher Henry Leland of the town's weekly newspaper, the *Signal*. If Leland despaired of the future, he seldom showed it. Like his father, Alonzo, who was known as the "eternal optimist," Henry could find some good everywhere. One evening his eye fell on the remodeled front of James Gage's general store and confectionery, and the new lantern shining brightly overhead, and Gage won the glad type for that week. M.M. Williams had almost completed encasing his log furniture store in planed lumber. That was progress, Leland pointed out in another issue. He was equally pleased to report that Wintsch and Wildenthaler had built a new board sidewalk in front of their bakery.

The columns of the *Signal* reflected not only the pleasure of the editor, but his impatience as well, for Leland prodded constantly. "We need simple manufactured products," he declared at one point, recalling that "one week only nine pounds of butter were available"—at

$1.50 a pound. "We can manufacture candles, soap, linseed oil, sugar from beets, simple farm implements, wagons, carriages, hats, woolen goods. We do not require luxuries." And he urged the townfolk: "Do less whining and grumbling. Have more hope and faith in our country. We will find no better elsewhere."

Leland was a doer as well as an urger. He was one of the promoters of the town's grist mill and of the water ditch that powered it. He not only cracked the whip; he worked in the ranks, and he was especially concerned about the streets.

Nothing much could be done about the dust and the mud, everyone agreed, since paving was out of the question. But there were hogs rooting here and there, and something could be done about the boulders in the streets and the trash blowing up against the sides of the buildings. And some way had to be found to get to the cemetery, which was practically inaccessible on the bluff in a spot that later would become Pioneer Park.

The bluff was creased by a gully at the head of Fifth Street. If this could be widened and deepened, and made into a street, it would provide easy access to the final resting place of the town's departed. There was no other reason to climb to the flat above downtown since there was nothing there but sand and sagebrush. The towns-people gnawed away at that gully for several years without much result, using the dirt to fill low areas in downtown streets where water collected. The diggers were still laboring, with primitive tools, when the Seventies ended. It would take another twenty years or so to dig enough of the gully out to accommodate a two-lane grade.

Meanwhile, people reached the cemetery by means of Snake River Grade, later called Prospect Grade, which was much steeper then, or by a roundabout route that skirted the bluff to the east of town and then climbed up to the flat on an easier slope. The Snake River Grade was much closer, but it was hard. Leland complained that the grade was so steep "a team of horses is required to pull an empty wagon up.''

Complaints of hogs running loose became so frequent in the early Seventies that the City Council had no choice but to act. On May 18, 1872, it passed an ordinance outlawing swine on city streets and imposing a fine of $5 to $20. It apparently did little good, for the complaints continued. Part of the problem was that Constable Dan McElwee had many hog-owning friends and arresting them would cause hard feelings. Besides, McElwee had no place to put any hogs and piglets that he might round up. So on July 1, the Council adopted another ordinance, this time providing that McElwee would be required to act on the complaint of any resident. The Council not only took the constable off the hook but provided him with some fencing. That evidently solved the problem, for the Council enacted no more animal ordinances in the next four years. By 1876, it was loose horses and cattle that had citizens aroused. According to the *Lewiston Teller*, ''cattle of all kinds roam the streets, oftimes taking possession of the sidewalks to the exclusion of pedestrians.'' And again, ''a cow treed several school girls on their way home to lunch.'' And this, also from the *Teller*: ''An anxious inquirer asks whether upon meeting a cow on the sidewalk, it is proper to give her the inside or the outside of the walk?'' On July 3 of that year, the Council outlawed loose horses and cattle.

But animals weren't the only problem. A sink hole developed on Montgomery Street and filled to the brim with sewage from the Globe Hotel. The locals quickly learned to avoid that spot but a stranger riding through town one night fell into it along with his horse—and for some reason neglected to sue.

Writing in the *Signal* of June 6, 1874, Henry Leland echoed the complaints of many Lewistonians: ''What a horrible condition some of our leading streets are in—boots, shoes, tin cans, shavings, paper, boxes, etc., etc., scattered about town in all directions. All these, together with the loose gravel and rock, make the streets look very bad. And a few bits would employ a Chinaman or two to make a decided improvement in the way of cleaning." Instead, the Council decided, on January 4, 1875, to put city prisoners to work cleaning the streets.

Downtown in the early Seventies consisted of ten short streets—the east-west A through E (or Montgomery) and the north-south First through Fifth. The town could scarcely afford to lose one of them but it did, as the Clearwater River gradually washed away A Street. As the water took away the beach and then the bank, one frail building after another slid into the river. Among the structures lost were Vic Trevitt's store, which may have been the first in Lewiston, and the headquarters of the Oregon Steam Navigation Co. During the several years it took for the river to destroy A Street, four weekly newspapers tried in vain to arouse the citizens to action. The last was the *Teller*, which warned on July 26, 1883, "Our city front along the Clearwater is too valuable to be wasted in this manner, and every foot of it will be required as the city becomes of commercial importance."

But it was far too late. The street by then was doomed, and perhaps was doomed from the start. Even if A Street might have been saved by timely action in the Seventies, the town's general malaise probably would have prevented it. Lewistonians had no way of knowing then that better times were coming.

*   *   *

It doesn't seem to have bothered any Lewiston property owner of 1872 that he couldn't legally own his piece of land. People behaved as though the Nez Perce Indians did not exist, although in fact they were the legal owners of the land that Lewiston sat on. The Nez Perces didn't complain much about this intrusion into their reservation, but property rights were clouded and would remain so until the legal issue was put to rest.

Lewiston had been settled in clear, uncaring violation of the Treaty of 1855, which forbade any uninvited white presence in the lands reserved for the Nez Perce Indians.

The reservation at that time extended roughly from the Blue Mountains on the west to the Bitterroots on the east and from the Palouse River in the north to a line south of Payette Lake. The Indian agent, A.J. Cain, made a half-hearted and futile attempt to enforce the law, but the pressure of immigration was simply too great; Cain finally said that the packers, merchants and others at Lewiston must not put up permanent buildings. That is why early Lewiston consisted mainly of tents, or canvas stretched over wooden frames. When Hill Beachey built his hotel, the Luna House, in 1862, he covered the hewn log walls with a canvas roof; that seemed to satisfy agent Cain.

By 1863, in time for the first meeting of the Territorial Legislature, Beachey had replaced the canvas roof with a wooden one. Nobody seemed to mind. By that time there were many wooden buildings on the flat between the river and the bluff, and nobody worried about them, either. Nor was there apparently any objection to the establishment of Lewiston as the first capital of the new Idaho Territory despite the fact it was perched illegally on reservation land. What worried the young city's civic leaders was the legal cloud that hung over their property rights. Technically, the whites could own none of these lots.

This hankering for a townsite free and clear was part of the pressure that produced a new agreement. The Treaty of 1863 shrunk the Nez Perce reservation to a fraction of its original size, squeezing the wide-ranging Nez Perce bands into an area along the Clearwater River and eliminating the high prairies and the mining regions as well as the city of Lewiston.

Unfortunately for everyone, Congress neglected to ratify the treaty immediately and property rights remained in limbo for four years. At Lewiston, people were buying and selling city lots without regard to treaties, putting up permanent buildings and otherwise behaving as though the Indians and the reservation weren't there. Congress finally ratified the Treaty of 1863, on March 2, 1867. But

Lewiston didn't automatically become legal even then. The City Council took no action to clear away the legal cloud until November 6, 1871. It then resolved, unanimously, "that His Honor, the Mayor, be and is hereby authorized to cause entry to be made at the proper Land Office, the quantum of land embracing the City of Lewiston to which the inhabitants thereof are entitled under the Act of Congress approved March 2, 1867, and to pay for the same and all expenses incidental thereto, and to draw warrants upon the city treasurer for said payment and expenses."

The Council meant well, but the mayor was Levi Ankeny, and his heart wasn't in it. Ankeny at this time was contemplating new business opportunities at Walla Walla and Portland. He had lost interest in the affairs of Lewiston to the point where he—and not only he—was no longer bothering to attend City Council meetings. For the remainder of his term as mayor, the Council was unable to enact business for lack of a quorum. Three years later, the city found a mayor with the ability and force to complete the task. Dr. Henry W. Stainton (pronounced as without the *i*) was a pioneer physician accustomed to handling emergencies. A man of action, he was prepared to help a sick man or a sick village. Stainton was elected in March, 1874, and attended his first Council meeting on April 6. Wasting no time, he hired E.B. True, a surveyor and teacher, to make the legally required survey of the city and agreed to pay him $660 for the work.

Stainton then called a special meeting of the Council, got Council approval of his contract with True and directed City Clerk Charles G. Kress to visit every property owner. The mayor also advertised all unclaimed city land for sale and found buyers for most of it. Some offered $3 an acre, some as high as $4.50. The properties were sold to the highest bidders and the city invested in unsold property with scrip authorized by the Council.

With all the t's crossed and i's dotted, the city of Lewiston became at last a legal entity, but it had taken eleven years after the signing of the Treaty of 1863 to bring it all to pass.

Because of Dr. Stainton's work for the city on this occasion, his friends thereafter insisted that he was the truly "first" mayor of Lewiston. In a sense he was. But the official roster names him as the fourth, after Dr. Madison A. Kelly (1863-'67), T.G. Wright (1867-'71) and Levi Ankeny (1871-'74).

Ankeny did not linger in Lewiston long enough to serve out his term. In 1873 he sold his retail merchandising business to the Loewenberg Bros. and his classy house on Snake River Avenue—then the "best" address in town—to Andrew Roux, the city's first barber, and moved to Walla Walla. He went into business there and at Portland, became a millionaire, and eventually won election to Congress.

12

Vive La France

People seeking the best in food and lodging in the 1870s and '80s called upon Madame Melaine Bonhore LaFrancois, who ran the finest hotel in the north country at Second and D Streets in Lewiston. But the Hotel De France was only one of two where French was the language of the kitchen and the counting room. The other half of this Gaullic rivalry was the Raymond House at Fifth and Main, built by Raymond Saux in 1879 when the De France was already flourishing.

Saux (pronounced Sue), an experienced hotelier from Paris, arrived with his family in 1874, apparently intent on showing frontier Lewiston how it was done. Saux first presented himself to Madame LaFrancois. Finding that she would welcome a long vacation from the trials of management, he arranged to lease the De France. When Madame returned after several months in California and Paris, she offered to sell the hotel to Saux, and Saux quickly agreed to buy. They were unable to come to terms, however, and after the negotiations had broken down Saux announced that he would build a hotel of his own.

Saux's health was failing, but he started construction nevertheless in February, 1879. Building proceeded on schedule, despite the illness of the builder, according to a plan that had become popular in small western cities. The first floor of the three-story building was surrounded by a veranda with supporting pillars. The veranda roof kept out much of the heat and dust in summers and the cold rain in winter, and the pillars made handy hitching posts.

As Saux's building was going up, Madame LaFrancois was undertaking an elaborate remodeling and expansion program at the Hotel De France. She established special units for families. She announced plans to encase the entire building in brick, but for some reason never did.

Saux dedicated his new hotel, the Raymond House, at a grand ball on September 5, 1879, to which he invited everyone who could come. It proved to be the outstanding social event of the year in the Lewiston region and many who drove in from distances made a weekend of it. There were speeches in praise of both the building and the builder. Dancers, singers and local musicians provided entertainment, and Ferdinand Roos and his string orchestra played for dancing until dawn.

Within a week, the Raymond House was registering guests for its 35 rooms, at $1.50 to $2.50 a night depending upon the room's location. The hotel quickly became a popular stopping place, but the builder did not have long to enjoy his success. Raymond Saux was dead within ten months of the opening, and Madame Saux undertook the management of the hotel. Although she knew little English, she was aided by her son-in-law, W. E. Timberlake, and together, in 1906, they built a brick annex that almost doubled the number of rooms from 35 to 54.

Meanwhile, Madame Melaine LaFrancois, twice widowed, was presiding graciously three blocks away at the Hotel De France. She had arrived at Lewiston in early 1862 with a sick husband, Paul Bonhore, and their young son, Eugene, after following the gold strikes in California. Madame was aghast at the condition of Lewiston's hotels. The best of them, the Luna House, still had a canvas roof over its log walls, and the others were mere hovels by her standards. She decided that she would build a decent hotel, and straightaway set about ordering lumber and other materials. Since there was yet no mill at Lewiston, Madame had milled lumber freighted from Mount Idaho, then a thriving town on the southern edge of the Camas Prairie. She imported expensive furnishings from Paris — draperies, carpeting, hand-carved furniture, blankets and bedding.

During this period, Paul Bonhore died and Madame married Charles LaFrancois, a former French army officer who had fled from the political troubles in France to the mountains of Idaho. He was a fine gentleman, by all accounts, and a popular figure around the hotel, but he was not of much practical help and Madame managed the business herself — and continued to do so after LaFrancois died in 1874. In the late '70s and '80s, at the height of its elegance and renown, the Hotel De France attracted a large and loyal clientele. Couples would travel for hundreds of miles to be married in its lavish parlor. Madame's guests marveled at the heavy silk, satin and brocade draperies, lounged on hand-carved divans fashioned in the style of Louis XIV, and sank their feet deep into red velvet carpets.

A former daughter-in-law, who had once been Mrs. Eugene Bonhore, managed the hotel for two years and later recalled that during those months, some sixty couples had been married in the sumptuous parlor. To a *Lewiston Morning Tribune* reporter, she described her mother-in-law as "the grandest woman that ever came into this country."

The dining room offered the best food available in the region, cooked by a Paris-trained French chef, Baptiste Escude, whom Madame had found at Walla Walla. This was the menu for a Sunday dinner in May of 1885, as advertised in advance in the *Lewiston Teller:*

May 24, 1885

Soup — Oyster a l'anglaise, relishes, radishes,
pate de Foi Gras de Strasberg.

Salad — Chicken Salade, Mayonnaise a la Richelein,
Lettuce, Romaine.

Fish — Young salmon, caper sauce.

Entree — Petit Pate a la Financier, Supreme.
DeVolaille a la Victoria.

Roasts — Spring chicken en pyramide, spring lamb.
Filet de Veau (veal) a la Renaissance.
Vegetables — Green peas a la francaise, new potatoes.
Dessert — Assorted cakes. Custard pudding,
vanilla ice cream.
Fruit — Strawberries, oranges.

Madame owned and managed a 25-acre farm on which she produced vegetables, milk, cheese, butter and beef. But unfortunately for her and the De France, the times were not good. Although she was a keen buyer and careful manager, the hotel began losing money. The panic of 1873 was being felt in Idaho as elsewhere, and business was hurting. The editor of the weekly *Signal,* his usual optimism sorely tried, wrote, ''We have waited through the winter with very little money-to-buy. Therefore, no trade . . . The miners have gradually left the land, and no money has come in . . . In quartz mining, money from the east is required to bring about prosperity, and none is coming in.''

Madame LaFrancois struggled to hold down expenses, and she found herself fighting to keep the stage office, a vital source of income. She gave up her plans to buy a new cart, deciding instead to refinish the old one and give the driver a new uniform. Her Parisian chef became expert at making a little food look like a lot. Madame was behind in his wages, but Escude, like the rest of the staff, was patient. The son, Eugene, was lazy and — worse — careless with money.

Money problems continued through the Eighties and Nineties. Things would improve for a while and then, just when Madame was able to relax a little, she would have bills she couldn't pay and payrolls she couldn't quite meet. At length, Escude's patience frayed and he began complaining about Eugene's idleness. Finally, in May, 1895, the chef came to Madame with a friend and a proposition. The friend was James W. Reid, then a leading Lewiston lawyer. The proposition was that Escude would buy the hotel with the back wages that Madame owed him.

Madame resisted, but her back was to the wall and she had no choice but to sign a promissory note and mortgage agreeing to pay her chef $6,800 in back wages at interest of 6 percent. She was unable to make her payments and died on April 14, 1897. In September, 1898, Escude moved to acquire the long-delayed wages. By then the estate owed Escude $10,072, and he was about to foreclose. Eugene Bonhore, the sole heir, had done nothing to protect his own interests until the announcement of the sheriff's sale in November. Eugene then rushed to retain a lawyer, but it was too late. Sheriff Thomas D. Barton called the sale for November 9, 1898, and Escude was the only bidder. He got the building for $10,167.97, but the furnishings, the liquor license and supplies went to Eugene. The business continued under the management of J. W. Davidson & Co., which had been leasing the hotel for ten months.

Escude, now in failing health, had not worked at the De France since the death of Madame LaFrancois and had moved to the home of a French friend, Louis Delsol, east of town. A month or so after the sheriff's sale, Escude drove to Lewiston for an overnight visit at the home of Eugene Bonhore. They dined at 5 and Escude retired at 8. He became suddenly ill at 2 a.m., and was dead before morning.

Dennis Holland, who had made fortunes in mining and cattle, came to Lewiston with money to invest and in 1899 he bought the Hotel De France and announced plans to remodel and enlarge it. He completed a twelve-room addition in October, 1903, and added a $30,000 brick annex in 1910. After Holland's death on May 26, 1912, two nephews, George and A. E. Smurthwaite, managed the hotel. Ownership later passed from the Holland estate to a man named Alexander, then to George Carnegie. Adam Schlee of Clarkston, a former Uniontown area farmer, bought the hotel from Carnegie in the early 1920s for $22,500, thinking it would make a nice living for him and his wife, Edna. The couple found that hotel management was not for them, and they leased the De France to a succession of managers who gradually drove the business into the ground.

By this time, automobiles were everywhere, and servicing them had become a good business. Adam and Edna Schlee decided to tear down the De France and put in its place a new building in which to sell and service cars. The hotel came down in 1945 and the new building, which the Schlees called the Evergreen, went up. Grove Barton and Harlan Hoyt, who already owned four service stations, rented the Evergreen, which then became their fifth.

The Hotel De France had served the Lewiston area for 82 years.

The stage office, which Madame LaFrancois had fought so vigorously to keep for the De France, was by this time at the Raymond, serving Greyhound bus passengers. Madame Saux, whose husband, Raymond, had built the hotel in 1879, continued to manage it until her death shortly after the turn of the century. Her daughter and son-in-law, Mr. and Mrs. W. E. Timberlake, managed it until 1910, when they sold it to another pioneer family, Mr. and Mrs. James McGrane. McGrane's father had been a steward on the sternwheeler, the Colonel Wright, on the vessel's first trip to Lewiston in 1861.

The Raymond House was badly damaged by fire in 1922, and the next year the owners modernized throughout, installing a new kitchen with a waffle iron that could turn out 360 waffles an hour. The hotel reopened in 1923 simply as the Raymond and without the veranda. After the death of James McGrane in 1941, F. H. (Ted) Ward, the son of Mrs. McGrane, managed the hotel until it was sold to Thomas W. Boise, a nephew of James McGrane, and his partner, A. S. (Sid) Johnson, in 1947.

Like the De France, the Raymond had seen hard times. It barely weathered the Great Depression of the Thirties, and in January, 1962, the Raymond and four small businesses were sold to the First Security Bank of Idaho, which had a branch across the street. Nothing was said about the sale at the time, but a month later the bank announced that it needed parking space for its customers and that the Raymond and the four small businesses had been acquired for that purpose. The four included the Maple Lounge, the Rendezvous Cafe, the Raymond Cafe and the Granada Theater.

The Raymond had been in decline for a long time when the wrecking ball finally leveled it. But it had fed and sheltered the hungry and the travel worn for 83 years, longer by one than the Hotel De France.

13

Wheels of Commerce

It is no coincidence that John P. Vollmer not only install-ed the first telephone in the Pacific Northwest, but also owned the first automobile in Lewiston, established the city's first bank, developed the region's first chain of general stores and ended up a millionaire. Had Vollmer chosen the military life, he would have become the nation's first five-star general. It would not be enough to say that Vollmer was the town's leading businessman in the Seventies and Eighties; in a sense he *was* the town's business.

The other citizens of Lewiston were less impressed by the telephone than Vollmer was. They saw it as an interesting gadget; he saw the future in this invention which was not yet even in production. Alexander Graham Bell had patented the device in March, 1876, after which he took his telephone to Philadelphia, then celebrating the nation's first centennial. Vollmer saw it demonstrated later that year in San Francisco and brought two of the instruments home with him. He had a line installed from his home on Snake River Avenue to the second floor of his store at Fourth and Main Streets. And on May 10, 1878, Vollmer made the first recorded telephone call in the Pacific Northwest. He invited any who were interested to come and hear it demonstrated, and many accepted. Later, the Raymond House installed a phone line from the hotel to the boat dock, so it could get the first word when a steamer arrived. For most, however, the telegraph was good enough, and the telephone didn't become widely used in Lewiston until the Nineties.

John P. Vollmer would go on to other things, but he is still remembered as the first in the Northwest to understand the importance of Bell's invention. It was typical of the foresight that made him the merchant prince of Lewiston and Idaho's first millionaire.

Vollmer's name first appeared in an ad in the Idaho *Signal* on March 16, 1872, as an "importer and jobber of foreign and domestic liquors and cigars." In July of 1873, Vollmer annouced that he would sell no more liquor because of "conscientious scruples." Some merchants had been selling the Indians skookum flour, which contained a small bottle of whiskey in each sack. Vollmer was 26 and had come to Lewiston from Indianapolis, where he had been employed by a large book company. He had developed an ink manufacturing process that brought him a good living, but after service in the Union Army in the closing days of the Civil War, he had succumbed to the lure of new opportunities in the West. He journeyed first to Walla Walla, where he became the manager of a wine company, and left Walla Walla for Lewiston upon hearing that the Nez Perce reservation might soon be opened to settlement. At Lewiston, Vollmer formed a partnership with Wallace Scott and John Fix. They established the Vollmer Clearwater Co., a retail store with branches in Grangeville, Mount Idaho, Genesee, Uniontown and Asotin. He decided the region needed a bank, and in 1883, the First National Bank of Lewiston opened with Vollmer as the first president. Still looking ahead, he became the agent for all northern Idaho railroads, even though there were not yet any railroads there. He brought to Lewiston its first phonograph and provided recordings at 10 cents a play. He took to the automobile without hesitation and in 1909 was driving the region's first White Steamer. In 1914, it was the town's first Baker Electric, a fancy sedan that ran on storage batteries.

The Republican Party offered him its nomination for governor in 1898 and the Progressives extended the same invitation in 1914. He declined both times. He was the first president of the Lewiston Board of Trade, later to become the Chamber of Commerce, was elected to the Board of Trustees of the Lewiston State Normal School in 1894, and he managed to serve terms on both the Lewiston School Board and the City Council. He took an interest in livestock, giving generous support to the Lewiston Northwest Livestock Show, and promised to put up "generous bait" to any lumber company that would locate at Lewiston.

With so many buckets in the well, Vollmer began to find his Lewiston store scarcely worth the trouble. The store was closed and the three owners broke partnership and went their separate ways.

*   *   *

If Lewiston could boast another merchant prince, it was J. Alexander, who referred to himself simply as "J" and who for 37 years operated one of the city's leading retail stores. He had seen Lewiston when it was packed with gold-hungry prospectors, and refused to acknowledge that it would not always be a trading center. The area was suffering severe economic pangs from the panic of 1873, but Alexander ventured boldly into the retail business anyhow and with the help of one M. Hexter, opened his store in 1876.

Alexander was a small man whose smooth and close-fitting suits made him appear even smaller. He was so splay-footed that people often thought he was wearing his shoes on the wrong feet. He wore a permanent, happy smile. He was a man of few words, with no gift for banter, and customers in his store found themselves always dealing with clerks while Alexander's smile hovered in the background. His smile never wore thin from the day he put up his sign: "Old Joe's, The Home of Satisfaction." Because times were hard, he was generous with credit. "J" carried many a farmer through his entire harvest season and nothing was ever said about charges.

Once the Lewiston store was well established, he branched out and opened the Alexander-Freidenrich store in Grangeville in 1879. The Grangeville store remained in business until 1988, outlasting the Lewiston store by many years.

*　　*　　*

The city's best-known jack of all trades may have been Joseph K. Vincent who, in his 87 years, by one count mastered or practiced sixteen different occupations. At 17, he left his birthplace at Salem, Massachusetts, for a life at sea. When he learned that there were riches to be had on the gold coast of California, he left the sea and tried his hand at mining on Feather River. He volunteered for military service during the Indian wars and was one of the first soldiers to arrive at Fort Lapwai in 1862. He was serving as a deputy U.S. marshal when the territorial seal and records were spirited from Lewiston to Boise in 1863.

Released by the Army, Vincent chose what seemed the easiest way to establish himself in a new country. He and a partner opened a saloon they named the Blue Wing. There they set up the city's first ten-pin alley. Like many others in the community, Vincent fell under the spell of Alonzo Leland, a lawyer, journalist, legislator and the father of Henry Leland. Alonzo Leland, as editor of the *Portland Times*, had helped to inspire the northern Idaho gold rush, later joined the rush himself and remained ever afterward the eternal optimist. Vincent became enchanted by Leland's daughter, Elizabeth, and under her influence he began edging away from the liquor business, referring to himself not as a saloon keeper but as an auctioneer. He conducted enough sales to justify the title, and he and Elizabeth Leland were married on Christmas Day in 1865.

After attending his first City Council meeting, Vincent became interested in city government. He was named temporary marshal, the chief peace officer in the city in 1872, during the illness of Marshal Dan McElwee. His instructions were to enforce the laws, provide a place to corral loose cattle, horses and mules, and to collect taxes. Vincent managed these assignments and accepted appointment as street commissioner in 1884.

He opened an auction house and commission store in 1872 and a year later founded the city's first recreational firm, an entertainment place he called The Tank, which offered soft drinks, candy, pastries and cigars, plus games for the children and magazines and cards for their parents. Vincent bought a large tract of land in the Tammany area southeast of Lewiston where he raised livestock, grew wheat and corn and experimented with peanuts. He went into the restaurant business briefly in 1883. On December 10, 1886, at an all-night dancing party, he and Elizabeth and their children (they had ten) celebrated the completion of a large family home.

J. K. turned to hotel management in the closing years of his life. He was the owner-operator of the Cottonwood Hotel for five years and later bought the pioneer Mount Idaho Hotel, where he died in 1909. The title "Judge," by which the *Lewiston Morning Tribune* referred to him, was earned, not honorary; Vincent had served a term as Idaho County probate judge.

*   *   *

Charles A. Thatcher, another of Lewiston's earliest entrepreneurs, bought the Alta House hotel from E. C. Mayhew in May, 1864, for $1,500. The price included all the furniture, bedding, restaurant equipment and the liquor on hand. Though Thatcher & Son remained in the hotel business briefly, C. A. plunged into other deals. He was the first in line to file at the U. S. Land Office when it opened at Lewiston in 1871. He bought the old Masonic Hall and began remodeling it into sleeping rooms. He took agencies for selling anything that came his way. Listed in his advertisements in the *Signal* were corn meal, bacon, shingles, nails, cabinet organs, flour, butter, grain, lumber, books and pictures.

When the City Council called for bids to fence the cemetery, then on the site of the present Pioneer Park, Thatcher was on hand with the lowest at $363.20.

111

One day during the 1890s, the small store at 704 Main Street where Thatcher sold newspapers, magazines and reed organs caught fire, destroying most of the stock and much of the building. Thatcher priced the ruins at $40. His son, Curtis, and Curtis's friend, Fred Kling, managed to raise the money and bought what was left of the business. On sunny days the young men spread their goods out. When it rained, the stock was stacked tightly under what remained of the roof. There was nothing to lock because the place had no door. The Northern Pacific Railroad completed its line into Lewiston at about this time and the contract for delivery of express was awarded to Thatcher & Kling for $75 a month. The railroad money proved to be just enough to keep the business going. By the turn of the century, Thatcher & Kling had become the depository for all school textbooks in use at Lewiston including those of the Lewiston State Normal School. The operators were quick to stock anything new. They sold the first automobile tires in town and invested heavily in fancy wallpaper. They carried the first horned Edison phonographs and featured new recordings at well-advertised and well-attended public concerts.

When Curtis Thatcher moved to Yakima in 1919, Fred Kling bought him out and the store became simply Kling's. Kling's son, William, joined his father in the enterprise in about 1926. The elder Kling served as Lewiston postmaster from 1933 to 1943 and died shortly thereafter. William Kling bought the business from his father's estate in 1945 and 20 years later, sold it to two former employees, Frank and Dorothy Miles.

*   *   *

The Weisgerber brothers and their brewery made major business news at Lewiston at least three times. They established the first brewery in Idaho Territory in 1863. They built the first brick building in Lewiston in 1879, and they introduced manufactured ice to the parched and baking town in 1898.

The brothers were born in Germany and emigrated to

112

the United States in the 1860s. Ernest arrived first, in 1862, and founded the brewery on a site overlooking the Snake River across the street from the present Lewis-Clark Plaza. John and Christ arrived in 1869 looking for their brother, whom they had not seen for many years. The three worked the brewery together for a while and then John and Christ (sometimes called Chris and sometimes Christe,) bought the business and renamed it the California Brewery. They continued to operate the business until John's death in 1890.

The brothers used their first brick building for a saloon operated in the German style, serving lunch and old-fashioned "steam" beer. They put up several other buildings downtown including a frame structure on Main at the head of Second Street where the W. E. Pinch wholesale house is now, in 1878, and a frame building at Fifth and Main in 1885. That one was replaced by the present Weisgerber Building, for many years the home of the Owl Drug Store, in the early 1900s.

Christ began manufacturing ice in 1898 by submerging tanks of water in brine in a building on First Street. In a town where people had to collect ice from the rivers in winter and store it for summer use — and where sometimes the winters were too mild to produce any ice — that was real progress.

Christ was the father of Philip Weisgerber, who retired in 1955 after serving twenty-four years as Nez Perce County clerk and recorder.

*   *   *

Ezra Baird, a miner, businessman, lawman and politician, was working in a San Francisco bakery when he learned of the Idaho gold strikes. He left immediately for the mines, arriving in the Lewiston area in April, 1862. After four years of mining and operating a hotel at Newsome, Baird bought the express line from Lewiston to Elk City, later extending it into Florence and Warren. He married Mary Alice Odle, the daughter of James Odle, the first farmer at Mount Idaho, on October 3, 1873.

He served as a mayor of Lewiston and three terms as sheriff of Nez Perce County. He served later as U. S. marshal for Idaho and in his later life continued to invest in mining ventures.

*   *   *

Despite the success of John P. Vollmer and a few others, Lewiston in the Seventies was not a good place to become a millionaire. The panic of 1873 shook the foundations of most of the country's financial empires, and the inland Northwest shared in the economic doldrums. Yet people continued to go into business and hope for the best.

Lewiston had its wheelwright, Lott Wiggin; its wagon builder, Charles Hatter; its metal workers, the brothers C.C. and D.D. Bunnell; its blacksmiths, H. P. Maginnis, John Story, James McDonnough and J. R. Yane; its jeweler-watchmakers, I. N. Arment, C. E. Spaulding and Charles G. Kress. George Glass advertised himself as a "fashionable boot-maker" and proved the point by decorating his shop with wallpaper. There were livery stables, some offering rubber-tired rigs for romantic outings. Among the saddle shops were those of T. S. Billings, Thomas Worden and Caleb Cooper.

Lewiston had its women crafters as well. When Dora Otter first went "on her own," she was apprenticed in the dressmaking shop of Mrs. M. A. White. Her work was so good that she was permitted to do some of the top, or outside, stitching, the stitching that on a respectable dress was presumed to be perfect. Every ball gown in that period was built on a foundation of muslin, and in the typical shop it was the apprentice's job to fit and finish the muslin. When the foundation was finished and approved, the dressmaker took over, building tiers of drapery or ruffling or pleating, which fell freely to the ankles.

Often a dressmaker and a milliner worked together as a team. In the Seventies and until about the turn of the century milliners actually made the hats they sold, decorating them with straws of various kinds, feathers and felts, flowers, bows, veils, fruits, streamers, buckles and emblems.

Mrs. Alida Anderson opened the first millinery shop at Lewiston in the early Seventies. Her advertisement in the May 2, 1874, *Signal* directed customers to her shop "opposite the Catholic Church." There she carried stocks of lace, embroideries, ties, scarves and fichues as well as millinery goods. Among other women serving the social leaders of the day were Mrs. A. L. Coffey, Mrs. M. Glover, Mrs. M. A. White, Mrs. J. B. Sprenger and Mrs. C. L. Stevens. Mrs. Stevens also had the agency for Wilson's Improved Sewing Machines.

Lewiston's early stores often carried a variety of wares, from groceries to axle grease. But Richard J. Monroe was the first to designate his small business as "variety." He featured garden seeds, shrubbery and trees. Monroe's financial rating and leadership in the community stemmed from his longtime position as receiver for the Lewiston Land Office. He served under Presidents Grant, Hayes, Garfield and Benjamin Harrison and later he and his family became political leaders in the Lewiston area.

S. G. Isaman was a pioneer teacher, druggist and hotel operator. Edmund Pearcy, whose ferry crossed the Snake River a short distance south of the confluence, was also a land manager. John Silcott was a road builder as well as the region's best-known ferryman. Thomas H. Worden was a housemover as well as the operator of a harness and saddle shop. Dr. Madison A. Kelly financed a lumber mill, a grist mill and livestock herds. He and Dr. H. W. Stainton, a pioneer physician, followed the small-town tradition of serving as mayors.

At least three women influenced the business life of the community in the Seventies: Mrs. Emma Bittner, Mrs. Hank Trimble and Mrs. Charlotte Vining. Forced financially out of three hotels, one at a time, Mrs. Bittner manged to open yet another. Mrs. Trimble followed her husband as manager of the saloon he had started. Mrs. Vining opened the first ice cream parlor.

Some 20 general merchandise stores were operating in

the city at some time during the Seventies and Eighties. They included Crawford Slocum & Co., Ross Demster & Co., Yates & Lane, R. Bailey, Fitch & Co., Sanborn & Co., Robbins & Vallard, James Flanagan & Co., Grostein & Binnard, Baldwin Brothers, Loewenberg Brothers, Ankeny & Sons, Townsend & Buker, A. H. Robie, W. B. Gerger, Kaufman & Rosenthal, Fleischman's, H. H. Snow, George H. Sandy, Slater and H. Leland, Bacon & Thompson, Belcher & Church, A. Gilman, A. Damas, J. Alexander, Slater & Co. and Scott & Vollmer.

John Proctor has been credited with opening the first assay office at Lewiston in 1862, but Richard Hurley had an assay office at about the same time. In October, 1863, *The Golden Age* quoted Hurley as boasting that he had weighed $78,000 in gold dust the previous month.

The Lewiston Grocery, which began in 1872 as the Lewiston Bakery, was the city's leading food store for nearly 80 years. It was founded by a German immigrant, Conrad Wintsch, and was unrelated to a firm by the same name that operated briefly in the Sixties. Another early bakery, the California, was lost in Lewiston's first big fire in 1868. The long-lived Lewiston Bakery owed much of its success to another German, Seraphin Wildenthaler, who had a talent for knowing just what his women customers wanted to buy. Wildenthaler first visited Lewiston in 1865 after knocking about the country for most of his youth. He formed a partnership with a man named C. Baker to open a bakery, but sold out and left a short time later for Montana. He returned to Lewiston five years later and bought into the grocery-bakery owned by Conrad Wintsch.

At first the store had a bar where liquors were served but Wildenthaler, sensing new strength in the town's temperance forces, announced that the Lewiston Bakery would no longer serve intoxicants. At the same time, he bought Wintsch's share of the business. Under Wildenthaler's management, the grocery-bakery prospered. The best groceries arrived first at Wildenthaler's, everything in prime condition, and he was the first to stock such new items as green celery, grapefruit and avocados. He was a demon for cleanliness and his store fairly sparkled.

Wildenthaler was joined in the business by young Orville Norberg, a native of Pataha who had come to Lewiston to work for "Peg Leg" Texier, a double amputee who operated a fruit stand and grocery. Norberg began investing in Wildenthaler's company stock and after Wildenthaler's death in 1908, Norberg managed to acquire a controlling interest in the Lewiston Grocery. The store thereafter became noted for its personalized service. Norberg made the rounds of his regular customers every morning, starting sometimes as early as 7 o'clock. He established a city-wide delivery service which made four trips daily through the town. He had eight teams of wagons, each wagon covered by an umbrella-like roof. In the late 1920s, Norberg replaced the wagons with autos. As the years passed, the chain groceries began to dominate the food business and personalized service no longer fit the pattern. The Lewiston Grocery closed its doors in 1950.

The frontier butcher's lot was not an easy one. Since there were no packing plants, he had to shop in the country for his livestock, then had to hang the meat and cut and package it, usually amid swarms of flies. The only refrigeration was ice cut from the river shoals in winter and packed in sawdust until summer. And in Lewiston's mild winters, it often was necessary to have it packed in from other, colder places. That may help to explain why only two butchers managed to stay in business for ten years at Lewiston in the Seventies and early Eighties. They were C. P. Coburn and Dan Wardwell. Their Lewiston Market was open between 1872 and 1882, and relied heavily on specialty meats like sausage, smoked or salted products with some staying power. J. B. Rowley bought Thomas Worden's Commercial Market in 1873 but tired of it soon and closed. A man named Davey opened a meat market in 1879, and closed within the year.

E. Norton and E. L. Bonner opened the city's first fruit stand in June, 1863. Wesley Mulkey followed in

1872, showing the good yield of his new orchard east of town. Fruit crops were surprisingly large that year and there were plenty of melons, berries and grapes as well as tree fruits. M. "Peg Leg" Texier, who had frozen both feet, opened a stand in his own building in July, 1872.

The Seventies were not a good time in the restaurant business, judging by the number that opened only to close. Every respectable hotel had its dining room and Madame Melaine LaFrancois operated the best at the Hotel De France, where an excellent three or four course meal could be had for 50 to 75 cents. The weekly *Golden Age* recognized only three cafes not attached to the hotels. They were the Barnum, the Cabinet Restaurant of Joseph K. Vincent and the Mexican Orleans Restaurant.

In 1873, Andrew Roux, a Frenchman, became the first permanent barber in Lewiston. He paid $2,000, then a handsome price, for the home of the wealthy Levi Ankeny on Snake River Avenue. The *Lewiston Teller* described his shop as "second to none in the upper country." Bonner and H. Jones had operated a barber shop and bath house in the 1860s, but it was short-lived. J. A. Hoag, who arrived in 1877, and Albert Bunker, 1879, were the only other barbers of the Seventies. They gave more shaves than haircuts, and the price of a haircut remained at 25 cents until 1907.

No one doubted, in the Sixties and Seventies, that there would always be a need for a livery stable. Anyone who owned or could lease a large building could make a stab at this lucrative business. Many did and many failed because the competition was keen.

The livery stables rented fancy rigs for special events such as community dances and private balls, but their main business was serving the traveling public. Many a weary traveler thanked his lucky stars for a good livery stable where his famished and exhausted beasts could eat, drink, and then rest on a bedding of soft, warm hay. With his animals cared for, he could go about his business.

Lewiston's first livery stable was an open-sided affair operated by Thomas J. Moore. There is mention of another, the Stevens Livery and Feed Lot east of Lewiston, in an 1862 issue of *The Golden Age.* At least four livery stables, counting Moore's, were operating at Lewiston in the early Seventies. The Luna Stable, associated with the Luna House, an early hotel, and the Pioneer, founded by M. Fettis, were the most prominent. Fettis was probably the first owner of a regular livery, on the north side of what is now Main Street. S. H. Crites of east Lewiston took over when Fettis decided to enter the stage business. Next was C. C. Bunnell, a metal worker. Bunnell sold the Pioneer to J. L. Schultz and J. L. Cook in April, 1872. Later that year, Cook bought out his partner and became the sole owner. Meanwhile, J. M. Curry and N. B. Holbrook were co-owners of the Luna Stable on C Street between Third and Fourth.

To build a wheel in the Seventies required a blacksmith's tools, so it was natural for the wheelwright, Lott Wiggin, to become the city's first blacksmith. Wiggin had arrived at Lewiston in May, 1861, aboard the Colonel Wright. Unfortunately for Wiggin, his shop and tool shed were too close to Lewiston's Chinatown, which had grown up in the Seventies on the lowland near the confluence of the rivers. Fire broke out in Chinatown on November 19, 1883, leveled 14 Chinese homes and engulfed the Wiggin shop and tool shed. The loss was a crushing blow to the elderly craftsman. Overwhelmed by the difficulty of replacing his aged tools, he abandoned his forge.

Some other early blacksmiths included Charles Knapp, who operated the Imperial at Seventh and D Streets; David Johnson, E. Darr, Elmer Luce, Billy Grimm and W. C. Mallory. Later came Charles Hatter, who also was a wagon maker; H. P. McGinnis, G. W. Gill, John Story and J. W. Benjamin. J. R. Yane and J. B. Finch, who arrived in 1878, found the Lewiston field too crowded and moved on to Grangeville. Pat Barton opened one of the last shops at Lewiston, on Fourth Street just north of the office of the *Lewiston Morning Tribune*, which was then at 0213 Fourth. Bill Crosley, who succeeded Barton, closed the shop for lack of patronage in 1918. After Crosley, D. D. Hoffer continued as the city's only blacksmith until his death in February, 1947.

Dr. H. W. Stainton may have been Lewiston's first physician. Or it may have been Dr. Madison A. Kelly. Both claimed the honor and each had his partisans, but the argument was never settled. Both devoted many years to the care of the sick. Dr. Kelly once announced his retirement and sold his drug store but later returned and re-established himself. Both men held city offices and both took active parts in other community affairs. Dr. Kelly has been called the first mayor of Lewiston, but he served by appointment during a time when Lewiston was still illegally squatting on Indian land. Dr. Stainton, the fourth mayor, led the campaign to abolish the legal cloud and give the city full rights to be where it was. Among the other doctors who practiced at Lewiston in the Seventies were F. H. Simmons, I. S. McIteen, L. Terry, H. B. Sanborn, J. B. Morris, C. A. Sears and J. Q. Moxley. Although he had worked for a medical degree and had practiced for ten years in his native Ohio, Dr. Moxley was unable to prove he had completed the medical course. He was licensed to practice in Idaho Territory and Idaho state anyhow since he had healed the sick in Ohio and had practiced for six months at Mount Idaho.

Moxley had bought Kelly's home and drug store when Kelly announced his retirement, and when Kelly returned and asked for his store and practice back, Moxley refused. Sears arrived in the late Seventies. After a short time at Lewiston, he left for the mines and died there shortly afterward.

A Mrs. Burr advertised in the Eighties that she "treats electrically all diseases of women." Others practicing medicine of one kind or another in that decade were Drs. Pierre Harmony, F. S. Stirling, J. C. Anderson and F. S. Easton.

An 1863 issue of *The Golden Age* carried an ad for a jewelry store that had been opened at Lewiston by G. S.

Neu, apparently the city's first. A second jeweler, William Hyde, had his notice in the *North Idaho Radiator* in 1865. Jewelry evidently was not a hot item in the Seventies, for each jeweler seems to have had a sideline to keep bread on the table or else abandoned business for politics. Charles G. Kress served as postmaster. Joseph Perrault sold his stock and store to Alfred Damas in 1873 and became territorial auditor and controller. Other jewelers of the decade, C.E. Spaulding and J. Walker, survived only briefly.

There was no shortage of saloons, from the very first, partly because saloon keeping was a good way to raise money for other enterprises. J. B. Rowley and W. Leach gave their drinking place the initials that were then on every tongue, N.P.R.R. No one could understand why the Northern Pacific was slow in stretching its rails toward Lewiston. On the Fourth of July, 1872, managers of the N.P.R.R. saloon erected a 70-foot pole beside the building and promised a prize to the first climber. Rowley had by then sold his interest to L. A. White.

Ferd Roos and the partnership of Stonebraker and Cole both sought to use the same railroad name, the O.R. & N., for Oregon Railroad and Navigation Co., but Stonebraker and Cole were first. Roos, the king of dance fiddlers, then named his place the Palace. Mae Kettenbach recalled many years later that she and some friends once persuaded Roos to play for them, over the telephone, from his saloon. She said the music came though quite well.

There also was the Board of Trade, the State Bar, the Casino, the Challenge Saloon and Billiard Room, the Club, the Log Cabin, the Elite, the Star Saloon and Beer Garden, the Idaho Saloon, the Cabinet, the Concert Saloon, the Miners Exchange, the Oro Fino Saloon, the Senate, the Glen Ellen and the bar of the Hotel De France. There was Jimmie the Mug, the Blue Wing, the Arcade, the Magnolia, the Cactus, the Gray Eagle, the Mint and the Owl.

Encouraged by a temperance movement among some leading citizens, the City Council strove to control the activities of the liquor interests. It prohibited saloons in the residential section east of Fifth Street and it boosted license fees to $500 a year. It ruled that drinking areas must be screened from public view, and several proprietors lost their licenses because they had served women.

14

The Chinese

This item appeared in *The Golden Age* on March 12, 1864: "A meeting of miners of the Oro Fino district was held February 14 at Pierce City for the purpose of inquiring into the expendiency of introducing Chinese labor into this mining camp." An important change was about to take place in the miners' attitude toward the Chinese and other Orientals — a change prompted not by moral insight but by harsh economics.

Until 1864, no Asians were allowed to work the mines of northern Idaho. According to Article 14 of the mining laws for the Nez Perce and Salmon River country: "Chinese or Tartars are hereby prohibited from working these mines, under any and all circumstances." A revision of the mining laws of the Oro Fino district, adopted on April 14, 1861, declared: "That the resolutions as passed at a prior meeting in regard to the complete exclusion of the Chinese and Asiatic races and the South Pacific Ocean Islanders from the mines, be confirmed." In August, 1862, the laws of the Warren district stated that, "All Chinamen are prohibited from holding claims or working in this district as hired men."

By February of 1864, however, these same districts were experiencing a severe labor shortage. The easiest money had already been withdrawn from the diggings and most of the prospectors had gone south to new gold strikes in the Boise Basin. To continue to work the old claims required hard labor and many hands. Since the Indians were disinclined to tie themselves to a miner's life, the only good source of cheap labor was the pool of Chinese who had come to the U.S. to work the California mines and build the railroads. Thus the decision by the Oro Fino miners to reconsider the Chinese exclusion laws. They elected John B. Lauck president and William A. Goulder secretary of a committee of inquiry.

The committee evidently recommended that the doors be thrown open, for the Chinese began arriving at Lewiston enroute to the mines in March of the following year. The *Daily Oregonian* of Portland reported on March 1, 1865, that 15 or 20 Chinese miners had arrived at Walla Walla on their way to the Snake River and Oro Fino mines. Altogether several thousand Chinese found their way to the mines of the Oro Fino, Florence and Elk City districts and to the towns, like Lewiston, that supplied them. At first, the Chinese came to the camps as simple laborers, to work the placers for wages; later, they began buying already well-worked claims from white miners seeking richer diggings. In the towns, they opened laundries and restaurants and offered their services as domestic help.

They lived on the edges of society and were relentlessly exploited. The Second Territorial Legislature in 1864 enacted a law taxing Chinese miners $4 a month; the Legislature of 1866 raised the tax to $5 and required that no person of the Mongolian race could take gold from the mines or work or own a claim without a license. The late Henry Telcher of Grangeville told historian Alfreda Elsensohn that his father, who was the Idaho County assessor in 1882, had to collect the $5 monthly tax. Telcher recalled his father returning from Warren with two buckskin bags of gold worth about $2,000 which he said had been virtually shaken out of the clothes of the Chinese, they hated the tax so much. In May of 1882, the Lewiston City Council levied a tax of $8 a quarter on wash houses and the Chinese hand laundry operators revolted. The Chinese said they would not continue to wash white people's clothes, and several of them were jailed. The *Lewiston Teller* of June 8, 1882, quotes one of the jailed Chinese as follows: "Too much hot. No likee workee this hot weather; me stay in jail. Me have enough to eat, no pay for it. No workee all rightee. American man clothes go dirty, all rightee, me sabe." In 1888, the tax collector visited one of the Chinese at Mount Idaho and took all the money he had, after which the impoverished victim apparently committed suicide, for he was never seen again.

In 1866, the population of the Oro Fino district included an estimated 120 white men and 550 Chinese. The Chinese moved into the Elk City district in the Seventies, and by 1882 there were only eleven white men still there. The Chinese remained in the Elk City district until 1888. A group of white men had come down from Coeur d'Alene in 1887 and started jumping their claims. The Chinese appealed to the court for help, but the court ruled that aliens could not hold mining claims under federal law.

For the Chinese in America in those days there was no such thing as naturalization. They were doomed by law to alien status. Chinese immigration was virtually prohibited until the builders of the Central Pacific Railroad needed coolie labor in 1865. Even then, no Chinese could become a citizen.

So the Chinese lived in a sort of limbo in both the mining camps and the towns, in enclaves of their own. That was partly the way they wanted it but largely the way their white neighbors demanded it. Indeed, some of their white neighbors would have preferred that they not live in the towns at all — though they were welcome to work there. When fire broke out in Lewiston's Chinatown on the northwest corner of the city on November 19, 1883, some white residents urged fire fighters to let it burn. The fire was fought anyhow, mainly in order to save Lott Wiggin's blacksmith shop. The shop was destroyed, along with a Chinese temple and the homes of fourteen Chinese families.

On November 30, 1888, the Idaho County *Free Press*

noted that "A steam laundry has been started in Lewiston. The Chinese must go." On December 11, 1902, the *Free Press* declared that Grangeville ought to have a steam laundry since "at present, all washing is done by Chinamen." In its issue of August 17, 1903, the *Coeur d'Alene Miner* reported: "The grass grows thick in the only street in Pierce City, on either side of which the dilapidated houses are occupied by the Mongolians, in which they uninterruptedly indulge in the vices that have made them a curse to our country." A Moscow hotel advertised, in one of the newspapers of that period, "No Chinese employed here." At Warren, a Chinese was arrested and hanged for stealing a pair of boots from a white man's house.

The Chinese were hard-working and frugal. On the wages of a restaurant cook, a Chinese man could support himself and save enough money to travel back to China, find a bride, and return. A Chinese called Ah Bing cooked at the hotel in Mount Idaho for some 35 years during which he traveled twice to China, buying a wife each time. Alonzo Brown, who went to Elk City in 1869 to run his brother's store, recalled later that "most of our trading was with Chinamen. This was a new business for me, and at first I did not think I would like it, as they all looked alike to me and the store had been crediting them from week to week and sometimes longer. But I got along very well with them. They proved to be good customers. They lived within their means. If they did well, they spent their money liberally and when they only made a little, they lived on that little. I did not lose any money by crediting them, and I have had a better opinion of Chinamen ever since . . ."

For many years the Chinese of the region maintained an important temple, or joss house, at Lewiston. It originally was on First Street, but was moved to Sixth and C streets when the Chinese community moved in that direction. There a Chinese miner could go to learn from the gods where he should search for gold or what might be the best day for traveling. The interior was ornately decorated with lanterns, brocades and a handsomely carved altar in front of which hung a peanut oil lamp. In ancient, lacquered cans were 90 joss sticks which, when shaken in the proper way, could answer important questions. Although not much used by then, the temple was still open and being cared for in the 1940s by a Chinese called Jim Wah, who every day lit the punks and peanut oil lamp and reverently dusted the altar. The old temple was bought and torn down in the late 1950s to make room for the building now occupied by the *Lewiston Morning Tribune.*

The Chinese had a fluctuating relationship with whites, usually civil if not cordial, but occasionally violent.

The Idaho County *Free Press* at Grangeville reported on February 17, 1888, that "the Chinese celebrated the arrival of their New Year with the usual display of fireworks and feasting. White people who visited their quarters were hospitably entertained and given handsome presents." At Lewiston the Chinese celebrated their New Year by prancing a huge dragon down Main Street accompanied by the popping of fireworks and the delighted screams of white children. And when the whites of Lewiston celebrated their own New Year's eve, a well-known Chinese called Jim Ye Ott would tell the city's fortune.

On the other hand, there were the grisly murders of Chinese at Douglas Bar on the Snake River in 1885. The Chinese were doing some mining on the Oregon side near the mouth of the Imnaha River one July afternoon when eight white cowboys rode into camp and opened fire, slaughtering thirty-two men — some as they lay napping, some as they ran for cover, one as he was swimming desperately for the Idaho shore. Bodies were strewn all over the beach, and rivermen running the Snake told of more bodies floating in the water. The white men found 18 flasks of gold dust and buried them near the camp, planning to return later and retrieve the loot. They never did get them all, however; in 1902, a couple of young men prospecting in the vicinity came upon one flask containing

$700 in gold. Three men were arrested for the crime, but no one was ever convicted.

*   *   *

The most well remembered of all the Chinese in the region is probably Polly Bemis, the subject of a romantic Western legend, who died at Grangeville in 1933 at the age of 81.

The legend was that Polly (no one knows her real name) was won in a poker game when she was 18 by a Connecticut Yankee named Charley Bemis. That is probably not true, but it doesn't matter; the real story is interesting enough.

She was born in China, sold by her parents — as many Chinese girls were then — and brought to the United States, eventually winding up in the mining camp of Warren in southern Idaho County. Charley Bemis operated a saloon in Warren, and what probably happened is this: Bemis got into an argument during a poker game with Johnny Cox, who shot him in the eye, and Polly nursed him back to health after cleaning the eye with a crochet needle. Bemis married Polly and the two of them moved from Warren down to the Salmon River. For the next 30 years they lived on a ranch there, entertaining wilderness visitors and old friends from the mining days. Bemis died in 1922 — of laziness, Polly said later — and she remained on the ranch, cultivating a garden, tending her stock, and frequently putting visitors up for the night. One of those visitors described Polly as a little over four feet tall, "neat as a pin and wrinkled as a walnut . . . full of dash and charm. She rolls from side to side when she walks — the strangest kind of gait."

She was connected by a telephone line to Charles Shepp and Peter Klinkhammer, who had a ranch across the river. Shepp or Klinkhammer would call Polly every day to make sure she was all right and row over if she needed help. She fell ill in late 1933 and Shepp and Klinkhammer decided she had to be taken out. As Sister Alfreda Elsensohn describes it in *Pioneer Days in Idaho County:* "They took her on horseback over narrow and

128

winding trails to the War Eagle Mine where they had arranged to have an ambulance waiting for her . . . She died on November 3 and was buried in Grangeville, although she had expressed her wish at one time to be buried near her old home where she could hear the roar of the Salmon River.'' In 1987, her house on the river was turned into a museum and Polly's bones were reburied there.

As for the legend: Either she or Bemis presumably would have disclosed to someone during their years together how much truth there was in the poker game story — had the question been asked. Since there is no evidence that it was, it is probably safe to assume that there was no such story until after Polly died.

15

Seeds of War

To the Indians of the mountain West, the whites were a source of wonder, amusement, profit and misery. When the Nez Perces met the Lewis and Clark party on the Weippe Prairie in the fall of 1805, it was, for all but one of them, their first sight of white men. (That one was a Nez Perce woman who had seen white people while living for a time with some plains Indians.) Yet they got along well immediately. The Nez Perces provided the Corps of Discovery with food, labor and priceless advice. Captain William Clark treated some of the Indians for minor ailments and Captain Meriwether Lewis gave them medals and other presents. The captains also presented two of the chiefs with American flags, one of which the explorers found flying from a pole in front of a longhouse at Kamiah on their return to the Clearwater the following year. After they had made canoes and resumed their journey westward, groups of Indians followed them along the banks of the Clearwater or floated with them in their own canoes and buffalo-skin boats, and at one stopping place, the explorers and the Nez Perces partied together. "It was verry mery (sic)," Clark wrote in his journal, and Private Joseph Whitehouse noted that "we played the fiddle and danced a little."

The white fur trappers and missionaries who visited the area in the first half of the century also found the Nez

Perces congenial and helpful — if not always willing to be converted. Groups of Nez Perces frequently camped with Jim Bridger, William Sublette and other fur-trapping mountain men in the 1820s and 1830s and whites and Nez Perces celebrated together at the annual trappers' rendezvous. When trappers were harassed by Blackfeet following the rendezvous at Pierre's Hole in 1836, both Nez Perces and Flatheads came to their aid. Gold prospectors who followed the fur trappers into the region often used the Nez Perces as guides and many lost whites were rescued by Indians during the brutal winter of 1861-'62. As long as the visitors seemed merely to be passing through or lingering only long enough to pluck some metal from the ground, the Indians didn't mind; it was the settlers who alarmed them and even many of these were treated with forebearance.

William Craig, an early-day trapper and frequent visitor, became such a friend of the Nez Perces that they gave him a sizable donation of land on Lapwai Creek (and Craig gave his name to a nearby mountain). When Captain E. D. Pierce was trying to find his way to the mountains north of the Clearwater in the fall of 1860, it was a Nez Perce chief, Timothy, who welcomed him to his camp on the Snake River west of present-day Clarkston. And it was Timothy's daughter, Jane, who volunteered to guide the party into the Clearwater mountains.

The Rev. Henry Harmon Spalding, who had established his mission on Lapwai Creek in 1836, was there for many years and his influence was widespread among the Indians. The ones he had converted were especially friendly to the whites, who by 1861 were intruding in massive numbers into their country. And it was largely Spalding's influence that divided the tribe into two factions: the so-called treaty and non-treaty Indians. The Christian Indians, such as Lawyer, Reuben and Timothy, Spalding's converts, signed the treaties of 1855 and 1863. Among those chiefs who refused to sign the more restrictive treaty of 1863, including Joseph, Looking Glass and White Bird, most were non-Christian Indians. The villages of the treaty Indians were scattered up and down the Clearwater between Lapwai and Kamiah — except for Timothy's, on the Snake River at present-day Silcott. The winter quarters of the non-treaty Indians were more far-flung — in the Wallowa Valley, on the Salmon River and on the Snake.

The Nez Perce Tribe was a loosely-knit group of bands that took their names from the valleys where they wintered. A band might contain as many as 500 people or as few as fifty. The bands all mingled freely. They traveled to the plains together to hunt buffalo, they camped on the prairies together to gather camas roots, and they traveled down to the Columbia together to fish and to trade with other tribes. In 1860, they numbered between three and four thousand people — by far the largest as well as the most powerful and richest tribe in the region between the Cascades and the Rocky Mountains. In 1860, they also were the only independent Indians left in that region; the Yakimas, Cayuses, Spokanes, Coeur d'Alenes and others had all been subdued in the 1850s by the United States Army and corralled on reservations.

Many of the tribes had acquired horses in the 18th Century from Spanish territories in the south. The Nez Perces had become expert breeders but it is not certain, as widely believed, that they developed the spotted pony now known as the Appaloosa. They may have, but as Alvin Josephy Jr. notes, in *The Nez Perce Indians and the Opening of the Northwest,* other tribes also had spotted ponies and the Nez Perces used non-spotted horses as well as spotted ones. Horses were so frequently traded and raided among the tribes that it may be impossible to tell where the Appaloosa came from. Certainly it was prized, then as now, for its good looks, speed and endurance, and was one source of the Nez Perces' wealth. Another was the tribe's herds of cattle fattened on the bunch grass that was abundant throughout the region. These Indians roamed widely, worked hard, and lived relatively well in a rich and beautiful country.

In the Treaty of 1855, the Nez Perces ceded a small

portion of the southern edge of their domain in return for a large reservation that extended from the Palouse River on the north to south of Payette Lakes and from Alpowa Creek on the west to the crest of the Bitterroots. Within this territory they were guaranteed freedom from encroachment by whites, but the guarantee proved worthless. The Pierce party found gold in large quantities in 1860 and by early 1861, the Nez Perce reservation was teeming with prospectors who paid no heed whatever to the treaty. A city was established at Lewiston, on Indian land, in violation of the law; other towns sprang up at Pierce, Florence, Warren, Elk City. Everywhere the miners settled, with their women and children, they sent for others. No power on Earth could keep the whites off the Nez Perce reservation. As William H. Wallace, the delegate to Congress from Washington Territory, put it at the time in a speech to the House: "It is idle, Mr. Speaker, to suppose that adventurous men can be kept off land so rich in gold as this is, where men are making from one hundred to one thousand dollars a day per hand and in some instances two thousand dollars per hand. It cannot be done. Were you to legislate from now to eternity, it could not be done." *The Golden Age* of Lewiston approvingly printed a little poem in January of 1863, written by a *Golden Age* carrier:

> Get out of the way, you Nez Perces,
> Keep out of the way, I tell you.
> The Anglo-Saxon has come
> For the gold that now surrounds you.

The only thing to do, the government decided, was write a new treaty reducing the reservation to "manageable" size. That would mean taking the mining areas and the towns away from the Indians and putting all the Indians in an area between Lapwai and Kamiah that was roughly a tenth the size of the 1855 reservation.

The Nez Perces said no. But in a council at Lapwai that

went on for several days, the government's negotiators managed to get the signatures of the so-called treaty Indians, chiefly Lawyer, in return for promises of money, schools, farm tools and protection. The treaty Indians would not much be affected since almost all of them already lived within the boundaries of the proposed new reservation. The non-treaty Indians, including the Wallowa band, refused to sign and went home. The government contended that the new treaty was binding on all the bands, arguing that Lawyer and the others had signed for all. Not so, argued Old Joseph, the head of the Wallowa band; nobody could sell his land but him. The government agents, insisting that Joseph's land had been sold, offered to pay for it; Joseph refused to accept the money. Meanwhile, white settlers had discovered the lush valley of Wallowa and were pressing to get into it. The Indians began losing cattle, then finding them shot. They continued to resist peacefully even though some settlers by this time were building cabins in the upper end of the valley, planting gardens and pasturing cattle. In 1871, Old Joseph died, imploring young Joseph, his son, never to sell the Wallowas.

The new chief called upon the government to honor the band's rights under the Treaty of 1855, reminding officials that his people had never signed the later one. President Grant responded in 1873, declaring that the Wallowas were Indian country and ordering the whites to stay out. It did no good. The splendid isolation of the Wallowa band behind its mountain barriers had been breached and there was no turning back. Rumors began to circulate among the settlers that the Indians were on the verge of violence. They asked for protection and meanwhile began mobilizing their men. Seeing nothing but trouble ahead, the Interior Department told the Indian Bureau that the Nez Perces would have to be moved onto the new reservation at Lapwai. In November, 1876, a federal commission heard Joseph's argument that if his people ever owned the Wallowa Valley, they owned it still since they had never sold it. But the commission, under heavy political pressure from the governor of Oregon, among others, ruled against Joseph. It decreed that all the non-treaty Nez Perces, including Joseph's band, would have to move to the new reservation within "a reasonable time" or be moved there by force. The Indian Bureau interpreted a "reasonable time" to mean by April 1, 1877.

The Nez Perces couldn't possibly move their women and children, their horses. cattle. lodges and other equipment over the mountains and across the Snake River in winter. They asked for another conference and General O. O. Howard, the commander of the Army of the Columbia, agreed to meet with them on May 14 at Lapwai. When the non-treaty chiefs arrived there, however, Howard refused to deal with them or even to discuss the commission's ruling. Instead, when the chiefs objected, he had one of them thrown into the guardhouse. That broke the spirit of the others, who realized then that there was no point in talking or resisting; they agreed to come onto the reservation within the thirty days that Howard demanded.

Joseph and his younger brother, Ollicut, returned to the Wallowa Valley and the Nez Perces began immediately to gather their herds from the mountains, round up their horses, and begin the evacuation. Well within the thirty-day deadline, driving their cattle and horses and pulling their lodges and other possessions, the Nez Perce men, women and children — probably about 180 people — arrived on the bank of the Snake River. They got the women and children across on skin rafts pulled by swimming four-horse teams, the horses ridden by naked young men. They got some of the cattle across also, but hundreds were swept away and drowned and some were driven off by white men following the Indians out of the valley.

Once on the Idaho side of the river, and with a little more than a week left before the deadline for arrival at Lapwai, the Nez Perces crossed the Salmon River and traveled to an old traditional council ground at Lake Tolo near Grangeville and paused there to savor the last few days of freedom. Gathering there also were other non-treaty bands enroute to the reservation. Chief White Bird and his people came from their winter home on the Salmon. Chief Looking Glass, middle-aged and imperious, brought his people from the mouth of Cottonwood Creek near the present town of Stites. Toohoolhoolzote, the one who had been thrown in the guardhouse by General Howard, came from the wild lands between the Salmon and the Snake.

The people were angry but they had no intention other than to follow General Howard's orders and move peaceably onto the reservation. Then on June 13, with one day remaining, all the good intentions turned to dust.

*   *   *

Years after that, a white woman on the Salmon River, pointing out to a reporter the ranch where Larry Ott had lived, said, "I remember Larry well. He was a nice man. He killed an Indian to get that place." The Indian he had killed was the father of a young Nez Perce named Wahlitits, one of White Bird's band, who on this June 13 was racing his pony, brandishing his rifle and playing war when an old man called out to him: "If you're so brave, why don't you kill the man who killed your father?" Young Wahlitits, badly hurt, retired to his teepee in shame, and then emerged angry and defiant.

"I would have killed Ott," he shouted, "except for you old people. You have stock and horses and families. I did not want to bring you into trouble. But if you want to see war, you will see war."

The next morning, Wahlitits and two companions — they called themselves the Red Blankets because they all wore red — rode out of camp and down to the Salmon River looking for Larry Ott. Had they found him, the trouble might have ended there. But Ott was not at home, so the three killed two other white men who were known for their hostility to the Indians. During this rampage, they encountered the wife of Wahlitits and sent her back to Lake Tolo on a stolen horse to report what was happening. Joseph and Ollicut were not there; they had recrossed the river to butcher some beef. But the elders there, and the women, were horrified. They knew the soldiers would come intent on revenge, but many of the young men wanted to fight. The next day, about fifteen of them rode down to the Salmon to join the Red Blankets, and the killing spree continued. It was not indiscriminate, however; each of the victims, with the possible exception of a white woman who died when her house burned down around her, had been known as an Indian hater.

Altogether 17 white settlers were killed by avenging Nez Perces. The word of the fighting spread quickly along the river, and up the draws to the Camas Prairie, and many of the white families, fearing for their lives, abandoned their homes and fled to places like Mount Idaho, a town south of Grangeville, for protection. From Mount Idaho, storekeeper Lloyd Brown sent desperate pleas to Fort Lapwai for arms, ammunition and soldiers.

Meanwhile, Joseph and Ollicut returned to Lake Tolo, with a supply of fresh meat, to find the camp in an uproar. The anger and bitterness of many years had erupted into a war fever. After an all-night council, in which Joseph sought to calm tempers and to persuade everybody to move quietly onto the reservation, the chiefs decided to run for the wild country between the rivers and prepare to fight Howard's soldiers. Joseph cast his lot with them. The Wallowa band, along with all the other non-treaty Indians except those of Looking Glass, broke camp and trailed down White Bird Hill toward the Salmon River.

Thus began the War of 1877, sometimes called the Joseph War or the Nez Perce War.

It was not a war at all in the usual sense, and it certainly was not Joseph's war. It was a 1,700-mile retreat interrupted by occasional battles involving at the most, some 250 Nez Perce warriors, many of them old men, and at times as many as 2,000 United States troops and volunteers. The Indians had with them their women and children, a dreadful handicap in fighting a running battle. For much of the time, they had no clear strategy or destination. Howard assumed, along with most other Americans, that the warrior leader was Joseph; he was the one who had dealt most often with the government on behalf of the non-treaty Indians and the most influential of the chiefs. Joseph got the credit for brilliant maneuvering in the wilderness and became, almost overnight, a national celebrity, but Joseph was not the strategist. His role was to care for the women and children and to keep all the parts of the tribe moving together. The generalship fell mainly to Ollicut, Rainbow, Five Wounds, and later in the campaign, to Lean Elk and Looking Glass.

16

The Long Retreat

In response to settlers' pleas for protection, General Howard sent Captain David Perry with two companies of cavalry to Grangeville and Mount Idaho. On the way Perry found a looted freight wagon and other signs of violence, and at Mount Idaho he was told that Indians traveling in small groups had killed several white people. The whole Camas Prairie was in a state of shock and families were barricading themselves in their homes. While at Mount Idaho, Perry learned that the Nez Perces were camped on White Bird Hill, and he set out after them that evening with eleven volunteers from Grangeville and a group of treaty Indians.

The troopers arrived before dawn on June 17 at the brow of White Bird Hill, and Perry decided they should move immediately down the slope in order to cut the Indians off before they could cross the Salmon. At first light, the troopers started down the hill with an advance patrol of eight men leading and the two companies following in columns of fours. The Indians, camped some three miles below, had posted scouts at the top and knew the soldiers were coming. They had put the women and children a mile to the rear and had dug in behind a couple of buttes to await the cavalry. They hoped to surrender, but were prepared to fight if necessary.

The advance patrol, under the command of Lieutenant

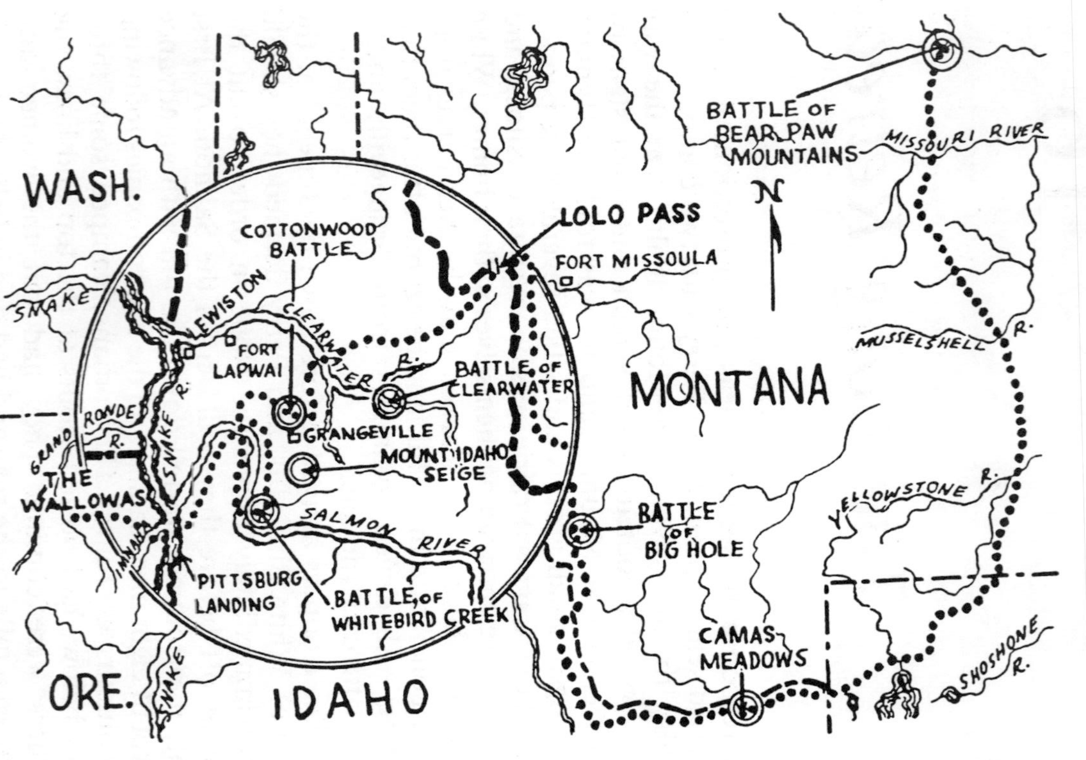

The route of the Nez Perces' retreat from Lake Tolo, near Grangeville, to the Bear Paw Mountains of Montana. (Drawn by Phyllis Budweg for the Lewiston Morning Tribune.)

Edward R. Theller, moved cautiously down the trail and halted when six Nez Perces appeared from behind one of the buttes carrying a flag of truce. Theller deployed his men and paused warily as the Indians continued to advance under the white flag. Suddenly, one of the Grangeville volunteers fired into the group of six. An Indian fired back, killing the bugler of one of the companies drawing up behind Theller, and pandemonium broke loose. Captain Perry attempted to form a battle line. He put the volunteers on a rocky knoll to his right, a company of dismounted men in the center and a mounted company on his left, but before he could get his people set a warrior named Two Moons, followed by fifteen screaming riders, galloped straight for the volunteers, firing as they came. The volunteers got off some shots then fled up a draw, leaving Perry's line exposed. Then Two Moons and his group galloped to the west and flanked Company F. Meanwhile, other warriors charged directly at the center of the line, driving the soldiers back and cutting Perry's troops to pieces. Nineteen of them sought to make a stand, with their backs to a rock wall, but were wiped out. The cavalry finally, in Two Moons' words, "turned and rode hard from that deadly mixing."

The troops fled from the field in disarray, leaving behind 34 dead, including Lieutenant Theller—fully a third of Perry's command. No Indians had been killed and only two wounded. And the Indians were able to retrieve 63 army rifles and a number of pistols from the battlefield.

Perry's defeat shocked Howard and sent new waves of panic across the region. It had been only a year since Custer's massacre at the Little Big Horn and memories of that horror were still fresh. It had been less than ten years since the tribes of eastern Washington were subdued. Settlers living between Walla Walla and Colfax began building stockades and gathering their families into safe havens. At Lewiston, a militia was quickly organized and volunteers began digging rifle pits on the bluff above Main Street in what is now Pioneer Park. The Lewiston City Council, which then included Mayor Noyes B. Holbrook, John P. Vollmer, M.W. Williams, S.P. Hutchings and Christ Weisgerber, voted to telegraph the mayor of Portland for 50 stands of rifles plus ammunition. At the same time, the Council voted to telegraph the president of the Oregon Steam Navigation Co. that "trade and commerce is threatened and we stand in need of immediate aid and protection commercially and personally." Marshal Joseph K. Vincent ordered rifle pits dug on what is now Prospect Avenue, to protect against assault from the Snake River, and in the present Pioneer Park—then the town cemetery— where the remains of one of them can still be seen.

Howard feared that the battle of White Bird might spark a general uprising among Indians of the Northwest and he sent urgent pleas for reinforcements. Before long troops began arriving from Alaska, from Oregon and California, and from the Southwest. On one occasion, the steamer Almota docked at Lewiston with 500 members of an infantry regiment from Georgia. The steamer New Tenino brought 107 infantrymen up the Snake River from Walla Walla. Howard called Colonel Alfred Sully of the 21st Infantry to Lapwai to help defend Lewiston.

Dr. J.B. Morris, a Lewiston physician, learned that there were wounded settlers at Mount Idaho without medical care, and he rode alone the 75 miles from Lewiston to treat them.

At Slate Creek, on the Salmon River below Florence, the residents built a stockade for protection. The people at Warren, a mining camp near Florence, built forts, as did those at Elk City on the South Fork of the Clearwater. The city fathers of Lewiston wired their delegate to Congress, S.S. Fenn, urging him to supply the city with government guns and ammunition.

Also at Lewiston, Captain Edward J. McConville organized a company of 60 men to protect life and property there. Then McConville led another group of volunteers up to the Camas Prairie to join General Howard in pursuit of the non-treaty Indians.

Near White Bird, meanwhile, the Nez Perces were joined by two small bands led by Five Wounds and Rainbow, who had been hunting buffalo east of the Bitterroots. Thus reinforced, they moved down to the Salmon River and crossed to the other side. The Nez Perces hoped to buy some time, assuming that Howard was in pursuit. As indeed he was.

With 227 troops, some twenty volunteers and a large string of pack animals and guides, the one-armed general set out from Fort Lapwai heading south. Reaching the Salmon, he found that the Indians had crossed ahead of him. Howard later recalled his thoughts as he sat on the river bank contemplating the enemy's position. "No general could have chosen a safer position or one that would be more likely to puzzle and obstruct a pursuing foe. If we make a direct pursuit, he can go southward toward Boise for at least thirty miles and then turn to our left. He can go straight to his rear and cross the Snake at Pittsburgh Landing. He can go on down the Salmon and cross at several places and then turn either to the left for his old haunts in the Wallowa Valley or to the right and pass our flank, threatening our line of supply while he has at the same time a wonderful natural barrier between him and us in the Salmon . . . "

Howard assumed that the enemy was Joseph and that Joseph had devised the strategy he ascribed to the Nez Perces as he sat there on the bank watching the Indians across the river watching him. But the crossing of the Salmon was probably the suggestion of Rainbow and Five Wounds, who knew the country well; and it also was the logical escape from General Howard.

Howard had no way to pursue the Indians because he couldn't cross until his boats arrived. When they did, Howard took his forces over, but by this time the Indians had disappeared into the south. After leaving Howard behind, they turned north, hustled along the west shore of the Salmon, and crossed again. The Indians were now on the north side of the Salmon and Howard was on the south side, dragging his cannon over some of the roughest country on the continent, in driving rain and with diminished forces. Before crossing the Salmon, he had sent part of his force north under Captain Stephen Whipple in response to an unsettling report. Word had come to him that Looking Glass was preparing to take his people off the reservation and join the warring bands.

The report was untrue. While Howard and his men were laboring over the steep trails south of the Salmon, Whipple led his troops into the village of Chief Looking Glass, who was sitting in his teepee eating breakfast, and began to fire. The startled Indians fled across the South Fork into some trees, followed by their outraged chief. Some attempt apparently was made to parley, but talks broke down and Whipple's troops killed an Indian woman and baby, destroyed the camp, and made off toward Cottonwood with 725 Indian horses.

The Army's position now was precarious. Howard was still south of the Salmon while the main body of hostile Indians was between him and Whipple, threatening Howard's supply line and all the communities of the Camas Prairie. To make matters worse, Howard could not recross the Salmon in pursuit of the Indians, but had to retrace his steps over rocky terrain to the place of his original crossing, where he had left his boats. As he was doing this, the Nez Perces were moving across the Camas Prairie. At one point they met a reconnoitering party of ten soldiers under the command of Lieutenant S.M. Rains and in a brief battle killed every man. They passed north of Cottonwood and dug in on the bank of the South Fork of the Clearwater at the mouth of Cottonwood creek near the present town of Stites. There they were joined by Looking Glass, who was still raging over Whipple's assault on his village.

"I tried to surrender every way I could," Looking Glass told the other chiefs. "My horses, lodges, and everything I had were taken away by the soldiers we had done so much for . . . The officer may say it was a mistake. It is a lie. He is a dog and I have been treated worse than a dog by him. I am ready for war.''

The Indians now had a fighting strength of 191 men, but they were burdened with some 450 women and children and they had no clear idea of what to do next. Howard was sure to find them. Should they stay and try to smash him here, or retreat and try to hide? Looking Glass urged that they retreat over the Lolo Trail into Montana where they could join their friends, the Crows. Joseph said he preferred not to die in Montana, ''that different place.'' Some of the others suggested withdrawing southward into the Seven Devils where it would be next to impossible to flush them out.

Looking Glass held out for Montana and union with the Crows, with whom the Nez Perces had fought against the Sioux and with whom they had many times hunted buffalo. Besides, he said, Howard would never follow them there. While the chiefs were mulling all this, Howard struck.

He had been traveling north along a high ridge east of the South Fork when one of his officers, looking back, saw Indian teepees across the river about two miles away and below. Howard turned and fired a howitzer shell into the camp and took the Indians by surprise. The Indians responded quickly. Toohoolhoolzote and 24 warriors leaped into the water, crossed the river and scaled the bluffs on the other side and there, using the rocks for cover, poured a heavy fire into Howard's position. The Indians kept the soldiers pinned down until others could get across the river and into the fight. As mounted Nez Perces appeared over the bluffs to the east, Howard found himself surrounded. He pulled his men into a tight square, with his headquarters in the center behind a pile of saddles. As night fell, the soldiers dug rifle pits in a semi-circle around Howard's post. The day had been hot, the soldiers had run out of water early, and the only spring in the area was covered by Indian fire. One of the warriors,

Peo Peo Tholekt, said later that during the night he could hear the soldiers, many of them wounded, crying from pain and thirst. In heavy fighting the next day, the soldiers gained the spring and by afternoon the Indians were retreating down a ravine under heavy artillery fire.

Joseph had left the battle and returned to the village in order to get the women and children packed and ready to move. As the warriors fought a delaying action in the ravine across the river, Joseph led the rest of the band out of the village toward Kamiah. The warriors had done their part. When they could hold the soldiers back no longer, they jumped onto their horses, forded the river and followed the main band. Howard and his troops crossed at a more leisurely pace and halted in the abandoned village. There the signs of a hasty departure were everywhere. Great caches of food lay around, fires were still burning and meals were warm.

The battle of the Clearwater was over. Howard had lost 13 troopers killed and 27 wounded. The Indians had lost four men killed and six wounded. Howard chose not to pursue the Indians and remained that night and the next day where he was. The Nez Perces, meanwhile, paused near present-day Kamiah, in sight of the Indian sub-agency, to rest. Then they crossed the Clearwater and traveled to a traditional Indian meeting ground on the Weippe Prairie and there the debate resumed as to what to do next. Looking Glass still argued that they should cross over the Bitterroots into Montana and join their friends the Crows. Looking Glass prevailed, and on July 27 the Nez Perces arrived at present-day Lolo, Montana, and entered the Bitterroot Valley.

It never occurred to the Indians, apparently, that Howard would follow them into Montana; they thought they would leave the war behind once they were out of Idaho. But Howard had learned from treaty Indians that the non-treaties would head for the Weippe Prairie once they left the Clearwater, and he was only a week behind them when they reached the Bitterroot Valley. Ahead of them was Captain Charles C. Rawn, who had come from Fort Missoula with 30 soldiers and 200 volunteers on the telegraphed instructions of General Howard. Rawn and his men were building a log barricade and preparing to stop the Indians there. But before Rawn and his men could get the barricade built, the Nez Perces arrived, in a good humor and feeling safe at last. Joseph, White Bird and Looking Glass rode into camp, dismounted, and shook hands with Captain Rawn. They told him they were passing through peaceably and would give no trouble to him or to any other white people. Rawn replied that his orders were to stop them there and he intended to do that. The civilian volunteers, finding the Indians friendly and having better things to do than linger there, departed for home. With only his thirty soldiers left, Rawn was helpless to halt the Nez Perces and they moseyed on past the place that has been known ever since as Fort Fizzle.

"No more fighting!" Yellow Wolf exulted. "We have left General Howard and his war in Idaho!" The pace was leisurely as the Nez Perces moved down the Bitterroot Valley. General Howard by now was far behind. But the Nez Perces didn't know that Colonel John Gibbon was at that very time hurrying over the divide with 163 troopers from Fort Benton, Fort Shaw and Fort Ellis plus 35 civilian volunteers. The Indians made camp on August 7 on the shore of the North Fork of the Big Hole River. They put up thirty teepees along the bank of this narrow stream and put their horses out to graze. Feeling secure, they didn't bother to post sentries that evening but cooked supper, watched the children playing in the river, and at dark rolled into their blankets and slept.

Shortly before dawn, the camp was awakened by a rifle shot followed by a fusillade of bullets that poured into the tents killing men, women and children in their blankets. Colonel Gibbon had arrived during the night and posted his dismounted troops in the woods across the stream. The first shot had been fired at an Indian crossing the river to check on the horses and then the battle of the

Big Hole had exploded in a rain of death.

Warriors dashed out of their teepees, firing, as women and children fled into the willows behind the camp. Wahlitits and his wife, both armed, threw themselves down behind a log and began firing at the troops. Both were killed. Five Wounds ran from his tent with a bow and sailed arrows into the line of soldiers until he was cut down. Casualties were heavy on both sides as the battle raged. Gibbon's troops had not expected so withering a defense and many of them were now as startled as were the Indians. Gibbon had taken a bullet in the thigh and was out of action. Finally the soldiers fell back and took a defensive position behind a knoll, where they were pinned down by Nez Perce sharpshooters. In the afternoon, with Gibbon's troops no longer threatening, some of the Nez Perce men returned to the village and began burying their wives and children, and the women who had been huddling in the willows emerged and set to work digging shallow graves for the fallen warriors. Joseph and White Bird directed the packing of the camp and the Indians moved out, leaving Ollicut and some others behind to guard their withdrawal.

For the past week, Howard had been racing hard from the north and on the night of August 8 he arrived at the Big Hole—too late to help Gibbon but in time to chase the Nez Perce rear guard off. The Indians withdrew slowly and in two days caught up with the main band. The Nez Perces had lost about 20 fighting men, including some of their best warriors, and some 60 old men, women and children had been killed or wounded. Gibbon had lost 29 men killed and 40 wounded.

The disillusioned Nez Perces, realizing now that they had not left the war in Idaho after all, told Looking Glass they could no longer accept his leadership. Rainbow and Five Wounds, however, were both dead and Ollicut was not familiar with the country. So they turned to a well-known warrior and buffalo hunter named Lean Elk (and known to the whites as Poker Joe) and asked him to lead the band through Yellowstone Park to the Crow country in northern Montana. Lean Elk had been hunting in the region and had joined the band when it entered the Bitterroot Valley. With Lean Elk leading, the Indians moved south, crossed the Lemhi Pass into Idaho and traveled east on the Idaho side toward Yellowstone. Gibbon was out of the war now but Howard was still behind them and hoping to cut them off as they crossed the Continental Divide at Targhee Pass. His hopes were dashed one dark night when a force of 28 Indians led by Ollicut rode quietly back to Howard's camp and ran off his pack string. While the general scoured the settlements for more animals, the Indians passed through Targhee Pass and into the five-year-old Yellowstone National Park.

The passage through the park was a curious one. The Indians ran across a lone prospector named John Shively, captured him, and took him along as a guide. Shively traveled with the Indians for a week and apparently got along well with them for he ignored several opportunities to escape. He reported later that the Indians by this time were armed with repeating rifles and that they were carrying a dozen wounded with them. They encountered several groups of tourists in the park and forced them to travel with them so that they could not report their whereabouts to Howard or his scouts. Several of the men tried to escape or turned out to be spies and two of them were killed. At one point, just for fun, the Indians commandeered a stage coach from which the frightened occupants had fled and drove it at the rear of the band for several hours.

At the eastern end of the park the Nez Perces found themselves pursued by cavalry coming from various directions and managed, by sheer desperation and superior knowledge of the terrain, to avoid several traps. There was a fight at Canyon Creek where a force under Colonel Samuel Sturgis overtook them. The warriors held off the troops with heavy and accurate rifle fire while the rest of the band ducked into a narrow, deep canyon. Then the whole band escaped through the canyon ahead of

Sturgis.

By early September the Nez Perces were in the land of their friends the Crows, but the Crows were now working for the Army and the Nez Perces had to fight them off as they made their way to the Missouri River. They crossed the Missouri as the weather turned cold and pushed on toward the Bear Paw Mountains of northern Montana. Thirty miles south of the Canadian border they paused to rest, confident they had left the soldiers far behind. In a couple of days they would move north into Canada and find safety with another refugee, Sitting Bull.

The pause proved to be fatal. Colonel Nelson Miles, with a force of some 600 men, was coming toward them from the east and General Howard was in hot pursuit from the south. On the morning of September 30, as the Indians were gathering their horses for the last few miles of their retreat, one of them heard frenzied shouting from the teepees. "Turning, I saw everybody in confusion," Black Eagle said later. "I heard a rumbling like stampeding buffalo to the south and I saw troops galloping toward us."

Miles had arrived first and ordered an immediate cavalry charge against the Indians, who were camped in a shallow basin. The Indians responded quickly, and the first line of troops ran into a withering fire which saved the camp for the moment. Although outnumbered, the Nez Perces had the advantage of terrain and the battle dragged on. According to the account of Captain Henry Romeyn, commander of Company G of the 5th Infantry:

"It was desired to deploy Company G by the right flank and the bugler was ordered to sound the deployment. 'I can't blow, Sir, I'm shot,' said the brave fellow, who was on the ground with a broken spine. By 3 p.m. it was evident the attack must become a seige." Desultory firing continued through the day from both sides. That night the temperature dropped and by morning the ground was covered by snow. As Joseph recalled later: "We could have escaped if we had left our wounded, old women and children behind. But we were unwilling to leave them. We had never heard of a wounded Indian recovering while in the hands of white men.'' On the first day of battle the band had lost 22 fighting men including Lean Elk, Toohoolhoolzote and Ollicut.

On the afternoon of October 1, Miles, eager to win the surrender before Howard should arrive, asked to meet with Joseph. A white flag was raised and Joseph walked to Miles' camp, where he was seized and imprisoned. The Nez Perces in return seized one of Miles' lieutenants and the prisoners were exchanged. Joseph returned to his own camp and the fighting continued until dark. The next day an Army pack train arrived with a 12-pound cannon but Miles found that the barrel couldn't be depressed enough to fire into the basin. The troopers managed to make a sort of mortar out of it by sinking the tail in a hole in the ground, aiming high and using a very low charge of powder. In this way they were able to lob shells into the basin, and in late afternoon Joseph raised a white flag. He offered to abandon the position to Miles if he was allowed to ride out with the women and children. Miles refused, Joseph returned to his camp, and the battle resumed. On October 3, Looking Glass was killed together with a woman and a child. On October 4, Howard arrived and on October 5, Howard sent a messenger to Joseph asking if he wished to surrender.

Joseph mounted a horse and with a rifle over one arm rode up to General Howard, dismounted and handed the general his rifle. To the interpreter (since Joseph did not speak English) he said, ''Tell General Howard I know his heart. What he told me before, I have in my heart. I am tired of fighting. Our chiefs are killed. Looking Glass is dead. The old men are all dead. It is the young men who say yes and no. He who led the young men is dead. It is cold and we have no blankets. The little children are freezing to death. My people, some of them, have run away to the hills and have no blankets, no food. No one knows where they are—perhaps freezing to death. I want to have time to look for my children and see how many I can find. Maybe I shall find them among the dead. Hear me, my chiefs. I am tired. My heart is sick and sad. From where the sun now stands, I will fight no more forever."

Both Miles and Howard had promised Joseph that if he surrendered they would see that the band got back to Idaho, but that was not to be. William Tecumseh Sherman, now the general of the Army, insisted that the non-treaty Nez Perces must never return to the Northwest. They were sent to a swampland in Oklahoma, where many died from malaria and the unaccustomed heat. At Miles' request, some remnants of the band, including Joseph, finally were settled on the Colville reservation at Nespelem in Washington, and died there. A few who had escaped from the Bear Paw battlefield and got to Canada eventually straggled back to Lapwai. The treaty Nez Perces wanted nothing to do with them and they ended their lives as did the others, in a sort of limbo, belonging nowhere.

In 1957, the late Jack Wilkins, a *Lewiston Morning Tribune* reporter, ended a series of articles on the war with these words:

"Those were days of glory for the Nez Perces as the previous year had been for the Sioux and the Cheyennes. In the ensuing decade, the Army was to have skirmishes like the Ute and Sheep Eater wars, but in 1877 for the last time painted war ponies flashed over the hills of America and the exultation of battle flushed the riders. They are silhouetted still, in the proud memories of the Nez Perces, in the history books that white children read . . . a memory and a symbol of the mystery of the passing of time."

On August 11, 1877, Alonzo Leland wrote in the *Teller*: "The two best months of the year for mining have been lost to the mining camps, save to the Chinese and a few others who remained and worked their claims, and as a consequence, the gold yield will be comparatively light the present year. But if Joseph has gone to Montana with all his warriors, we can say with much propriety, 'good riddance.' "

17

Jawbone Flat

The place the settlers called Jawbone Flat, which was to become Vineland and the village of Concord, later renamed Clarkston, for many years was simply barren land that had to be crossed to get to someplace else. The Indians spurned it. They made their camps in more likely places such as the mouth of the Alpowa Creek, where Timothy had his band, or the mouth of Asotin Creek, the winter camp of old Chief Looking Glass. The first settlers considered it a wasteland of sand and jackrabbits; they preferred the higher country to the south and west where there was grass for livestock, timber for building, and enough moisture to grow grain. They called it Jawbone Flat, some say, because its terrain gave it a shape that resembled the biblical jawbone of an ass. Another story has it that one winter when the snow was unusually deep, stockmen in the uplands drove their cattle down to the confluence of the rivers. But it was a bad winter there, too, and when spring came there were so many dead cattle on the ground that some riders were muttering ''jawbones, jawbones,'' and calling it Jawbone Flat.

One homesteader who was able to make a living there, and quite a good one, was Edward Pearcy. He operated a ferry that crossed the Snake River to Lewiston. But for many the Flat was a losing proposition and most of those who had taken up homesteads there either left for higher ground or hung on in hopes of someday selling out.

The region at that time was still a part of Walla Walla County, as was the rest of eastern Washington. Columbia County, including the present Asotin, Garfield and Columbia Counties, was separated from Walla Walla County in 1875 and Garfield County, then including the present Asotin County, was separated from Columbia County in 1881. The residents of the region between the Snake and Grand Ronde Rivers began almost immediately to campaign for a county of their own—largely because they hated the long drive to the county seat at Pomeroy. Leaders of the movement, including Theon Welch, founder of the town of Theon, traveled ceaselessly throughout the region getting signatures on a separation petition, and Jackson O'Keefe took the petition to Olympia. The Territorial Legislature was agreeable, and Governor W.A. Newell signed the bill creating the territory's southeasternmost county on October 27, 1883.

The first Asotin County Commissioners, appointed by the Legislature, were J.D. Swain, John A. Weissenfels and William Critchfield. Their first task, and not an enviable one, was to select a county seat. It was to be the temporary seat, but everyone recognized that "temporary" has a way of becoming "permanent," and so the bidding was brisk. The prime competition was between the towns of Asotin and Assotin City, which were about a half mile apart in the Asotin Valley. Alexander Sumpter, who had platted the town of Assotin City, offered the county the free use of his store building plus free fuel, free lights, a safe, desk and tables. T.M.E. Schank, who had platted the town of Asotin, offered his new four-room dwelling, among other blandishments. Since Schank's house lay midway between the two towns, the Commissioners decided that it would make a good compromise. Schank won the bid. The two communities eventually became one, sharing the name Asotin.

A year later, when it came time to name a permanent county seat, the town of Anatone and the now-extinct towns of Theon and Silcott put in bids. The towns of Asotin and Assotin City, by now united in the cause, had little trouble winning the election. There were so few people living at the time on Jawbone Flat that it was not in the running. The first county courthouse was completed in July, 1899, at a cost of $3,975. It burned in 1936, under circumstances that strongly suggested arson, and was replaced by the present courthouse, a remodeled former hotel building, at a cost of $20,642.

.   In 1916, the young city of Clarkston made the first of several attempts to snatch the county seat from Asotin. The vote favored Clarkston but fell short of the necessary 60 percent. Clarkston tried again in 1936, after the first courthouse had burned, and lost by eight votes. In 1946, a group of Clarkston advocates launched still another attempt, arguing that the county seat should be where most of the people were. Asotin countered that the taxpayers already had a courthouse building there and to build another one in Clarkston would be foolish. The economy argument won, and Asotin remains the county seat.

In 1887, a well-known railroad engineer named C.C. Van Arsdol—who was later to engineer the route of the spiral highway on Lewiston Hill—visited the valley and found himself imagining what the Flat would look like with irrigation. He was kept occupied by other projects, however, and did not return to Lewiston until his employer, the Northern Pacific Railroad, went into receivership in the depression of 1893. After a couple of unsuccessful attempts to get financing for an irrigation system, Van Arsdol found the key in another newcomer to the region, E.H. Libby.

Libby, a member of a wealthy Boston family with excellent connections, had been advised by his doctor to go West for his health. In the Yakima Valley, he had seen irrigation at work and, impressed, he had studied several possible tracts in Washington and Idaho to develop and sell. These included Jawbone Flat, and he and Van Arsdol joined forces. They both were acquainted with Charles Francis Adams, a wealthy railroad man who owned a ranch opposite Lewiston on the Clearwater River and had been thinking of running a railroad through the area. Libby approached Adams and persuaded him to join the development team. Thus Adams became the financier, Libby the promoter and Van Arsdol the engineer of the triumvirate that watered the desert of Jawbone Flat.

Their plan was to bring water from Asotin Creek through a big ditch connected by wooden aqueducts. It was an ambitious scheme that involved blasting through much rock and tunneling through a portion of the so-called Swallows Nest—a huge cliff rising up from the bank of the Snake River south of present Clarkston. It took less than six months for laborers to build the 14 miles of flumes and open ditch that brought water from Asotin Creek, about nine miles up from its mouth, to what is now Clarkston.

Van Arsdol moved his family onto the Flat in 1896 and that year his son, Maurice, became the first white child born there. His home, which adjoined an old settler's cabin, was later placed on the National Register of Historic Places.

By 1899, the twenty-five homes on the Flat were being served by water from this ditch both for irrigation and for drinking. At each house, the water for drinking was diverted from the ditch through a sand filter into a concrete cistern.

The original development company was reorganized several times over the years and the open ditch was replaced by a closed wooden pipe, located much higher along the canyon wall, which increased the flow and capacity of the system.

The town was platted in 1899, the year the first interstate bridge was built, and by 1900 Clarkston was a thriving little city with a hardware store, a livery stable, lumber yard, grocery stores, drug store, a bakery, a saloon, a hotel and a newspaper, the *Vinelander*. Orchards were planted in the unincorporated area south and west of town known as Vineland in the late Nineties, and in 1903 two companies shipped 200,000 boxes of fruit.

The former Jawbone Flat could still be dusty in a hot summer and the sprinkler wagon was an every day sight as it drove through the streets, spraying delighted children on the way. People said the horses knew the route so well that G.B. Kidwell could sleep most of the time under the umbrella that shaded the wagon seat.

18

The Green Years

Lewiston baked in the summer sun of the Sixties, surrounded by bald hills and treeless except for the scrub willows that grew along the river banks. But by 1870, the little city's residents had planted the poplar trees for which the town became famous. The first, on western Main Street, were stretching their arms toward the sky and shaking their leaves in a fluttering green welcome. A well, drilled especially to water these trees, was creating a demand for irrigation water to support other greenery as well. And other pressures were building.

A bad livery stable fire prompted a group of volunteers to organize the first company of fire fighters. The volunteers soon lost interest and abandoned their buckets, at least partly because of the futility of fighting fires by dipping water out of shallow wells. At about the same time, certain events at Walla Walla convinced the people of Lewiston that they could no longer get by without a flour mill. And they couldn't operate a mill without a controlled flow of water.

Until the winter of 1871-'72, the mills of Walla Walla had faithfully supplied the homemakers of Lewiston with flour for bread. The city and the mining camps it supplied by this time were using some 15,000 barrels a year. At $5 a barrel, that meant that $75,000 a year was flowing from Lewiston to Walla Walla for flour alone—despite the fact that Lewiston was virtually surrounded by wheat fields. The merchants apparently didn't mind for they were buying at wholesale and selling at retail and making a tidy profit. But for reasons not clear today, the supply of Walla Walla flour somehow fell short in 1871 and '72 and there was talk again about a grist mill at Lewiston and a water ditch to run it. There was much discussion of the kind of ditch that was needed and how much power it might provide. The men argued vigorously about that. The women talked longingly of water for flower gardens and lawns. How much would a flour mill cost? some people asked, and Editor Leland of the *Signal* answered that Lewiston could build two flour mills with the money paid out to the freighters who hauled the flour from Walla Walla.

On a sizzling August 24 in 1872, as Lewiston lay drowsing in the heat, a bank of dust appeared across the river and from it emerged five teams, each pulling a wagon and trailer toward the ferry. It was a shipment of flour from Walla Walla, greeted at Lewiston with great relief. "There will be no flour shortage this year as there was a year ago," Editor Leland wrote in the *Signal*. "Shipments are continuing in, and a new grist mill will go into operation on Camas Prairie." The Camas Prairie grist mill had been set up as a lumber mill a few years earlier by Dr. Madison A. Kelly, Lewiston's first mayor. Noting that the people needed flour even more than they needed lumber, Dr. Kelly had ordered heavy milling equipment brought in.

At Lewiston, the flour shortage was over, at least for the moment, and talk of the ditch and the grist mill subsided. But in the fall of 1873, the millers of Walla Walla turned the key that unlocked the door to Lewiston's independence. They agreed that they would raise the price of flour to $6.50 a barrel.

A group of Lewiston businessmen responded by forming the Lewiston Water Ditch and Milling Co. and arranging for the sale of 400 shares at $10 each. Those in a position to know insisted that the ditch could be built for

$4,000, and if there were additional costs, assessments could be made. "The construction of this ditch and the erection of a flouring mill will infuse new life into both merchant and farmer," Leland wrote in the *Signal* of November 15, 1873. But the beginning of the ditch did not end the arguments about it. Indeed, they continued more heatedly and led eventually to lawsuits.

Wesley Mulkey, a man of action, force and imagination, and a prominent fruit grower, won the first construction contract. E.B. True did the survey, and work began on a project that would change the face of pioneer Lewiston. The plan for the four-and-a-half mile ditch called for the water to be admitted at a point about four miles up the Clearwater River east of Lewiston. From there the ditch would cross the eastern end of the city—then well outside the city limits—in a southwesterly direction until it reached the eastern part of the bluff that edged the city on the south. From there it was to follow the curve at the base of the bluff and enter downtown Lewiston at the foot of the present Fifth Street Grade. From there, the water would move underground below the sidewalk on the south side of Montgomery Street, later to become Main. It would end in a short waterfall into the Snake River near the present eastern end of the Interstate Bridge. Where it passed through the business district, the ditch was to be covered with heavy planking.

The contractor told the *Signal* in late November that work on the ditch and the grist mill was "progressing finely" with a construction crew that numbered 78 men, 65 of them Chinese. But from the start, the ditch was plagued with difficulties of every kind. During the digging there were frequent cave-ins. Walls had to be repeatedly straightened, widening the ditch and increasing the work. Troubles mounted once the water began to flow. There were leaks and flooding. Repairs sometimes cut off the water even on the hottest summer days. Garbage and other refuse often choked the flow.

The newspapers of the time were peppered with

Lewiston in the Eighties and Nineties was known as the City of Poplars. This is a view of Main Street at about Ninth, looking east, at that time a residential area. (*Lewiston Morning Tribune*.)

Polly Bemis, perhaps the best remembered of all the region's Chinese residents. (*Nez Perce County Historical Society, R.G. Bailey collection.*)

The Raymond House, on the northeast corner of Fifth and Main, in summer 1905. The site is now a parking lot. (*Lewiston Morning Tribune*.)

The Hotel De France, at Second and C Streets, in about 1915. The view is to the southeast, with the Normal Hill bluff in the far background. (*Lewiston Morning Tribune*.)

A quiet summer afternoon at Lewiston in the 1880s. In the foreground is the gully that would later become the Fifth Street Grade, leading to the intersection of Fifth and Main Streets. (*Lewiston Morning Tribune*.)

Joseph Alexander, who established long-lived department stores at Lewiston and Grangeville. (*Lewiston Morning Tribune*.)

Main Street in 1891, looking east from between Third and Fourth Streets. (*Lewiston Morning Tribune*.)

The main street of Clarkston in 1915, looking south. The brick building, as this is written, is occupied by Boyer's Clarkston Furniture Co. (*Nez Perce County Historical Society, Betty Rudfelt collection.*)

The irrigation flume that carried water to Clarkston from Asotin Creek is shown where it tunneled through the Swallows Nest. (*Nez Perce County Historical Society, Henry Fair-Dole collection.*)

The first interstate bridge can barely be seen in this photo taken in about 1900 looking north past the confluence. At the left is Concord, later to become the city of Clarkston. (*Nez Perce County Historical Society.*)

These Nez Perces were photographed at a council at Lapwai in May of 1877, at which they asked for more time to move onto the reservation. General O.O. Howard refused their request, and war broke out shortly thereafter. (*Nez Perce County Historical Society*,)

Receding waters of the Great Flood of 1894, when the Clearwater, full of spring runoff, overflowed its banks and covered much of downtown Lewiston. This was Fourth and Main streets, looking east. (*Lewiston Morning Tribune*.)

Fifth and Main streets, looking west, in January, 1930. (*Nez Perce County Historical Society, Gray-Dole collection*.)

Downtown Lewiston looking north from the bluff in 1890. The building at far left, under the arrow, is the Raymond House. (*Lewiston Morning Tribune.*)

The hardware store of C.C. Bunnell on Main Street near the present Young Women's Christian Association building, probably 1882. (*Lewiston Morning Tribune.*)

complaints about the condition of the waterway. "The stench which arises from some portions of the covered ditch that runs through the town is very offensive. There must be dead carcasses or other putrid matter lodged along its margin." And this: "The plank covering the ditch needs repairing. A sober young man fell through it the other night and got a severe wetting." And on another occasion: "Tuesday morning the Lewiston ditch broke and the water entered the shed of Grostein and Binnard and damaged wheat and flax stored there." From the *Lewiston Teller* of August 6, 1886: "The street sprinkler was greatly missed during last week while the ditch was being repaired. Water was turned into the ditch again on Monday." In the same issue is a notice over the signature of Benjamin Booth: "I have finished the cleaning and repairing of the ditch and all persons are hereby forbidden to throw or dump any offal, filth or garbage of any kind into said ditch . . . I am determined that the water in this ditch will be kept fresh and pure for those desiring to use same." There is still another notice signed by Benjamin Booth in the *Teller* for June 13, 1889: "Notice is hereby given to all persons living on the line of the Lewiston water ditch to refrain from throwing anything into or cutting wires for the purpose of letting stock of any kind into said ditch. Some of the things thrown in are wash boilers, iron pots, oil cans, fruit cans, vegetable cuttings of all kinds, dead hens, dead cats, and dogs. The water of this ditch is expected to be clean and fit for human use so far down as where the saloons commence. I am aware of a number of families using it above this point. This is my last call before the hammer falls."

The ditch seemed to create more problems than it solved, yet it transformed the dusty little city into an oasis of gardens, flowers and lawns edged with picket fences, with here and there a splashing water wheel. In summers, towering poplars shaded it.

The open ditch was abandoned in 1902 when the city bought its own water system, and over the years the traces of it have gradually disappeared.

Meanwhile, the grist mill that was the reason for it all began grinding out flour in April, 1874. It was the first of four flour mills that served Lewiston in the years that followed.

*   *   *

The ditch is remembered now for having given Lewiston—a nondescript village on a hot, dry river flat—the means to prettify itself. Because of the ditch, the Seventies and Eighties have been called the green era, a time when tall poplars shaded the dusty main street and lawns and gardens flourished behind neat picket fences. The villagers had begun planting Lombardy poplars in the late 1860s and eventually almost every street was lined by these sky-climbing trees with their fluttering leaves. According to an account in Elliott's *History of Idaho Territory*, Lewiston looked from a distance like an oasis in the desert. It's not certain how these trees came to be planted, but an explanation given by Charles G. Kress, a pioneer jeweler, may be as good as any.

It seems Lewiston was headed for an unusually hot summer in 1867. By May, the sun was beating mercilessly down on the hot dust of the streets. People stayed at home and commerce died in the heat. A group of storekeepers gathered under a partial awning at the combined drug and variety store of R.J. Monroe at First and Montgomery. Monroe sighed and wished aloud for a shade tree. One of the group doubted that a tree would grow on a Lewiston street. Another thought it might not hurt to find out. He passed a hat around town and collected $210, the estimated cost of sinking a well that would irrigate a few trees.

Wesley Mulkey, who later was to build the Lewiston ditch, donated three trees from his grove east of town. According to Kress, "The trees seemed inspired with a due sense of the importance of their mission." The first three lived, the idea spread, and soon poplars appeared all over the place. To ease the burden of drawing and carrying water, some householders devised a shortcut. They used empty five-gallon kerosene cans carefully washed and punched full of holes. They sank each can in the ground near a tree and simply filled the cans when they became empty. For some fifty years the trees were the pride of the city; a Lewiston ordinance made it a misdemeanor to mutilate one of them.

Oldtimers believed that the trees had health-giving qualities, and in this they had the backing of certain pseudo-medical authorities of the time. William R. Smith, superintendent of the Botanical Gardens in Washington, D.C., gave it as his opinion that the poplars prevented malaria by "absorbing the miasma." The town not only put up happily each fall with a sea of leaves, it bore with good grace the broken windows that resulted whenever a high wind sent poplar branches flying through the air.

Business expansion west of Fifth Street, together with cracking sidewalks and bulging pavement, eventually doomed the poplars in that part of town. For every tree that was taken out a newspaper item would include an apology and an explanation to pacify the mourners. "One of the oldest poplar trees in the city was taken out from in front of the C.C. Bunnell hardware store last Friday," the *Lewiston Teller* announced sadly in 1888. "It was taking up too much room on the sidewalk. Other trees along Main Street must be cut down soon for the same reason." By the 1890s, the poplars' ranks were thinning in the business district although their lines remained unbroken on East Main. For many years one lone giant stood at the corner of Third and D Streets, in front of the Bollinger Hotel, a last green sentinel against the sky. Fears of a destructive windstorm finally drove the owners to cut down the old veteran, but they refused to make a complete sacrifice. A ten-foot stump was left as a monument to the past. The *Lewiston Morning Tribune* of May 10, 1922, commenting on the amputation, reported: "The tree measured three feet across and was planted more than fifty years ago by pioneer Warren P. Hunt." Because the stump continued to live and grow, bulging the sidewalk, it, too, was later cut out but the circular opening where it grew remained in the sidewalk for many years.

For survivability in difficult circumstances, the townsfolk could hardly have picked a better tree than the poplar. A story is told of a freight wagon driver who cut a poplar switch for a whip in a hundred-mile run. After reaching his destination, he pushed the branch into a sand bank. On his next trip through, the freighter was surprised to find it had sprouted branches and leaves and was firmly rooted.

The last of the city's poplars to come down, in 1923, stood at Eighteenth and Main Streets, once a country crossroads.

Even before the poplars grew tall, the householders of Lewiston struggled, sometimes successfully, sometimes not, to coax a little beauty from the dirt. Mrs. Levi Ankeny, who had lived previously in Portland, planted portulacas in the sand of her dooryard on Snake River Avenue. Nothing happened. But the next spring she prevailed upon her husband to have a well dug, and by summer her place was ablaze with flowers. As Genevieve Bonner, a Lewiston pioneer, wrote later, "Those fortunate ones who had wells upon their places could indulge their love for flowers as ardently as their arms were strong enough to pump the water to sprinkle the plants, or just as long as the faithful Chinaman could be induced to work." Among the favorites were petunias, verbena, portulaca, abutilon, amaryllis, fuschias, begonias and calla lilies.

After the ditch was dug along the bluff, the adjacent householders installed water wheels to lift the water onto their lots and irrigation suddenly was relatively easy. Thus the homes along the south side of East Main—that is, roughly from Seventh Street eastward—soon were surrounded by profusions of perennials including peonies, canterbury bells, roses and flags, as well as some hardy annuals. Climbing roses and honeysuckle graced the porches and the chicken yard fences. At the back of each yard, bordering the ditch, were berry bushes and in the front, between the house and the picket fence, was likely to be a well with a community dipper and an apple tree shading a hammock. There would be baskets of flowers hanging on the porch and still more plants in the bay window.

Genevieve Bonner recalled that one of the women had a century plant in a tub on rollers. "She tenderly rolled it in and out of the sun, nursing it like a baby, for fifteen years, and then one night it inconsiderately froze to death . . . I remember being taken to see a night-blooming cereus, the loveliest thing that had ever happened in Lewiston, and all of the school children were allowed to stay up that night long enough to see the wonder of the town."

19

Golden Harvests

The Egyptians are said to have planted wheat by throwing the seed directly into the mud left by the flooding waters of the Nile, then running cattle over it in order to trample the seed into the ground. The Marmaduke Jeffreys family, early settlers in the Peola area about 30 miles west of Lewiston, did much the same as the Egyptians. After scattering the wheat seed over their first small field, they looked about for a way to trample it in. They noticed large burrs growing on a hedge near the house and they saw that the branches were heavy and that the burrs pointed in many directions. To the Jeffreys, it seemed like a message from Heaven. Marmaduke Jeffreys, the father, cut off the burr branches and let his horse pull them back and forth over the field, with Marmaduke Junior, then a lad of 15, helping. Later, Marmaduke the elder, who had been a blacksmith "back in the states," set up a forge, and using metal from wagon wheels, built a harrow which all the neighboring homesteaders were happy to borrow.

Tiffany Floch, the son of Ben Floch, a pioneer of Asotin County, recalled hearing his elders tell how they used the branches of a wild plum tree to force the wheat seed into the ground. Virgil Flock (who changed the spelling of his name to match the spelling on a paycheck and never changed it back) was 100 years old in 1984 and still remembered the first wheat harvests of his youth. His father, Ben Floch, and three of his father's brothers went into the field at daybreak, each carrying a heavy scythe—the old-fashioned kind with the long wooden handle and the curved blade. He remembered the rhythmical swish, swish, swish of the swinging scythes continuing until dark as his father and his uncles cut the wheat. Younger men followed the reapers, gathering and binding the stalks into sheaves which they stacked in upright groups called shocks, for drying and threshing.

The trick then was to coax the wheat kernels out of the heads. The Egyptians would have done it by spreading the stalks on hard ground and driving cattle over them to knock the kernels loose. The American homesteader would spread the stalks on a wooden floor, or hard-packed earth, and beat them with a wooden flail. The beating resulted in a crushed mixture of straw, chaff and grain, but only the fine wheat grains remained whole. Then everybody waited for a good, brisk breeze. When it came, the harvesters threw the mixture of straw, chaff and grain into the air and let the wind carry off everything but the grain, which fell at their feet. The ancient Egyptians would have recognized the wheat harvest of 1865 in the Lewiston country, so little had it changed over the years.

More modern methods were a long time coming to the frontier homesteads of the inland Northwest. While the scythes were swishing through the wheat fields of Peola and the Palouse, many eastern farmers already were cutting wheat with machines. Rufus Hall McCormick sold his first seven reapers in 1843 and by 1845 some 50 of McCormick's reapers were cutting grain in the eastern U.S. But even in the fields above the Snake, the reaper did in time replace the scythe and the steam thresher replaced the threshing floor and flail.

For many of the homesteaders, wheat was not the crop of choice. They planned to grow corn, as they had in the Midwest, where warm nights encourage quick growth. The cooler nights of the Lewiston country made for disappointing harvests and the farmers rather quickly switched to wheat. It proved the ideal choice for the region's soil and climate, but it required more land than corn. A wheat farmer couldn't make money on 160 acres. The homesteads had to be enlarged and gradually they were, frequently through the purchase of pre-emptions from the Land Office at $2.50 an acre. The federal government also was offering homesteaders an additional 160 acres in timber claims, but timber was not attractive to farmers who already had worked themselves weary clearing their land of trees. Neighbors sometimes enlarged their farms by buying each other out; it was a hard life, and not every homesteading family found itself suited to it.

By the mid-1880s, mechanical methods of harvest were transforming the agriculture of the Lewiston region. Not only was the horse-drawn reaper cutting the wheat and binding the sheaves on the typical large farm; bundle wagons were carrying the sheaves to a big stationary thresher, powered by horses walking in a circle, which shook out the grain. Skilled specialists of the art sacked the grain and sewed the sacks closed, their hands moving almost faster than the eye could see. Then drivers hauled the sacked grain to warehouses along the Snake River to await shipment by steamboat to markets on the coast. To harvest the wheat on a large farm might take as many as forty horses and their drivers, producing huge threshing crews that moved from farm to farm.

When the steam engine replaced the ever-circling horses in powering the thresher, a new and romantic era began. Ask an old-timer what he best remembers about harvesting wheat near the turn of the century and he is likely to close his eyes and see once again the huge, iron engine, belching smoke and steam, its fire box glowing, its long belt carrying the power to the thresher; and hear again the flap-flap-flap of the belt snapping above the stubble. One of these 20-ton engines, moved laboriously from field to field, could serve a whole farming area. It was easy to fall in love with these huffing, puffing giants and one who did was Chris Busch, who tended a steam thresher as a boy growing up on a farm near Colton. Busch understood the benefits of the combination reaper-thresher, which would replace the steam engine, but he hated to see the old machines go. Many were sold for scrap but some were simply discarded and left to rust, and Busch began collecting these and putting them in working order. Over the years he gathered quite a few and eventually he devoted part of his farm to a sort of steam engine zoo, where he put the extinct behemoths on display. He discovered that his love for steam was shared by others, and in 1947 he held the first of a series of old-time threshing bees where other "steam fiends," as he called them, could relive the old days.

A combination reaper-thresher was developed in California in the 1860s, and the first combine, as it came to be called, appeared in the Lewiston region in the Eighties. It meant the end of the steam thresher and the beginning of the spectacular 32-horse teams that pulled the

Harvesting grain the old-fashioned way, on the Palouse near the turn of the century.

combines over the rolling hills of the region. The teams were carefully organized and trained. The fastest and smartest horses were placed in lead positions in which they were coached to turn the others. Thus the driver, using only two reins from his high seat on the combine, directed the team by directing the two lead horses. The teams were so large that in rolling country some of the horses might be out of sight of the driver. Working horses, like working men, often shirk when they can, leaving more of the work to others. When the teams were small, the driver could easily remind the shirker of his duty with the end of a whip. But with 32 horses pulling, that was not possible. That is why the typical combine driver kept a box of rocks handy and from time to time threw one at a lazy horse.

As tractors became better, farmers began to realize that their horses were costing too much. They began selling horses and buying tractors, and by 1915 or so, the 32-horse teams were on the way out. By 1930, there wasn't one left.

Farmers on Union Flat in Whitman County were among the first in the region to introduce farm machinery. Reese Reynolds and Wert Willoughby bought an early reaper, called a "dropper," whose only service was cutting; the raking and binding was left to the men. Wiley B. Hatley became the first owner of a self-propelled combine in 1887. George Ausman and Ben Floch were the first in Asotin County to use a self-propelled combine. K.L. Brown, a farmer whose first interest was machinery, built his own self-propelled combine in 1911 and used it to harvest the field of his friend, Dewey Scheibe, a teacher who was later to become the Asotin County school superintendent.

Three generations of the wheat-growing Prince family in Whitman County each harvested with different equipment as improvements were made. Henry A. Prince reaped with a header and threshed with the help of a steam engine in 1906. His son, Burdette Prince, used a tractor-powered combine to harvest the same fields in 1940.

Burdette's sons, Eugene and Hubert Prince, harvested with modern, self-propelled combines beginning in 1950.

Muriel and John Williams were the first combine owners on Fix Ridge. They waited until 1927 for a combine small enough to be pulled by 27 horses. By 1951, all the farmers on Fix Ridge had joined in the ownership of the area's one self-propelled combine.

The rolling hills of the Palouse Prairie threatened to block the use of the combine there until engineers developed a leveling device that could hold the machine in line with any slope.

*   *   *

"The threshing machine has made its rounds," reported the *Idaho Signal* on October 19, 1872, "and the farmers now have their grain in salable form." Well, not quite. Warehouses, in which to store grain prior to shipment, were few and small and space was frequently unavailable. There were no agricultural firms in the region and no grain buyers. There was not even a grist mill nearer than a small one at Colfax; a larger mill, on the Camas Prairie, was not yet ready to produce. The only decent market was the mining camps and in that October they were preparing to close for the season. It had not been an easy harvest, either. Primitive methods and equipment made the task laborious, and there was no pool of farm labor in the region; farmers had to draft their wives and children. Yet new settlers arrived nearly every week through the summers of 1872 and 1873, marveling at the huge crops they saw. Everywhere more land was being cleared and plowed and seed was in great demand.

When two-week-old newspapers arrived from the East, merchants and settlers searched them eagerly, hoping to read that the railroad was coming. Instead, they found business floundering in the national panic of 1873. Their transportation troubles, as it turned out, were just beginning.

If the two or three stern-wheelers then operating on the Snake River at Lewiston had been able to operate without interruption, they might have carried off a good fraction of those early crops. But the danger of grounding kept them docked during low water in summer, and during late spring floods, debris in the river made navigation hazardous. During the coldest winter months, boatmen had to contend with ice floes and possible freezing. Even though the crops weren't large by the standards of a later time, the steamboats fell ever further behind in their effort to carry the grain to market.

What was needed was a railroad. Henry Villard, the president of the Northern Pacific Railroad Co., advertised that his company would pay 45 cents a bushel for wheat, considered a good price at the time, and hold it in storage until the railroad came to carry it away. The growers would get their money then. The price was right, but Villard was unable to promise exactly when the railroad would reach Lewiston. He managed to convey the impression that it would be "next year," even though railroad engineers had not yet surveyed a feasible route. Meanwhile more fields were cleared and planted and more sacked wheat was heading into Lewiston for storage.

Villard ordered warehouses built at Juliaetta, Moscow, Vollmer, Kendrick, Lewiston and Asotin, but there was no sign of railroad tracks.

Still dependent on river boats, the growers continued to move their grain from the uplands where it grew to the banks of the Snake River where the docks were. For farmers on the plateau high above the valley, the drop was precipitous. Yet they managed somehow to get their wagon loads of sacked wheat down the steep canyon trails. Most of the drivers carried large logs which they dragged behind them down the steepest slopes as extra brakes. Some added special metal brakes that locked the wheels. Thus locked, the wagons practically coasted through rock-strewn dust. In harvest season, daytime temperatures were sometimes over a hundred, and blinding clouds increased both the misery and the danger.

There had to be a better way, and Major Sewell Truax

found one. An engineer and former commander of the Army post at Fort Lapwai, Truax decided in 1879 to harness gravity. He built a tramway consisting of an all-wooden pipeline on his land on the southern side of the Snake west of Lewiston. It led 3,200 feet from his wheat fields on the plateau down to within 1,700 feet of the boat docks. He poured the wheat in at the top and it flowed through the pipeline to the bottom. The system moved the grain rapidly but it damaged it in the process; the wheat was crushed and scorched by the high-speed friction and the pipeline itself was damaged. The idea of gravity flow caught on, however, and before long metal chutes were appearing along the canyon. Farmers found various ways to slow the destructive fall. Crossbars inserted at intervals in the pipeline could slow or stop the plunge.

An even better arrangement was a series of buckets on an endless cable that was looped from the headhouse on the top, then down to the river warehouse and return. The cable ran over pulleys supported by towers built into the cliffs and speed was controlled by heavy brakes. Each bucket carried a sack of wheat and each had an automatic trip that unloaded the sack at the bottom. There were two of these bucket tramways, one at a bend of the river north of Wawawai and one at Kelley Bar, about 20 miles west of Lewiston. These two tramways shot wheat down over the cliffs for more than 80 years.

The best remembered is probably the Mayview tramway between Granite Point and Wawawai, built in 1891 and closed in 1942. Its large buckets, or cars, could hold several sacks each. Each sack of grain was dropped into a chute at the top of the tramway and caught by a man standing in the chute who tossed it into a car. One of these men, John L. Morrison, could load 3,700 sacks a day, each sack weighing 130 to 140 pounds. The tramway's drop was so steep that the people at the upper end could not see the lower end, and a system of signals had to be devised. An operator at the bottom raised a flag on a tall post to signal the operator at the top when an empty car was on the way up. Since the tram couldn't move the grain as fast as it arrived from the fields, the operators laid out a series of short tracks back of the headhouse on which the grain sacks were packed on cars that later would move them to the chute. Fred Matthies, who owned the tramway for 20 years, later recalled that as many as 40,000 sacks might be waiting on the siding, as it were. "It really kept us hopping to handle all the grain before the sun ruined the strength of the gunny sacks," Mattheis said. "Sometimes it rained on the wheat but very little damage resulted because the wind blew so hard out on that bluff that the grain was dry almost before the rain had stopped falling."

The Mayview tramway, which carried sacked wheat from the Palouse Prairie to a landing on the Snake River.

The heavy cars descending put such a load on the brakes that the braking power had to be doubled after an accident in the first year of operation killed two people.

Tramways continued to serve the growers on the high plateaus after the coming of the railroad. The *History of North Idaho*, published in 1903, mentions a tramway on the Clearwater between Kamiah and Greer as being "one of the principal progressive movements of the year" of 1902. "The cable used is an endless coil of steel wires 13,200 feet long, suspended on rollers and carrying a thousand steel cages or buckets." A tramway was built in 1903 from Summit to the railroad in Agatha, also on the Clearwater. And the Kooskia Farmers Independent Tramway Company boasted that its tram "will be the first directly to serve the great Camas Prairie country. It will have a daily carrying capacity of 150 tons." In January, 1904, the farmers on Big Bear Ridge began asking for a tramway from the ridge into Kendrick but by this time the demand for tramways was decreasing on the Clearwater. When the farmers near Stites began talking of a tram, one of them changed the subject to roads. He said one tenth of the cost of a tram would build a "first class macadamized road" from Stites up Cottonwood Creek.

Henry Villard's railroad didn't reach Lewiston until 1898, when the NP came snaking from Juliaetta down the Clearwater. The bulk of the grain from the region was moved by rails until 1975, when a series of locks and dams made the lower Snake navigable for barges. Since then most of the wheat has once again been going down the river.

*　　*　　*

The harvesting crew of the 1860s may have been only a handful of family members. Nowadays it is again. It takes only two or three skilled people to make a crew. A strange quiet prevails. The excitement and confusion of 30 or more men and perhaps twice as many horses is only a memory of the "good old days." For more than 60 years, harvest was the main event of the year on every wheat farm of the West. When the fields began to turn gold, working men carrying bedrolls began to appear along the country roads looking for work and a good meal ticket.

Dora Otter Fleener of Moscow, in her book *Palouse Country Yesteryears*, has described the ritual of harvest at the ranch home of her parents, John and Myrtle Otter. When the alarm jangled at 3 or 3:30 a.m., the cook and her helpers arose from their beds in a pup tent near the cookhouse. They made their way in semi-darkness to the kitchen, lit a kerosene lamp, and soon had breakfast on the stove or in the oven. At the shout of "Roll out," the workers crawled from under the straw stack where they had been sleeping in their blankets, wagon wheel style, with their heads sticking out. On the Otter ranch there was always plenty of soap and cold water for washing off yesterday's grime. The morning meal usually included "a heaping milkpanful of beefsteaks, fried spuds, bacon and eggs, cooked cereal, probably oatmeal, with fresh cream; hot biscuits with butter, honey and jam—and last, doughnuts with lots of hot coffee."

It was no ordinary kitchen. This cookhouse was on wheels so that it could follow the harvesters about the ranch. Though there might be violent protests when the cookhouse was moved during baking hours, it had to be moved even so, usually with somebody holding the oven door shut. Equipment hung on hooks and storage was in a long box whose lid served as a seat for the diners. Breakfast was only the beginning of a cookhouse day. Besides two more "squares," at least three batches of bread had to be baked and cookies and coffee made ready for mid-morning and mid-afternoon "quartering time." Pies, cakes, fruits and cookies had to be off the stove early. Space on top was needed to keep potatoes, gravy, coffee and vegetables hot.

The cook had a flunky, or roustabout, who brought in the milk morning and evening, setting the large containers in the coldest water he could find. He kept chopped wood in the box and water in the barrel. Every day was wash day. Hand towels, tea towels, scrub brushes and hot pads all had to be washed every day. Because there were no home bleaches, everything had to be boiled, and that also on top of the stove. A five-gallon oil can, with one side cut out was the boiler. Since harvesting continued until dusk, supper had to be served late, sometimes after dark. And after supper the women scrambled to get everything ready for the morning rush.

For many years the thresher operator or "machine man" was the top hand on the crew, going about his business with an oil cup in one hand. In second place were the sack sewers. There would be two on a large crew as well as a "jig." It was the duty of the jig to fill the sacks with wheat from the spout, then pass them carefully to the sewers. As a three-man team they tried to find a sheltered spot so they could work out of the dust but that was often impossible. Each sack sewer zipped across the top of the bag, catching the ears on each side without a lost motion. A fast man could sew closed as many as a thousand sacks a day and his pay, in 1908, was around three dollars a day. Young men paying off mortgages sought jobs as bundle carriers for they could then count on pay for their horses and rigs as well as for themselves. The bundle carriers hauled the stalks to the thresher where, if it was a straw burner, two men would be feeding straw into the firebox, taking fifteen-minute turns.

Some of those steam engines could gulp four thousand gallons of water a day, and the crew had to include a "tankee" or "water buck" to satisfy that burning thirst.

The changes came gradually, but somewhere between the scythe and the self-propelled combine the man-hours needed to transform an acre of planting to wheat fell from eighty-three to two. Every wheat farm still has its annual harvest, and though it may be as exciting economically as ever, it is a pale and quiet contrast to the noise, confusion and human drama of the harvests of years ago.

20

A Bounty of Fruit

The late Miss Phoebe Bloom Taylor, when she was well into her nineties, still recalled vividly a three-day trip her family made to Lewiston from the Taylor farm near Pullman in the 1880s. The Taylors had driven some 35 miles to town to buy apples because their own land was too high for fruit.

The Taylors left before dawn and were well on their way when the first rays of the sun came slanting across the Palouse. When they reached the top of the Uniontown Grade, Judith Taylor put on a bold front lest the child Phoebe discover how frightened she was at the thought of the long descent. The child's father, Benjamin Franklin Taylor, got down and stood near the heads of the horses to allay their terror at the scene below. Once down the hill, there was the ferry, and neither the child nor the horses had been on a ferry before. Sometime after dark the family reached Lewiston, found a cabin for the night, and the next day bought red apples by the box and piled them in the wagon. After some shopping and another night in the cabin, the three arose in the dark and Phoebe was carried, still in her nightie, to the wagon and onto the ferry. There in the dim light of a lantern, as the boat crossed slowly to the north shore, Phoebe's mother helped her get dressed and told her how wonderful it was going to be to have apples to eat all winter.

And it was. Fruit was highly prized by the early settlers of the Lewiston country because there was so little of it. Once the trees that had been planted in the river bottoms began producing, families living in the uplands, like the Taylors, thought nothing of taking three days out of their busy lives to buy apples.

When Judith Taylor got her apples home, she had to guard against spoilage. The few that seemed ripest she set aside for eating fresh. She laid some others by for pies. But most of them she washed, cored, peeled and cut into uniform pieces for drying. She strung the pieces together and hung them up around the fireplace, and she rearranged the strings occasionally so that all the apples dried at the same rate. Some other farm wives used shelving, frames, boards and even wood spikes to help with the drying. Once they were dried, Mrs. Taylor stored them carefully away in a cool place to be used in the months ahead.

The river flat east of Lewiston was planted to fruit in the 1860s and the first, and perhaps the best, of the orchards was the 15-acre tract originally known as the Mulkey and Martin Orchard. Wesley Mulkey and his wife, Mary, had lived among orchardists in the Willamette Valley for eighteen years before moving to Lewiston in 1862. Their homestead lay near the Clearwater River with all of Lindsay Creek available for irrigation. Because the Mulkeys had trouble finding good nursery stock, Mary Mulkey planted hundreds of trees from seed. She watched and watered them carefully and most of the varieties flourished. The early orchardists weren't troubled by worms and insects because they hadn't been growing fruit long enough yet to attract them. People came from as far as a hundred miles away to sample and buy the fruits of the Mulkey orchard. In 1872, when his orchard was ten years old, Mulkey opened a fruit stand in Lewiston and the next year he expanded it into a grocery store. In 1874, he added a blacksmith shop with a regular smithy in charge.

It was Wesley Mulkey whose energy and foresight

were most responsible for the construction of the Lewiston ditch, the man-made canal that carried water from the Clearwater River through the backside of Lewiston and into the Snake. The ditch helped turn the dusty, sun-baked little town into a veritable oasis, but it almost buried Mulkey in community battles and endless litigation. Mulkey was in charge of construction, and through a torrent of problems he fought for his ditch with all his energy, his money and finally his credit. The Mulkeys were forced to sell their home and their livelihood, and in 1887 they gave up and moved back to their native Kansas.

The Mulkeys were only the first of many attracted to East Lewiston by the rich soil, the water and the long growing season. Gardens and orchards blossomed there, some under the guiding hands of immigrants from Italy. They began to be nudged out after the turn of the century when the area became the site of the Northwest Livestock Show, and their displacement was completed in 1927 with the purchase of the land for a lumber mill.

The region's fruit basket moved downriver, to the flats along the Snake between Lewiston and Wawawai. Orchards thrived on the lowlands interspersed along ninety miles of river bank. The almost continuous steep hills above the stream blocked the extreme winter cold of the highlands and the moderating effect of the water lessened the danger of biting cold at blossom time. As in East Lewiston, the first orchards got there before the insects did, if not by much.

Alexander Canutt of Penawawa, some 48 miles downstream from Lewiston, was the first among the river families to begin marketing fruit in a big way. He studied box making and learned how to pick the time when the fruit was ripe enough to sell and still firm enough to ship. Other orchardists along the river began following Canutt's example. Before long they were sending for help, and ranch crews grew larger and larger. Year-around crews handled the sprayings, the irrigation, the fertilizing, cultivating, pruning and thinning, and seasonal workers came to do the picking, packing, box making and hauling. The forty-hour week was standard but workers often put in sixty-hour weeks when picking and packing perishable fruits like peaches, plums and apricots. The workers on a typical downriver fruit ranch lived in rows of weatherbeaten, unpainted board shanties furnished with box bed frames and ticking designed to be filled with hay or straw. Each dwelling had a small stove with an oven, wall-mounted boxes for cupboards, single-bulb electric lights (after electricity became available), and running water. The tenants got this shelter free but furnished their own bedding and cooking and dining equipment.

Summer work opened in late June with cherries, the most difficult crop because they could be easily damaged by rain at the wrong time. Then came apricots, followed by early peaches and summer apples, then plums and prunes. After that came later peaches and pears and, finally, winter apples.

The work was hard and the days were long, but people found time during the summer for picnics, swimming parties, wiener and marshmallow roasts and rowboat excursions to pleasant groves. There was much singing by moonlight, since people had to make their own music, and on many a summer evening the cliffs echoed with laughter and two-part harmony. There was a dance every Saturday night at the Wawawai Hall, and summer romances bloomed. Many of the pickers still remember those summers in the fruit as the happiest of their lives.

Wawawai, with its 168 acres of orchards, was the largest of the Snake River fruit ranches. It had a good boat dock, so it became the packing and shipping point of many nearby orchards.

Besides Wawawai, there were large orchards at Truax, at Bishop and Penawawa on the north shore and at Alpowa, Kelley and Offield or Lakin on the south. Wawawai, which once had been platted as a town, had its own post office from 1885 to 1967 and was served by a cable ferry from 1895 to 1959. The owner discontinued the ferry then, saying that new federal regulations would prevent him from making a profit.

The cherry fruit fly, which invaded the region in the 1940s, ended cherries as a commercial crop, but the downriver fruit ranches continued to produce apricots, peaches, apples and pears until the mid-1970s, when the orchards were covered by the waters of Lower Granite Reservoir. After that, the Clarkston Flat became the most heavily fruited of the riverside orchards.

Clarkston had originally been platted to include orchard tracts, and by 1899 the orchards, mostly cherries, extended through western Clarkston from the Swallows Nest on the south to Bridge Street on the north. The first boxed Bing cherries were brought in for shipment in June, 1905, and in the following year Clarkston shipped the first carload of Bings in the United States. The Bing, a large, dark, firm and juicy cherry, became an immediately popular sensation and a commercial success. Cherries from those first trees, which were larger and firmer than later plantings, won twelve first prizes at the Alaska-Yukon-Pacific Exhibition at Seattle in 1909 and won awards at fairs wherever they were shown. In later years, the Clarkston orchards became better known for their production of tons of brining cherries, the small, bright Maraschinos used to garnish desserts and cocktails. The cherry fruit fly helped to end the cherry harvest and so did "progress." As the town developed, the trees came out to make room for houses, and Clarkston ceased to be a significant producer of fruit.

Much the same thing happened in the Lewiston Orchards, a large bench above and south of the city whose rich soil proved ideal for orchards and truck gardens. The large tracts were subdivided into building lots and by 1989 only a few commercial orchards and truck gardens were left.

*　　*　　*

There was a moment when the Lewiston country almost became a leading producer of fine wines. It had the climate, the soil, and the devoted energies of three remarkable men who gave Lewiston wines a reputation for excellence. They were Louis Delsol, Jacob Schaefer and Robert Schleicher.

Delsol was born in France, came to the United States in 1860 and arrived in Lewiston in 1866 on his way to the gold mines of the Salmon River. He evidently made some money at mining, for when he returned to Lewiston in 1870 he was able to buy 335 acres of land in east Lewiston, most of which is now occupied by the Potlatch Corp. and the switching yards of the Camas Prairie Railroad. Here he put in a two-acre vineyard stocked with varietal grape plants imported from California. He built a winery, and before the Seventies were out he was selling the first locally grown wines in Lewiston.

Schleicher, also a Frenchman, arrived in Lewiston in 1872, got a job as clerk at the Hotel De France, and in 1883 bought land four miles east of Lewiston on the south shore of the Clearwater River. He planted his first grapes shortly thereafter. He established a winery on the place and, along with Delsol, was selling wines to restaurants and individuals by the early 1890s. Schleicher was of a scientific bent, and experimented in his vineyard with some forty varieties of wine grapes. In 1906, he wrote that the wines produced on the Clearwater could match the quality of any grown in California, Europe or Asia, and invited anyone who doubted that to come see for himself.

Schaefer was born in Germany and learned wine making on his father's farm. He arrived at Lewiston in 1896 and in 1903 bought 160 acres near Lenore, on the north side of the Clearwater, plus twenty acres at Vineland, adjacent to present day Clarkston. He was unable to establish a winery at his Clearwater vineyard because the Interior Department forbade the manufacture of alcoholic beverages on the Indian reservation, so Schaefer built his winery instead on the Vineland property. By 1906, he too was producing reputable wines in commercial quantities from classic European grapes.

Schaefer, Schleicher and Delsol, together, were supplying wines for the whole Lewiston region and within a few years their wineries had become well known and respected throughout the Pacific Northwest. Schleicher, because of his writings and his numerous gold medals, attracted visitors from as far away as California and the wine-growing regions of the East.

Another who saw a future in wine grapes was H.L. Powers, who launched the development of Lewiston Orchards in 1900 largely as a grape-growing area. When Powers looked at the dry plain south of town, he saw row upon row of flourishing grape vines producing red and white varieties for a winery that he would build nearby. But first there had to be water on the land, and an irrigation system was born in Powers' mind along with the vineyards. He organized the Sweetwater Irrigation Co., and the Lewiston Land & Water Co. was formed to buy land and water rights for development. The water would come from the Craig Mountains some fifteen miles to the south by diversions from Sweetwater, Webb and Mission creeks. Powers' plan was to irrigate some 9,000 acres.

Looming on the horizon, however, was the dark threat of prohibition. A national temperance movement was gaining force, and in 1908 the Idaho Legislature passed a local option law permitting counties to vote themselves dry if they chose. Every two years for the next eight, the people of Nez Perce County fought over the legalization of alcohol, the drys on one side and the wets on the other. The battles divided families, destroyed friendships, set neighbors against one another and created a general mayhem every other year. The Lewiston First Ward, the area downtown west of Fifth Street, was the main battleground, and it became known as the "Bloody First." The drys and the wets won two each of the first four elections and the wets won the fifth and last, in 1916. The late Thomas J. Campbell, a *Lewiston Morning Tribune* reporter for many years, covered those elections. He recalled, many years later, that in 1916, when the drys won, "Dr. Susan Bruce, later the city health officer and opposed to prohibition, appeared on Main Street carrying an umbrella. Its covering had been removed, leaving only the handle and ribs. She was beseiged with inquiries. 'Why,' explained Dr. Bruce, 'it's going to be dry for two years. So why any protection against moisture?' "

It would be dry for longer than that. Two years later, before the county had a chance to vote again, the Volstead Act went into effect and the whole nation was dry. By then it no longer mattered to Delsol, Schleicher and Schaefer. The back-and-forth seesawing between legal and illegal alcohol had already badly damaged the wine industry in Nez Perce County. In 1911, Schaefer sold his vineyards on the Clearwater and at Vineland to a Portland vintner, J. E. Moore, who said he planned to market 30,000 gallons that fall. But the die was cast, and the Lewiston country's promising wine industry was as good as dead even before national prohibition formally wiped it out.

Powers' dream went a-glimmering too. In the ten years after 1906, when the Sweetwater Canal was completed, only 6,000 of the 9,000 acres had been sold and planted, and only 4,500 had been irrigated. The Lewiston Land & Water Co. was unable to sell enough land to sustain the project and in 1916 it went into receivership. Two years later, the Sweetwater Irrigation Co. also failed and it was reorganized by a holding company which put it into operation as the Lewiston Valley Water Co. By now, with the country in the grip of prohibition, there was no point in planting wine grapes. Instead, the Lewiston Orchards soon became covered with fruit trees and truck gardens on large tracts divided by narrow dirt roads. The Lewiston Orchards Irrigation District, largely financed by the Bureau of Reclamation, succeeding the water company, and in the Thirties, developers began dividing the tracts into building lots. What H.L. Powers saw as a sea of grape vines on country acres became instead a residential section of the city of Lewiston.

The house that Delsol built in the French provincial style still stands at this writing in a small, shady enclave surrounded by the grime and bustle of industry. It is, without much doubt, the oldest occupied dwelling in Lewiston. The land on which Schleicher planted his prize-winning vineyard is the ranch home of Bert and Gloria Teats. Schaefer's Vineyard winery has become a private home on the northwest corner of 22nd Avenue and Schaefer Drive in Clarkston.

21

Churches and Schools

The members of the first Territorial Legislature must have been more than a little shocked at the way the frontier capital of Lewiston honored the Sabbath. They put up with the saloons, the dance halls and other hilarious amusements for a few weeks and then, on January 23, 1864, they passed the Lord's Day Act.

It provided that "No person shall keep open any play house or theatre, race ground, cock pit or play any game of chance for gain or engage in any noisy amusements on the first day of the week, commonly called Lord's Day." Violators were to be fined not less than $30 or more than $250. The act was unenforceable, of course, and there is no record of anyone being convicted of violating it. As W.J. McConnell, an early-day Idaho governor, pointed out many years later: "To have attempted to enforce a Sunday rest law at that period of our territorial history would have resulted in vacancies in some of the offices."

This raw and boisterous mining town was much too preoccupied by other things to spend much time in prayer and contemplation. There was no regular house of worship at Lewiston until 1867, when the Rev. Joseph Cataldo built the first Catholic church. Some Presbyterians were holding meetings by this time but the first Protestant church, the Universalist, didn't go up until 1869. The Rev. J.D. McConkey, who arrived at Lewiston in 1881 as the first resident pastor of the Episcopal Church, had this to say about the town in a letter written in 1885:

"Here will be found a free and easy people. They are perfectly indifferent in the matter of religion and religious teaching. If there be preaching or religious teaching, well and good. They will not seek it but when it comes they will not directly oppose it. They regard religion as a good thing in its place but not indispensable, for they live by the theory that they can subsist without it, although when they come to die or be buried they cannot do without its consolation . . ."

Still, the first of the preachers—the circuit riders— were more than welcome in many of the homes of the region. They brought not only religion but news of other settlements, and they were much sought after for weddings, funerals and christenings. But the preachers who are remembered still are those who came and stayed and strove mightily to bring the gospel to the frontier. These included Henry Spalding, Joseph Cataldo, Daniel Tuttle, S.E. Stearns, Marcus Whitman, Father DeSmet and the McBeth sisters, Susan and Kate.

A Belgian priest, Pierre Jean DeSmet, arrived in the Bitterroot Valley in 1840 and preached there among both the Flatheads and the Nez Perces. He soon crossed over the mountains into what is now northern Idaho and within a few years had established a mission at the present town of Tensed, baptized large numbers of Indians and caused great consternation among the region's Protestant missionaries. The Rev. Henry Harmon Spalding and his wife, Eliza, had established their Presbyterian mission on the Clearwater at the mouth of Lapwai Creek in 1836. Another Presbyterian couple, the Rev. Marcus Whitman and his wife, Narcissa, had built a mission near Fort Walla Walla at about the same time. Spalding, Whitman and Asa Smith, another protestant missionary of the period, kept one another informed of the progress of the "black robes," as the Indians called the priests. The priests told the Indians to beware of the Protestants and the Protestants protested that the priests were bringing "popery" to the Northwest. As for the Indians, they never did understand why the Christian sects could not get along. The Catholic missionaries had some advantage because it was their practice to baptize the Indians first and then instruct them in the faith; the Protestants gave the instruction first and baptized only those they deemed ready for it. One sweep through the region by a "black robe" might produce a lot of converts, and it upset Spalding whenever he saw a Nez Perce carrying beads or a cross.

But Spalding had other troubles as well. He caused much resentment among the Nez Perces by forcing them, sometimes with a whip, to labor in the construction of mission buildings. It was his aim to teach the Indians to live more like white people, and that was bound to cause frictions. Yet despite his sometimes harsh measures, Spalding inspired intense loyalty and devotion among many Nez Perces, and his strong Presbyterian influence is evident among them today. He ministered not only to the Indians but was a frequent visitor to Lewiston, where he officiated at weddings and funerals and occasionally preached. The Whitmans' mission was short-lived. In 1847, with the Indians of the Walla Walla country becoming more and more fearful of white intrusion into their lands, a measles epidemic broke out, killing roughly half the Cayuse tribe. When the Indians saw that no white people were dying, they assumed the whites had poisoned them, and that apparently was one reason why the Whitmans were massacred along with their aides and their guests. This so frightened the Spaldings, who had also been targeted, that they left Lapwai to live and work on the coast. They were back at Lapwai in the early Seventies, however, but by 1873, Henry Spalding had become feeble and ill. It was at this point that Susan McBeth, a frail little dynamo of a woman, arrived at Lapwai to carry on his work.

She had been a missionary among the Choctaws of the Indian Territory and in hospitals of the Civil War before arriving at Lapwai to teach in the government Indian school. (The school was part of a package the government promised the tribe in negotiating the Treaty of 1855, and the government had turned its operation over to the Presbyterian Church.) Susan McBeth taught there for a year. In 1874, upon the death of Henry Spalding, she moved to Kamiah to continue his work of Christianizing the Nez Perces there. General O.O. Howard, the one-armed "Christian general" who fought the Nez Perces in the War of 1877, visited Miss McBeth at Kamiah and later described her this way:

"In a small house of two or three rooms, I found Miss McBeth living by herself. She is such an invalid from partial paralysis that she cannot walk from house to house, so I was sure to find her at home. The candle gave us a dim light so that I could scarcely make out how she looked as she gave me her hand and welcomed me to Kamiah. The next time I saw her was by daylight, which showed me a pale, intellectual face above a slight frame . . . Her work seems simple. Just like the Master's in some respects. She gathers her disciples about her, a few at a time, and having herself learned their language . . . she instructs them and makes them teachers. There is the lounge and the chair. There the cook stove and table. There, in another room, is the little cabinet organ, and a few benches. So was everything about this little teacher—the simplest in style and work."

When fighting broke out between whites and Indians in 1877, Miss McBeth fled Kamiah, accompanied by an escort of forty-five Indians, and returned to Lapwai. From there she went to Portland and at the end of the war, in the late fall of 1877, she returned to Lapwai and worked there until it was deemed safe for her to go "home" to Kamiah. Like most dedicated missionaries, she was a hard and unrelenting woman. She insisted that the Indians must settle down on the land, learn farming and proper housekeeping, and give up the traditional Indian ways. She was part of a determined effort to destroy the Nez Perce culture, and the effort was largely successful. Social historians now believe that it may also have been mistaken, but there can be no question of the courage and sincerity of those missionaries. Susan McBeth's greatest work may have been, ironically, the preservation of part of the Indian culture she was trying so hard to uproot: its language. Over the years she managed to compile a Nez Perce dictionary of 15,000 words. Because of failing health she was unable to complete the task, but the Smithsonian Institution asked her to send it there anyway. Susan's sister, Kate, took the manuscript in a box to the express office in Lewiston, and it was stowed with other mail and freight aboard the steamer Annie Faxon. Some miles down the Snake from Lewiston the Annie Faxon blew up and the box of manuscript went overboard. A settler farther down the river spotted it floating by, rescued it, and because he happened to be a friend of the McBeths, recognized the contents. He laid the wet pages out in the air to dry and got word to Kate that her sister's work was safe. The Smithsonian eventually got it—a miracle, Kate said.

Kate had come out from Ohio in 1879 to join her sister and remained at Kamiah until 1886. She then moved to Spalding and from there to Lapwai, where she continued to work as a missionary. Susan stayed at Kamiah until 1885, then moved to Mount Idaho and worked there until her death in 1893. Kate died among the Nez Perces in 1915. Susan had trained ten Nez Perces for ordination in the Presbyterian Church and Kate had trained four. Through these fourteen men and their successors, the sisters' work continues even now.

It was Father Joseph Cataldo, a big, tough, lantern-jawed Sicilian, who built the Catholic congregation at Lewiston. He also managed to baptize some 300 Nez Perces even though the Presbyterians had been on the scene well ahead of him. Cataldo built the Mission of the

Sacred Heart, near the present town of Cataldo east of Coeur d'Alene, in the early 1860s, and was there when his bishop asked him to do something for the Catholics of the Lewiston region. In 1867, he and a helper built a clapboard church on Fifth Street at what is now the Tribune Plaza parking lot. It was the first Catholic church for white people in northern Idaho. He later built a log church for Indians on the Clearwater River near Spalding and St. Joseph's Mission at Slickpoo between Lapwai and Culdesac.

He celebrated his diamond jubilee at Lewiston in 1927 and in 1928, at the age of 92 and confined to a wheelchair, he was transferred to Pendleton. He died within a year, still working.

The Salvation Army made its noisy debut in downtown Lewiston in 1895. Two officers, Ensign Shea and Lieutenant Morris, together with a musical group called the Crusaders, came down from Spokane that year hoping to establish a new Salvation Army post. In an article written for the *War Cry*, the Army's magazine, the two described a hair-raising trip down the Lewiston Hill by stage coach and their first visit to the town.

The Crusaders had come down the day before and hired a hall, sleeping there that night, and Shea and Morris had come down the following midnight, sharing the coach with the Crusaders' musical instruments. "The boys sold *War Crys* and the newsmen gave us a big sendoff, so we went to work. We visited all the homes and business houses, including the saloons, fourteen of them. At our open air meeting in front of the Silver Dollar Saloon, one man came out and joined us. He also stayed with us during our Saturday march down the street and sang with us. We were able to add four more to our collection of saved ones, collected eleven dollars, and had a record crowd on Sunday night. The proprietor of the saloon said he would pay the rent on the hall if we would return the next month."

The next year Captain Lydia Burton and Lieutenant

Jessie Long opened a headquarters in the basement of an old wooden building and the Salvation Army was in Lewiston to stay. It moved frequently from one rented space to another until 1920 when it acquired its first permanent headquarters, a building on Fourth Street.

S.E. Stearns, the "Baptist on Horseback," preached throughout northern Idaho and much of Washington in the 1870s and '80s, but he never had a church of his own. He sold land in Oregon to finance an itinerant ministry that took him from town to town over a period of some thirty years. Once while he was in Moscow he heard that there were four Baptists in Spokane without a church. He got on his horse, rode directly to Spokane, organized the congregation and bought land on Sprague Avenue for a building, selling his horse for the down payment.

By this time, Lewiston was a much quieter place than the frontier legislators of 1864 had found. If church bells didn't yet quite dominate the Sabbath, they tolled the end of the rough and ready town that Lewiston had been. It had turned its attention not only to churches but to schools.

*   *   *

Lewiston went for ten years without a school building and that was only partly because the Indian agent, A.J. Cain, wouldn't allow "permanent" buildings put up on Indian land. It was largely because schools require teachers and on the frontier a teacher was often hard to find.

Occasionally a teacher would come around (it's not clear who the first one was), and a few pupils could be housed in a tent or some other available space. The first schools, if they could be called that, were private affairs: A teacher would come to town, rent a classroom somewhere, and advertise for pupils. The parents would pay, per pupil, and if there were enough paid pupils the teacher would stay for a while. According to the late Dr. H.L. Talkington, a professor of history at the old Lewiston Normal School, the first teacher in Lewiston was

W.H. Farrar, a longtime resident of Moscow and a respected citizen. According to C.P. Coburn, an early day school board president, it was "a middle-aged man of professional appearance and quiet demeanor (who) appeared in the blackest of broadcloth . . . and a white tie . . . all bearing unmistakable signs of long usage. After diligent canvassing, he secured a few pupils and opened his school. Everything progressed satisfactorily until the teacher drew his first month's pay. He set out to double his money at the gambling table. But his wages passed into other hands . . . In the face of his ignominious downfall, he quietly departed."

As Coburn recalled it, Lewiston continued without any school at all until the fall of 1864 when P.H. Howe opened a subscription school in a small frame building on Fourth Street. Howe taught school for three months. He was an ardent Unionist, whose patriotism interfered somewhat with his lessons—he was fond of leading the children in singing "John Brown's Body"—but he was credited with awakening a spirit of education in the town.

The first public school in Nez Perce County was established at Lewiston in 1863 and it used up all of the available county funds. Whenever these funds fell short of the need, the school would be closed. Once when a closure was imminent the superintendent appealed to the City Council and the Council agreed that any money collected by the police in fines would go into the school fund.

This plan led to some angry commentary in the *Signal*, which noted on one occasion: "A series of fights has been occurring, but no arrests were made. We think the school fund ought to have a chance when such cases occur. We are creditably informed that there is less than one dollar in that fund, and not much prospects for any increase right away. It is true that the holidays is some excuse, but when people have to seek the street to get out of the way of flying bottles and tumblers, something ought to be done for the benefit of the school."

Another appeal was made to the City Council, which

responded by increasing the property tax by 35 cents per $100 of assessed valuation. The taxpayers exploded. Some insisted the boost was illegal, others were defiant and rebellious. Finally the unfortunate Marshal Dan McElwee was assigned to collect the tax. After heroic efforts, he was able to bring in $164.47, leaving $100 still outstanding. Three more men each took a turn at trying to collect for the school, but with little success.

The school didn't need much. About the only expense, aside from the rent, was the teacher's salary—up to $80 a month if the teacher was a man, somewhat less if the superintendent could find a woman—and wood for winter heat. There were no grades (Lewiston didn't have a graded school until 1881); the children of various ages all sat together on plain wooden benches and the older pupils helped to teach the young ones. The earliest schools had no blackboards, no paper and pencils, and no books other than those the pupils brought from home. An enterprising teacher named Eckels introduced blackboards and chalk in 1867 and the first textbooks came into use in 1879. The typical school term was three months, but it varied according to the available money and prior commitments of the teacher. Although the three-month term was not uncommon in the United States at that time, the *Signal* objected. In June of 1874, the editor complained that "it is certainly a shame that the youth of our town cannot be going to school." In November, 1876, the *Teller* noted, "We are told by one of the directors that the public school in this city will not open 'til about the middle of the month instead of the first Monday, as contemplated." That term of school opened on November 20, 1876, and closed on the following February 14. A proposed special tax to extend the term was rejected by the voters. Community leaders then rallied to the cause and the city was able to finance a four-month term next time. The first nine-month term of school was not achieved until 1878-'79.

Meanwhile, the civic leaders and socialites of the town were busy raising money for a genuine school

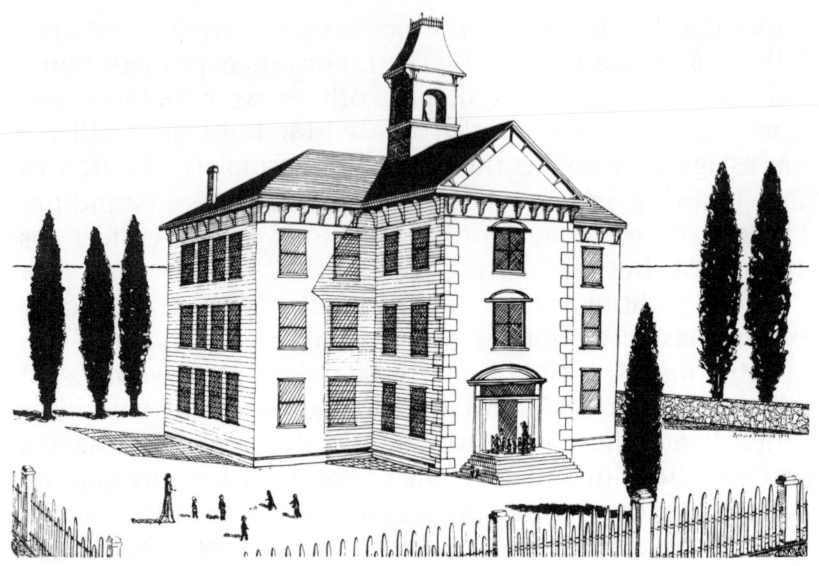

Lewiston's first public school building opened in 1873 at Tenth and F streets. It was quickly outgrown and was replaced, on the same site, by this larger building in 1882.

building, one especially designed for housing students. Their first move was to obtain the land at Tenth and F streets without having to pay for it. C.P. Coburn found a way. He knew that the owner of the property, Albert Ripson, had won title to it at the gambling table. Coburn went to Ripson and reminded him that the land had cost him nothing and would make a wonderful gift to all the children of the area. Ripson not only agreed to the donation; he also lined up two minor co-owners of the property, James W. Hays and L.W. Bacon, and got them to sign also. As new owner of the land, the school board could now advertise for bids. A carpenter named Mann presented the low bid of $1,450 and even though many thought it too low, Mann got the contract, put up a bond, and went to work.

The building committee, fearing the contractor would run out of money, sponsored an all-community dance and party at the newly opened Florence Hall and collected several hundred dollars. Mann did run short, but the bonding company paid the difference and Lewiston had its new school building. The cost was $2,000. One Boise educator called it "the best school building in Idaho," and J.W. Huston, a candidate for Congress, told a Lewiston audience that theirs was the only school house "worthy of the name" in the whole territory. The two-story frame building prompted a jump in the city's school enrollment in the spring of 1873 to fifty-four. Within nine years the city had outgrown that building, and it was replaced by a handsome three-story edifice in 1882.

Two of the most prominent of Lewiston's early teachers were Ellen Kelly and William A. Goulder. Miss Kelly was the daughter of Milton Kelly, one of President Lincoln's last appointments to the Territorial Supreme Court. Miss Kelly taught at Lewiston for two years and then opened a private school of her own. Goulder, who taught at Lewiston from 1869 to 1871, was a territorial legislator, journalist and historian.

Three Catholic Sisters of St. Francis opened the town's first parochial school in 1884, offering instruction in music, German, French and ornamental needlework as well as religion. They called it St. Aloysius Academy, and by the fall of 1885 it had an enrollment of 40 young ladies who paid board of $20 a month. The school was forced to close in 1887 for lack of teachers but reopened in 1888, closed again and reopened again. It closed for the last time in 1893. However, a group of Sisters of Visitation bought a tract of land on Normal Hill in 1897 and opened Visitation Academy there in 1898. In 1904, finding this property inadequate, they moved to the outskirts of Lewiston and the Sisters of St. Joseph of Idaho opened St. Stanislaus School on the Normal Hill site in 1905.

Meanwhile, the public grade school at Tenth and F Streets flourished. By 1883, J.A. Gardiner, the principal (whose duty it was to also teach the older students) had begun calling his upper class studies "high school." In 1888, the principal was M.L. Johnson, but Johnson was not to be there much longer. He got into trouble with the

School Board and was fired with three months still to go in the term. The boys in Johnson's class rebelled and refused to go to school, so Johnson opened a private school in the Grostein & Binnard Opera House and enrolled his former pupils. There they learned, among other things, algebra, geometry and American history. As a result of the student strike, the upper grades in which these courses were taught became officially known as the high school. High school was a two-year course, although third-year classes were occasionally taught. The high school graduated its first students in 1890, but there was no high school building until 1904—and even then the rooms were shared by grade school students who lived on Normal Hill.

The first institution of higher learning in Lewiston was the Lewis Collegiate Institute. The Methodists founded the tiny church college in 1882 in a little dwelling on the corner of Tenth and Idaho streets with the Rev. Levi Tarr as its president. He and his two teachers taught algebra, Latin, theology, literature and the principles of music. In 1883, the Methodists bought an old linseed oil mill on the Wesley Mulkey property east of Lewiston and moved it down to the corner of Seventh and Main. Storey Buck, who attended the institute there, wrote later: "On one side was the Presbyterian Church, on the other the Episcopal, with the Methodist Church and school between—'Piety Corner' they called it." The founders had named it after Meriwether Lewis, but when the college slid into debt and faced closure, they renamed it Wilbur College in honor of a wealthy churchman in Washington Territory. It did no good. The honoree failed to rise to the occasion and the Methodist Church closed the college after only four years of operation.

Thirteen years later, the Lewiston Normal School, a teacher training institution, opened on the upper floor of the Grostein & Binnard Opera House, on the site of what would later become the Lewis-Clark Hotel. The big open hall was partitioned off by walls of canvas into four classrooms. Although it was a state institution, it had no land on which to build. Lewiston donated ten acres of its city park for a campus, and the Legislature assigned to the Lewiston Normal ten thousand acres of income land. In September of 1894, the directors accepted the bid of Frank Clapp to erect a building, hoping to pay him with certificates issued against the land fund. All they got from that contract was the foundation, but the next Legislature appropriated $37,500 for a building, furnishings and maintenance, and in 1896 the Lewiston State Normal School opened in its own quarters.

The enrollment, when the school moved out of the opera house, was forty-three; in the second year in the new building it had reached 137. A training school was opened in 1899 in one wing of the building, and in 1917, some restless older pupils weary of going to class set a fire that destroyed the administration building's east wing and whole top floor. A new administration building was built in 1921. The normal school had become Northern Idaho College of Education when the Legislature closed it, citing a lack of money, in 1951. It had an enrollment of some six hundred students at the time. When it was reopened in 1955 as Lewis-Clark Normal School, a two-year branch of the University of Idaho, it managed to attract only 126. The branch arrangement proved impractical, and two years later it became Lewis-Clark State College, a four-year, independent institution. Under the new arrangement the college gained strength and prestige, and in 1990 had an enrollment, both on and off campus, of some 2,500.

*　　*　　*

It would be a mistake to suppose that the lack of organized schooling in Lewiston's earliest days meant the people were indifferent to learning. When school didn't keep, much learning took place in the home. In the mining camps, the most prized amenities were books. Teachers were honored above most others in the rough frontier settlements, and in every town there was a committee running a library or trying to start one. The Rev. Henry

Spalding's printing press was the first in the Pacific Northwest. Within a few months of its founding, Lewiston had a newspaper and it has never since been without one. And it isn't true, as legend has it, that northern Idaho got the university only because Boise wanted the prison.

The conditions under which pupils and teachers labored in the first schools—no books, no paper, no blackboards and frequently no heat—made formal education a hard-bought thing. Yet teachers opened schools and pupils went to them, to sit on hard benches and practice their writing on cumbersome slates. Their parents, like the parents of today, hoped their children would grow up to be smarter than they were, and most of them did their best to make it happen.

22

Longhorns and Short

The Nez Perce Indians were raising beef cattle well before the gold rush of 1861 brought the miners, and their miners' appetites, into the Clearwater country. The Indians had been introduced to livestock raising by the missionaries Henry Spalding and Marcus Whitman, among others, in the 1840s, and some of them had gone as far south as California to find cattle that would form the bases of their herds. So when the miners got hungry for something more than beans and bacon, there often was Indian beef to be had in return for their gold. When Captain E.D. Pierce, the father of the Idaho gold rush, was trading with the Nez Perces in 1852, he wanted both cattle and horses. As he wrote later, the Indians had horses and cattle in abundance but they made trading for cattle difficult by insisting that the animals be dickered for one at a time. Pierce decided to buy only horses, which the Indians were willing to trade in lots of six to ten.

The first large herd of cattle in the Oregon country, some 1,300, had come in with a covered wagon caravan under the leadership of Marcus Whitman in 1843. Whitman's friend and colleague, the Rev. Henry Spalding, had brought twenty-four of these cattle to his mission on Lapwai Creek, and these are believed to have been the first cattle in what is now Idaho. They were mixed-breed cows and bulls from the mid-West. The first longhorn cattle from Texas arrived in what is now southern Idaho in 1854, and longhorns became increasingly the cattle of choice throughout the region. They were lean but they were tough, able to fend for themselves on the open range and adaptable to most climates.

Many of the gold miners who reached the Lewiston country from 1861 onward were farmers at heart and when they surveyed the lush grass of the Camas and Weippe prairies and the valleys of the Snake and Salmon, they dreamed of becoming stockmen here someday. A veritable sea of grass stretched in a belt 300 miles long and 150 miles wide in a vast semicircle from Lewiston southeastward to the Bitterroots. It was easy for a newcomer to believe what one ·of the boosters of the period claimed—that "The profits of raising stock in this region may well be imagined when the cost, including taxes, of raising a full-grown steer worth $30 is no more than $3." But it wasn't quite that easy, as some early white stockmen discovered. Killing winters on the high prairie could decimate herds of even tough longhorn cattle. The harsh winter of 1861-'62 wiped out a lot of cattle along with a number of miners, and that helped to convince stockmen that there was little point in improving the herds. As long as they were letting the stock fend for itself, finding winter shelter in the gullies and under streamside willows, it would be foolish to import expensive new breeds. For many years, the stockmen of the Lewiston country settled for inferior beef from tough cattle that were expected to survive on their own through the coldest winters.

Tom Beall was perhaps the first large cattle operator in the Lewiston country. During the years of the open range, he ran herds of a thousand head between the Culdesac and Spalding areas. Bob Bracken may have been the first cattleman in what is now Asotin County, which was settled somewhat later. Bracken began raising cattle, horses and sheep on Asotin Creek in 1864, and in the Eighties was running sheep on the Grand Ronde. He later returned to Asotin Creek, where he raised horses and operated a general store.

J.M. Pomeroy brought 140 head of shorthorn cattle into what is now Garfield County in 1864, but he is better remembered there as founder of the town of Pomeroy and operator of several popular hotels and eating places. Others running cattle there in the early days were the Owsleys, in 1868; Mac Tatman, 1869; Newt Estes, who recorded the first brand, on May 2, 1882, and ran the first large herd of 1,500 head on Deadman Creek. Some of the prominent names among early Nez Perce County stockmen, besides Beall, were Caldwell, Fountain, Heitstuman, Jain, Lambert & Lathrop, Meacham, Madden, McCann, Paris, Reeves, Taylor, Thiessen, Trimble, Webb, Wilson and Wittman.

Hank Trimble was only 17 when he arrived at Lewiston in 1861, the year of the gold rush. He did some prospecting, opened a saloon, and with the saloon's profits he bought some good cattle. He let his wife manage the saloon and Trimble branched out into wheat and his ranch became one of the most admired in the country. Ben Jain ran cattle in the Lapwai district until he was 88. J.G. Shissler, according to the *Lewiston Teller*, was "one of the wealthiest farmers and stockmen" and had sold several hundred cows in Montana for $20 a head. He ran cattle in the Waha area south of Lewiston.

Some made money in cattle, but many went broke. The market was unsteady. Some parts of the range were ruined by overgrazing. Drought in the 1870s caused ranchers on the Grand Ronde to seek new pastures in the Wallowa Valley, and this pressure on the Indian inhabitants of the Wallowa helped sow the seeds of the Nez Perce War of 1877. Sheep were multiplying and competing for pasture. Cattle wandering loose year around on the open range were easy picking for thieves. Some winters were devastating even to the hardiest of cattle. The winter of 1861-'62 was especially bad, and in the winter of 1889-'90, more than half the cattle in Idaho froze to death. In their haste to sell what they could, stockmen with surviving cattle cut prices until animals were going for next to nothing.

Two factors saved the cattle industry from complete destruction, according to historian Edward Rinehart. One was the settling of the land and the growing practice of raising enough hay to winter all the range cattle. Another was the creation of the U.S. Forest Service, which assigned some range lands to cattle that otherwise would have been used for pasturing sheep. Cattle ranching was no longer a "free" enterprise. The rancher now had to lease his range and fence it, and he had to provide winter feed and shelter for his stock. Since there wasn't enough streamside drinking water for all his cattle, he had to dig his own well. All these things were too expensive to waste on lean flanks. So the Texan longhorn, once prized as hardy and adaptable, had to give way to fatter cattle that matured more quickly—cattle that could pay somewhat better for their keep.

That didn't take the risk or the adventure out of ranching in places like the Snake and Salmon River country. The isolation alone was daunting. John Platt, in a reminiscence called *Echoes of the Salmon River*, recalled some years ago how he built a house for his bride, the former Emma Batdorf. The newlyweds began housekeeping in a rock dugout with a smokey fireplace, but Platt had better things in mind.

First, he ordered foot-wide rough planks from a sawmill near Keuterville on the Camas Prairie. To get the lumber from the mill to Platt's ranch on the Salmon, a boat had to be built to carry the planks down the river. The lumber was first hauled to Maloney Point on a wagon, then down the point to the river on skids. There it was loaded onto the boat. A mile below the mouth of Maloney Creek, Bob Starr, who was making the delivery, arrived at China Rapids. The boat was unloaded and the lumber was tied to the bank while the boat was led through the rapids by rope. Then the lumber was corralled into rafts and the rafts were released one at a time to find their way through the rapids. After the lumber was reassembled, the rafts were nudged down the river again, arriving the next day at the ranch. From there it was hauled another mile to the building site. When the cabin was completed, the Platts made cupboards out of boxes and a bed out of willow branches over which they laid a mattress filled with bunch grass. That was a typical home on the Salmon.

"We raised six children on the Salmon River," Platt wrote. "All our transportation was by horse. We soon learned that carrying a child was tiresome to a parent. After a long trip the baby would be sore for days. We found that an oil box, lined with blankets and carried by a gentle pack horse, was a cozy nest for baby, and an immense relief to us. When we had two children, two boxes were used, balancing each other. When we had three, the larger child balanced the two smaller. By the time the fourth arrived, the older was able to ride alone. As we journeyed home, leading our pack horses loaded with children, we attracted much attention. One day a farmer ran across the field to tell us his opinion of persons who so treated their children. Jail, he said, was the proper place for us."

The loss of much of the open range to homesteaders brought complications, not the least of which was the introduction of barbed wire. A racing rider could mutilate himself and kill his horse on the cruel barbs of an unseen fence. James Reuben, the son of an Indian leader, was cut as he galloped home after dark, shredded by the barbs of a fence newly built. Next morning he was found unconscious and bleeding from wounds that proved fatal. An 8-year-old boy was dragged through a barbed wire fence near Lewiston by a frightened cow and was badly mangled. Wire fencing outraged many who simply resented the cutting up of the open range. Gangs of young fellows wearing bandanas or other disguising gear attacked fences with wire cutters, working at night and concentrating on water holes and springs. Settlers retaliated and tempers flared.

Although it meant the end of the open range, wire fencing helped to save the livestock industry in Idaho. It inhibited overgrazing. It made it possible for the stockman to grow hay, and thus to winter feed his cattle. And it helped cattlemen upgrade their herds through regulated breeding. The stockman could afford to buy a registered high-grade bull only if he could control its movements and those of his cows. Barbed wire helped to bring the livestock industry of age, and one mark of that achievement was the first Northwest Livestock Show at Lewiston in December, 1912.

The adult men of this village of 6,250 people—women didn't vote then—overwhelmingly agreed to furnish a permanent home for the show and to pay most of the cost of providing the first wagon bridge over the Clearwater River. Lewiston voted to put up $43,000 for a site on the eastern outskirts of town that was then occupied by orchards and truck gardens. Civic leaders considered it a grand undertaking since the town, as headquarters of the show, would become associated throughout the Pacific Northwest with purebred livestock. Draft horses along with highbred equine, registered sheep and hogs, also would be featured and the show and fair would draw vast throngs of people to a town that was badly in need of the business.

Getting ready for the first show was a hectic affair. For many days crews of volunteers dragged off orchard trimmings and cleared away underbrush and weeds. Pioneer Architect J.H. Nave designed a central building with a fifty-foot tower, a ground floor that included a circle of fifty stalls, and sleeping quarters on the balcony for grooms. Frank Rainville offered to do the building and "do it right," and he got the job because there was no time to call for bids. The directors leased a large circus tent to house the big show and sales ring and twenty-five sections of seats. Eighteen giant flags and patriotic bunting formed the background for the exhibit pens. Strings of bright lights helped transform the grounds into a winter circus.

To bring all the people in, the railroads offered special excursion fares. The Camas Prairie Railroad turned its line into a ten-cent jitney between Lewiston and the fair grounds, making sixteen trips a day at half-hour intervals. "This is a god-send to this western country," declared John Norwood, a Grangeville banker. "It means a new era for the livestock industry in the Northwest. No longer will we have to go East to see fine stock." Two days before the opening, some two hundred men were at work on the grounds (and none too soon; four carloads of exhibit stock arrived early from the Willamette Valley of Oregon). Carpenters were completing construction. Grooms were brushing and trotting their animals. Railroaders were tidying the tracksides and switching cars. Volunteers on ladders were fastening lights to tall poles and spreading whitewash on buildings and fences.

By opening day, 3,200 animals were on the grounds. Turnout on the first day of the show was 1,500. That number doubled on the second day and tripled on the third. Every hotel and rooming house in town was fully booked, and when the housing committee called for help, nearly every family opened its doors to a houseguest. A touring musical company, finding no rooms available, put up in a Pullman sleeper supplied by the Northern Pacific.

The Grangeville delegation brought along a cowboy band to enliven things. Seth Jones Jr., known on the Camas Prairie as "the biggest cowboy in the world," was the band's 350-pound drum major. Portland's delegation of sixty-five businessmen was met at the railroad depot at 7:30 a.m. on the opening day by the rousing strains of the Lewiston brass band. P.R. Bevis, with his fife and drum corp, led the way to the Masonic Temple, where a big breakfast was served. Spokane's delegation of eighty-one received the same welcome in the same way on the following day. The noisy parade that moved down Lewiston's Main Street on the final day of the show included a pack train of burdened mules, a resurrected prairie schooner, a stage coach and six and a mock holdup that punctured the air with the pop-pop of blank cartridges. After the parade there was an hour-long exhibition of purebred livestock valued at $250,000 and worth in today's money about three million.

In the sales ring that night, a fourteen-month-old Hereford steer entered by Robert Jones of Wisdom, Montana, sold for a record $1,328.75. At $1.05 a pound, that compared with the ten cents a cattleman might expect at the time on the market. W.H. Bristol of Lewiston's Cold Storage Market paid about double the market price for the reserve champion steer entered by Sweet and Overman of Grangeville. Other sales prices were almost as spectacular.

The first of a series of Northwest Livestock Shows was considered a huge success. Former Governor F.R. Gooding, a livestock man of note, uttered words of glowing praise. C.E. Arney, the western immigration agent for the Northern Pacific, was "never so agreeably surprised." W.W. Weeks, general manager of International Harvester Co., declared, "The livestock collected here was beyond comparison." Said Henry Albers of the Albers Milling Co. of Portland, a bit cryptically: "Your show get-up is astounding."

Prominent among the breeders were Augustus Schroeder of Keuterville for his Herefords, the Broadview Dairy Co. of Rosalia for dairy cattle, and James Kaylor of Peck for Holstein bulls. Lewiston area winners for sheep and swine included E.W. Sweet of Grangeville, Gus D. Thiessen of Lewiston, Daniels and Wallace of Tammany and E.N. Peaslee of Clarkston.

The grand climax of the event was a joint banquet in the Lewiston High School gymnasium of the Idaho-Washington Development League and the Northwest Livestock Association. H.L. Powers, sometimes called the "Irrigation Wizard" because of his guidance in the development of Lewiston Orchards, was the toastmaster.

That first show included Durham, Shorthorn,

Hereford, Aberdeen-Angus beef cattle and Holstein, Brown Swiss, Guernsey, Jersey and Ayrshire dairy cows. Among the draft horses were Percherons, Shires, Belgians, Clydesdales, Standard bred and Hambletonians. The sheep included Oxfords, Downs, Shropshires, Dorsets, Rambouillets, Hampshires and Lincolns. The hog breeds were Duroc, Jersey, Berkshire, Poland China, Hampshire, Chester White and Tamworth.

The day of the longhorn was over.

23

Going Up

The view from the rimrock high above Lewiston was as spectacular in the 1870s as it is now. But there was no real road there then and for most Lewistonians the view was out of reach. Worse still, the lack of a passable road made it next to impossible to move produce and supplies between the valley below and the prairie above. That irritated both the homesteaders on the Palouse and the merchants of Lewiston. The homesteaders had begun looking for a source of supplies nearer than Walla Walla, 150 miles away, and on March 30, 1872, some of them asked Lewiston for help.

With surprising speed, the Nez Perce County Commissioners chose John M. Silcott, a carpenter and longtime ferry operator, to supervise the building of a road up the Lewiston hill. And on April 27, Silcott announced that he had completed the first survey.

There already was a sort of trail there, used only by the most daring of wagon drivers. The procedure in coming down the hill was first to find the sturdiest wagon possible, test the brakes thoroughly, throw a couple of logs in the back, then find the trail. The logs would be used later, under the wheels, to hold the wagon on the steepest parts; or a tree might be dragged along behind to slow the descent. It wasn't a trip one wished to make often. Silcott's first plan was based extensively on this trail, which by then had gained the status of a "road," but making it less steep. As described in the *Idaho Signal*, Silcott's route would take the new road up the hill for 1,203 rods of one and a half foot grade (that is, a rise of a foot and a half every sixteen and a half feet), and ninety-five rods of one foot grade, plus 240 rods from Silcott's ferry to the beginning of the grade—a distance from the ferry to the summit of 1,538 rods or just under five miles. Silcott told the county commissioners that on much of the route the grading could be done with plow and scraper.

Silcott estimated that the whole road, nine feet wide, could be built for under $4,000 with turnouts and curves sufficiently generous to safely accommodate a wagon and eight yoke of cattle. "Will the money be raised to build the road forthwith as soon as practicable?" Silcott asked, and answered: "We shall soon see who is public spirited."

He had at his disposal twenty laborers, a team of horses, a scraper and plow, and the promise of $3,000 in tax money. Silcott offered to pay the laborers $3 a day, good pay for the time.

His first hurdle was to get around the cliff directly opposite Lewiston. As his starting point he chose the northern approach to his ferry landing, giving him three quarters of a mile of good road without even biting into the tax money. He had already begun to fear the tax money would not meet expenses. To make the money stretch, things would have to go smoothly, but they didn't. Some of the farmers on top wanted him to put the road closer to them. Some people down below accused Silcott of feathering his own nest by terminating the road at his ferry. His answer: Did they want to cross the river or didn't they? Some of his workers stalled because they disagreed with the route, others because they were behind in their fencing, their seeding or their plowing.

Silcott had presented his plan within the first month of his appointment, but that was only the beginning. Two conflicting boards of county commissioners and three differing committees of viewers—road district advisers—quarreled over five distinct routing plans. Three months after the county commissioners had accepted Silcott's original route, another was proposed by N.B. Holbrook and H.H. Hannaman, two viewers. Still others were presented in 1873 and 1874. One group proposed that the project be abandoned entirely and that the road be built several miles to the west. At their October meeting in 1873, the commissioners voted to pay Silcott $250 for his services. Those commissioners—J.T. Silverwood, J.M. Crooks and Moses Hexter—were defeated in the following month's election and the new commissioners—J.B. Menomy, D.H. Howser and George Dempster—ordered that Silcott's pay be stopped. It apparently was, for there is no mention in the *Idaho Signal* of those years that he had received any pay for his road work. In one sense, however, he stood to be rewarded no matter who built the road since it was he who owned the ferry.

Silcott stayed on the job and the work progressed, with occasional encouragement from the *Signal*. On May 4, 1872, it noted that "The road up the north hill is planned to pass two springs on the climb. These are all important in slackening the thirst of both man and beast." On May 25, the paper urged more public support of the project: "It behooves the people to encourage him (Silcott). By this means we can soon have a road up an ascent of 2,000 feet which will not find its equal in the country, and will be a source of pride and comfort to all who travel it."

June 1: "Supervisor John Silcott is beginning to grade the road uphill. He thinks the first mile will not exceed 75 cents, with a twelve-foot roadbed and a grade of eighteen inches per rod."

June 8: "One mile on the north hill road finished."

April 19, 1873: "Men have been engaged in repairing the hill road for the last two weeks."

May 17: "Progressing slowly but surely."

Thus was built the so-called Uniontown Grade. It was

completed in 1874 and remained the best road up the hill for forty-three years. It became even more important in the 1880s, when the Northern Pacific Railroad reached Uniontown, and it remained something of a thrill for travelers using it for the first time.

There were, for example, two officers of the Salvation Army, who came clattering down the hill in a stage coach one night in 1895, wedged in among various musical instruments. Ensign Shea and Lieutenant Morris were enroute to Lewiston, hoping to establish a Salvation Army post there and the musical instruments were for a group called the Crusaders, who had reached Lewiston the previous day. As Shea and Morris described the trip later in the *War Cry*, the Army's magazine:

"Because of the fruit fair excursion, our train did not leave (Spokane) until night and (we) found ourselves in Uniontown, Washington, at 11 p.m. We took the four-horse stage for a ten-mile drive down to Lewiston, which we reached at 1:30 a.m. Talk about the Alps and the bottomless pits, that wonderful Lewiston Hill was a fright. Down we went at breakneck speed for 1,200 feet in the middle of the night, turning first to the left and then to the right around the edge of that high point until five miles were behind us. The stage driver yelled blood and fire at the ferry man to get him to take us across to Lewiston, sleeping peacefully in the forks of the Clearwater and Snake rivers . . . "

Scary as it must have been to go tearing down that road in the middle of the night, the old Uniontown Grade wasn't outgrown until the automobile began to revolutionize highway travel after the turn of the century.

*   *   *

Pressure for a new road on the north hill began to build in 1902 when W.E. White of Walla Walla, an early day auto enthusiast, visited Lewiston as part of a "good roads" campaign. White had motored from Pomeroy to Lewiston in four hours and thirteen minutes. That was surprising enough; the people he addressed were even

213

more surprised when he suggested that an automobile road be built up the hill. Idaho had no highway department then and there was no state money for road building and improvement; each district was expected to plan and build its own roads and bridges.

Farmers coming down from the north complained that boulders on the hill road were stalling traffic. Starting in 1904, the Lewiston Commercial Club sponsored spring work days, called "good road" days, when businessmen in groups would spend hours at a time pushing boulders down into the canyons and filling the deep ruts left by wagons. The *Lewiston Tribune* of April 3, 1905, records that "more than 100 men spent the entire day removing boulders from the road leading to Uniontown." It remained an annual spring ritual for two decades. Club members believed they were promoting neighborliness with their friends to the north. J.T. Ray, founder of the Owl, Lewiston's largest and longest lasting drug store, reminded his co-workers, "This is Lewiston's gateway to the north."

As the number of autos increased, so did pressure to build a new road to Uniontown. There wasn't much anyone could do about it, however, since there was no state money for such a project and county budgets were too lean. The undertaking was obviously impossible. Then, Washington state highway authorities made a surprising decision and turned all that around.

Those were the days when the highway planners aimed to pass through as many towns as possible, in order to serve as many taxpayers as possible. And Washington wanted a good road to connect the two largest cities in the eastern part of the state, Walla Walla and Spokane. A straight line would have provided the shortest route. But the map show-ed that a straight line would serve almost no towns at all while a route from Walla Walla that curved into Idaho along the Snake River and then went north would pass through one town after another. The difference was nine-teen persons per mile on one route and 168 persons per mile on the other. Washington Highway Commissioner William R. Roy had no trouble deciding which route to take.

Another factor influenced the decision. Lewiston and Clarkston, Idaho and Washington, had recently won the struggle for free passage over the interstate bridge, which

The first interstate bridge in about 1920, with the Snake River Avenue steamboat docks in the background. Crossing the bridge is a Lewiston-Clarkston electric trolley.

had been built as a toll bridge by the Lewiston-Concord Bridge Co. in 1899. Washington would buy out the company if Idaho would improve the Uniontown Grade. For the road to be negotiable by the faltering autos of that period it would have to be held to a rise of four or five percent. For a year nothing happened. Then, on July 15, 1915, the Commercial Club voted to throw all of its effort into building a new Lewiston Hill state highway grade. Club President R. S. Erb claimed the town had found "unanimous sentiment in favor of united action back of its responsibility."

Eugene E. Booth, then Nez Perce county surveyor, was inspired. He declared a four percent grade could be built, adding that it should not cost more than $50,000.

His right hand assistant, J.J. McCreedy, made the survey. In accordance with Idaho law, a "good highways" district was formed and the new district agreed to pay two-thirds of the cost. Booth shortly thereafter became the state highway engineer and began pouring money into the Lewiston hill project—so much so that the state had to finish the highway or suffer a loss.

C.C. Van Arsdol of Clarkston, who won fame as the engineer planner for the route of the Canadian Pacific Railroad through the Rocky Mountains, was put in charge. The grading of the spiral highway was completed in 1916 and the highway was opened to traffic in November of the following year. The total cost was $100,000, in those days a staggering sum.

As Lewiston lawyer Eugene A. Cox put it at the time, "South Idaho screamed, but it was too late and Booth escaped into the Army."

It was a truly spectacular example of highway engineering, incorporating some of the circular bends suggested by E.A. White, a prominent fruit marketer and civic leader who had taken an interest in the project. From the top it gave a sweeping view of the Seven Devils mountains in the south, the Bitterroots in the east and the Blue Mountains to the west. And directly below, the city of Lewiston and Normal Hill, the confluence of two great rivers and white ribbons of pavement leading into the still rural Lewiston Orchards. Tourists loved it. "The finest piece of highway and surely the one affording the grandest view," according to W.F. Ashton, a visitor from California. A tourist from New Jersey called it "the scenic masterpiece of the world." And "It is comparable to anything Switzerland has to offer," declared a tourist from New York.

The people of Lewiston knew they had something here and they guarded it carefully. Women's clubs formed vigilance committees to keep out billboards. The Lewiston Commercial Club added $1,000 to its annual budget for spiral highway promotion. Families treated out-of-town guests to a view from the top. One of the garden clubs planted and maintained an iris garden in the embrace of a hairpin curve near the top. Over the years the road was improved bit by bit. Some of the sharpest corners were widened and some of the steepest climbs flattened. And in time the whole route was paved.

Perceptions change, however, and what seemed at first a great connector began to be seen as an impediment to easy travel. Truckers and others who had to drive for a living came to resent the sixty-four curves on the spiral and to wish for more speed and less scenery. Commerical travelers began to speak of the spiral as a "scenic monstrosity." It was not unusual in the Thirties and Forties to find a dozen steaming autos lined up at the spring, a little beyond the halfway point, as the drivers awaited their turn for water.

Agitation for a better highway began in the Sixties and by the early Seventies the talk had turned to which of several proposed routes it should take. The so-called ridge route was chosen and construction began in 1975. The highway was officially opened on October 28, 1977, and on the following January 23 it claimed its first victim, a Spokane truck driver who lost his brakes going down, turned into an escape ramp to slow his rig and instead sailed over the top.

The new highway reduced average travel time for passenger cars from twenty minutes to eight, but at a cost in lives and property. It was so much steeper that several escape ramps were required for runaway trucks, and more had to be added later. And still truckers continued to lose their lives or their loads either on the way down or at the bottom where the new road ended in a fairly sharp curve. The worst accident in the highway's first ten years involved not a truck but a passenger car which skidded in the fog on wet pavement, killing six people.

The first hill road, the Uniontown Grade, had cost about $6,000. The second, the spiral highway, cost

$100,000. The third and latest Lewiston Hill grade cost $15,150,500.

The old spiral highway remained open but the state discouraged its use, saying it did not intend to maintain both roads. Some truckers continued to use it anyway because it was safer than the newer, steeper grade. And in the early Eighties, some people sought to have it turned into a road racing route, lining the sharpest curves with bales of hay. It would be a great tourist draw, they said, but the idea got nowhere.

24

Trolleys, Trains and Taxicabs

Would the railroad never come? It must have seemed so to the farmers and merchants of the Lewiston country in the years when the gleaming rails were always just over the mountain. It is hard for us to realize, in the 1990s, how much the railroads meant to the white settlers of the region a hundred years ago when the mountains were so much higher and the places so much farther apart.

Farmers had only one means of shipping their produce to market: by steamboat down the Snake and Columbia Rivers. But the steamboats could operate only part of the year, when the water level was right, and even then the vessels were frequently laid up for repairs to their cantankerous steam engines. And even when all the boats were running, there weren't enough of them to carry the wheat downriver at harvest time. Besides the lack of shipping, there was the awful isolation when the boats weren't running, for they were the only convenient link between the frontier settlements and the outside world. So it is no wonder people listened ever more eagerly, even prayerfully, for the sound of the locomotive whistle.

There was a flurry of excitement in early April, 1883, when word came that Henry Villard, the president of the Northern Pacific Railway Co., would visit Lewiston aboard a sternwheel steamer on the 26th. When the day arrived, a large delegation of Lewiston businessmen, accompanied by the town's brass band in full regalia, went down to the docks to meet the boat. There was no sign of Villard. After a long wait and the passing of several messages, Villard sent word that he was indisposed and intended to remain in his stateroom. He said he had promised the town nothing, adding that he considered Lewiston well served by the steamboats. Next day, after Villard had left, the citizens learned that the great man's sole purpose in coming to town was to find out what the Oregon Short Line was up to in that region. The OSL had sent surveying crews through but had done nothing more. Charles Francis Adams, a former president of the Union Pacific and one of the developers of the Clarkston Flat, owned land in the valley and hoped to get a UP line surveyed down the Snake River and through Clarkston but nothing came of that dream, either.

Still, Alonzo Leland and others kept their spirits up and dreamed. And what dreamers they could be:

"Hurrah! Railroad for Lewiston This Fall," cried the *Teller* on March 21, 1887. "J.R. Stevens, OR&N surveyor, with a party of twelve men, is making camp today at Alpowa Ridge to view and locate a railroad from Pomeroy to Lewiston. It is expected that this line will be constructed between these two points in time to take off this year's crop. They have an outfit with them and orders to survey through as fast as possible."

On November 15, 1888, the *Teller* suggested that the yearning for a railroad might not have been unanimous. It reported, "There can now be little doubt that both Lewiston and Camas Prairie will have a railroad within a year and perhaps two roads. Are the people prepared to appreciate the advantages of a railroad? Will the mossbacks change and their skins become more soft and pliable?"

On October 2, 1890, the *Teller* announced as fact the hope that "Lewiston will be the center of operation of a number of branch lines to be built this year and next." And that same month: "Two new railroads for Lewiston this week. We will soon be a metropolis." Then: "The first whistle will blow at Lewiston before the citizens have eaten their Christmas dinners."

By this time, Editor Leland had been expecting the railroad momentarily for ten years and the first whistle was still almost a decade off. Nor would Leland and the others be satisfied with one. "Five railroads are pointing their way to Lewiston," said a seed company ad in the *Teller* in 1890. The Lewiston people assumed that the OR&N would lay tracks down the Snake River from Huntington, Oregon, and that the Northern Pacific would soon come down from Spokane Falls. They knew that the Union Pacific and the NP were both surveying a route from Montana to Lewiston through the Bitterroot Mountains, but they didn't know that the two lines were about to become one and that hard times and railroad economics would doom even that.

The lines of the OR&N, coming from the west, reached Pomeroy in 1883. The OR&N tracks reached Moscow from Colfax and Pullman in 1885. The Spokane & Palouse, a subsidiary of the Northern Pacific, stretched its rails south from Spokane by way of Pullman and reached Genesee in April, 1888. "The track was laid to Genesee Saturday in the new town," reported the *Teller*, "and great rejoicing was had in that section." A traveler could now leave Lewiston by stagecoach and connect at Genesee with the train to Spokane Falls. That cut the isolation down considerably. In 1889, the Spokane & Palouse reached Kendrick and Juliaetta, and farmers were told they would be able to ship their next crop by rail from Lewiston.

Meanwhile, survey crews from the NP and UP were busily locating lines through the Clearwater mountains and occasionally engaging in pitched battles. Out here, there was a race on to see which road would reach Lewiston first, but back in the board rooms of New York and St. Paul, railroad executives were adding up costs and declaring a truce. First, the two roads agreed to a joint venture that would punch one railroad through the Bitter-roots. But before they could get it launched, the country slid into a business slump that halted rail building everywhere. There also was the problem of crossing the Nez Perce Indian Reservation, which lay athwart the route. In 1888, an Indian agent ordered surveyors of the OR&N off the reservation. But in 1891, the Nez Perces agreed to permit the railroad to cross Indian land at a cost of $20 for every acre it crossed. That led the *Teller* to predict that Lewiston would have its railroad within 60 to 90 days.

Railroad executives continued to grumble about costs, and that led Lewiston citizens groups to offer the railroads subsidies of cash and right-of-way. At one committee meeting, in February, 1890, the citizens agreed to make "urgent demand" upon first one railroad and then another, with offers of subsidies. Two months later, Lewiston was prepared to offer the NP $50,000 in cash plus right-of-way for seven miles from the reservation into Lewiston. (Someone circulated a rumor, never verified, that Moscow was quietly offering the NP $150,000 to stay out of Lewiston.) On the Camas Prairie, citizens were prepared to accept a special tax on property in order to raise money to lure one of the railroads there. In 1891, the Lewiston group named the city's ten biggest taxpayers to a committee with orders to raise enough money to bring the most reluctant railroad to town. Nothing worked. The city even made room for a railroad depot between Third and Fourth streets, clearing the land and moving buildings out of the way. Still no whistles blew.

Throughout this period, the farmers were being assured that by next year they would be shipping their crops in railroad cars. They continued to send them down the river by boat. Then the panic of 1893 struck and grass began to grow between the rails already laid. All over the country that year businesses failed, farms were lost, banks closed, construction halted, the Northern Pacific went into receivership, and the price of wheat fell so low that it could not profitably be shipped out of Lewiston by any means.

Within a couple of years the panic eased and times improved, but the first rails weren't laid into Lewiston until 1898. The Northern Pacific came down from Juliaetta and along the Clearwater River in August of that year, and on September 15, a warm late-summer evening, the first train rolled into the depot, precisely on time.

It may have been the most joyous event in the history of the town. NP's Number 840 was due at 11 p.m. and the whole city, including many who had never seen a locomotive, turned out to welcome her. School children were allowed to stay up for the occasion. As 11 o'clock approached, the saloons closed, houses emptied, and buggies, horses and people clogged the streets downtown. In front of the depot, the kids laid their ears against the tracks, listening for the first sound of the approaching train. Two bands lined up along a picket fence, and took turns playing martial airs while couples danced on the station platform. Suddenly someone shouted and everyone grew quiet. Then, in the ensuing hush, it came—the sound of the whistle they had waited for so long. At exactly 11 o'clock, NP's Number 840 came around the bend and whooshed up to the station platform. She stopped, the steam hissing around her drive wheels and her bell clanging, and the crowd closed in on her in a spasm of excitement.

In the coaches were some two hundred businessmen from Spokane who had made a gala excursion out of this maiden run. They were greeted with cheers and hustled across the tracks to the saloons and private homes. For three days the city celebrated. There was a parade, an exhibition of area produce, house parties too numerous to count and dances in all the hotels. Then the crowds returned to the depot, the businessmen got back into their coaches, and another noisy gathering sped the train on its way back to Spokane.

By the close of 1898, the two railroad giants, UP and NP, together with their subsidiary lines, had strung a network of rails throughout the inland Northwest, the result of a vigorous contest for the region's shipping and passenger business. In 1881, the OR&N, a subsidiary of the UP, extended lines from Walla Walla to Waitsburg, Dayton and the mouth of the Tucannon at Turner, and built lines from Walla Walla to Milton, Oregon, and north through Riparia to Spokane. In 1882, the OR&N completed a line from Umatilla to Pendleton and in 1883 it ran a line from Starbuck to Pomeroy and completed its line from Walla Walla to Pendleton. In 1885, the OR&N built from Colfax to Pullman and Moscow. In 1886, it built from Colfax through Garfield and Tekoa into Wallace and the Coeur d'Alene mining district.

In 1887 and 1888, the Spokane & Palouse, a subsidiary of the Northern Pacific, built its branch from Spokane to Pullman, Uniontown and Genesee and another branch from Spokane to Davenport, Wilbur, Almira, Worden, Connell and other points in the Big Bend country of Washington. In 1889, the OR&N closed the gap between Riparia and Lacrosse, completing the line between Spokane and the main line connection at Pendleton. In 1890, the Spokane & Palouse built from Pullman to Moscow, Troy, Kendrick and Juliaetta, and in 1898, as we have seen, it extended its line from Juliaetta to Lewiston. And the competition continued.

In 1899, the NP built a branch line from Arrow Junction to Orofino, providing daily service to Agatha, Lenore, Contact, Ahsahka and Orofino. Another NP branch line went up the Lapwai Valley to Culdesac and a third went up the Clearwater to Kooskia and Stites. That fall, the UP and NP called a truce that restricted construction of the UP's line from Lewiston down the Snake to Riparia and ended UP's plans to build a line up the Snake from Clarkston to Huntington. Both railroads had depot sites in what is now Clarkston and plans to build more lines out of Lewiston-Clarkston in every

The so-called Uniontown Grade, built by John Silcott, can be seen in this picture of Lewiston looking north. It was taken in about 1900. (*Nez Perce County Historical Society*.)

John Silcott, an early-day ferryman and the builder of the first Lewiston Hill road. (*Nez Perce County Historical Society, R.G. Bailey collection*.)

The original interstate bridge under construction in April, 1899. The view is to the west toward Clarkston, then called Concord and still barren land. (*Nez Perce County Historical Society, Betty Rudfelt collection.*)

The toll bridge that connected Lewiston and Clarkston in 1899 nears completion. It was built as a profit-making venture by the Lewiston-Concord Bridge Co., which sold it to the state of Washington in 1913. The state removed the tolls. (*Nez Perce County Historical Society, Betty Rudfelt collection.*)

Near the top of the then-new spiral highway in 1918. (*Nez Perce County Historical Society.*)

Lewiston is across the river in this photo of the spiral highway, taken in about 1918. (*Nez Perce County Historical Society, Elsie Webster collection.*)

Downtown Lewiston at Fifth and Main, looking east, in about 1915. The R.C. Beach store later became C.C. Anderson Department Store, still later the Bon Marche, and after that the Towne Square mall. (*Lewiston Morning Tribune.*)

The first streetcar to cross the old interstate bridge pauses at the top of the arch on May 1, 1915. The man with the wheelbarrow went along in front of the trolley and shoveled sand on the tracks to provide enough traction to get the car up the slope. (*Nez Perce County Historical Society.*)

This was the scene at Lapwai in August, 1895, when security guards and bank representatives prepared to pay the Nez Perce Indians prior to the opening of the reservation. (*Nez Perce County Historical Society, Henry Fair-Dole collection.*)

The frail but indomitable Susan McBeth, the missionary teacher who worked among the Nez Perces for many years at Kamiah. (*Lewiston Morning Tribune.*)

A harvest crew at work in the Colton-Uniontown area before the turn of the century. The horses at the right are turning the shaft that powers the thresher, in the left foreground. Other teams are pushing two reapers, and horse-drawn wagons are carrying the stalks to the thresher. Visible in this picture are forty horses and twenty-one men. (*Lewiston Morning Tribune.*)

A twenty-horse team pulls a combine over Palouse hills during a turn-of-the-century wheat harvest. Before the advent of the tractor, 32-horse teams were not uncommon, and on the rolling prairie, the lead horses were frequently out of sight of the driver. (*Nez Perce County Historical Society, Betty Rudfelt collection.*)

This old Case steam engine was typical of the big machines that powered the threshers in the wheat fields of the Lewiston country prior to the arrival of the combine. (*Lewiston Morning Tribune.*)

The wanigan, a cookshack and bunkhouse on rafts, followed the log drives down the Clearwater River to Lewiston in days before the construction of Dworshak Dam blocked the North Fork and ended the river drives. (*Potlatch Corporation.*)

Before the first sawmill, lumber for sluice boxes and cabins was whipsawed by hand from whole logs, as in this photo. (*Nez Perce County Historical Society, R.G. Bailey collection.*)

direction. The truce brought a temporary halt to an orgy of railroad building and spawned the Camas Prairie Railroad, a unique experiment in railroad operation.

In a meeting at Lenore in 1899, officials of the UP and NP agreed that if they should ever build a line through the Bitterroots into Montana, they would share shops, bridges and tracks. At that meeting they also talked about a possible future branch line to the Camas Prairie that would be owned jointly. The Camas Prairie Railroad was formed ten years later with 150 miles of track. The UP's OR&N line from Riparia to Lewiston was made part of the CPRR, as were the NP's tracks to Stites and to Grangeville. A 999-year agreement between the UP and NP called for joint ownership of track, shops, rolling stock and personnel; the CPRR itself would own no track or rolling stock. Both parents would solicit business independently but they would share in the cost and upkeep of the Union Station in Lewiston.

The line from Spalding to Culdesac had been built in 1899 by the Clearwater Short Line Co., a branch of the NP, and the UP had completed its branch from Riparia to Lewiston in 1906. The UP and NP together completed the line from Culdesac to Grangeville in 1908. In the beginning, the CPRR hauled mostly cattle and grain from the farmlands of the Camas Prairie and upper Clearwater either north via the NP or west on the UP. It began hauling logs and lumber products on January 1, 1928, after completion of the line from Orofino to Headquarters.

Construction of the line to Grangeville was a daunting task. To reach and cross the Camas Prairie from the Clearwater River valley required 52 bridges, including high trestles, and seven tunnels, and the finished project was considered a feat of railroad engineering. It was not unusual for timorous passengers, riding the CPRR for the first time, to faint on the highest trestles. The company later replaced nine of the bridges with fill and "daylighted" one of the tunnels. The Culdesac-to-

The locomotive and crew of a construction train used in the building of the Camas Prairie Railroad's Lewiston-Kooskia line in 1899. From the left are Engineer Shorty Moyer (above), Brakeman Joe Albright, Conductor George Phillips, Brakeman Mark Windus and Fireman Bill Sisson.

Grangeville branch was no money maker, largely because of the high cost of maintaining all those bridges, and the railroad found it necessary to reduce service on the line in 1986, a few years after a motion picture company had used the spectacular track as the location of the movie, "Breakheart Pass."

* * *

When Lewiston's Main Street was paved in 1909, the city fathers had the good sense to install streetcar tracks even though the city had no streetcar and no immediate plan to get one. Every town of consequence had streetcars, and if Lewiston and Clarkston hoped to amount to anything they would have to have streetcars too.

First to use the tracks was the Lewiston Terminal Company, which operated a noisy gasoline motor car up and down Main Street for a time before going out of business in 1913. Shortly thereafter, Robert A. Foster, president of the Lewiston-Clarkston Improvement Co., which was promoting Clarkston, invited another transit firm to take over the operation of a scheduled trolley service. The bait was the franchise of the old Lewiston Terminal Co. plus, of course, the track. The Lewiston-Clarkston Transit Co. was formed and accepted Foster's invitation. The new company set itself a deadline of May 1, 1915, to begin service. During that week, the city would join in a celebration marking the opening of the Celilo Canal and an "open river to the sea," and there would be lots of people in town. The company had competent people experienced in street railways, but it faced a serious problem in meeting that deadline: a nationwide shortage of trolley cars. As Henry C. Hartung, the superintendent of the line, told the *Lewiston Morning Tribune* years later, "The streetcar industry was enjoying its greatest boom that year. It was just impossible to secure cars. We tried to get them from the Pullman Company and all the large and small manufacturers in the East, but orders were booked for months ahead."

Finally, the Lewiston-Clarkston Transit Co. was able

The car barn of the Lewiston-Clarkston Transit Co., which operated the electric trolley system from 1915 to 1929.

to persuade Spokane United Railways to let it have three of its old cars for $300 each. "They were already old and almost worn out, and too heavy and large for our needs," Hartung said, "but they served the purpose until we were able to secure new ones in April, 1916." By starting with a shorter line than planned—from Sixth and Sycamore in Clarkston to Thirteenth and Main in Lewiston—and by using the heavy, old cars, the company was able to meet its deadline. On May 1, 1915, Lewiston had streetcars to ride and just about everyone was riding them. Of an estimated 25,000 out to attend the Celilo celebration two days later, 4,780 rode on the streetcars. Superintendent Hartung himself drove the first carload.

That first car stalled trying to climb the high arch in the old interstate bridge because the flanged wheels couldn't get enough traction on the rails. Finally, it was necessary for John Dean, a company employee, to shovel sand on the rails from a wheelbarrow, moving along in front of the car, until it reached the top. Despite that minor handicap, the trolley had made an auspicious start. Hundreds rode the cars to and from work morning and evening, and in a few months the company extended the line from Thirteenth and Highland in Clarkston to Twenty-first and Main in Lewiston. Business was so good there was talk of extending the line to Asotin and putting rails on Normal Hill. In its best year, the company reported a gross of $30,000 and employed fourteen men. Cars ran every twenty minutes, making the first trip at 6:10 a.m. and the last at 11:40. Three cars were regularly used and a fourth was kept in reserve. There were turnout switches for passing at Sixth and Poplar in Clarkston and in front of the Temple Theater, now the Masonic Temple, in Lewiston. It took an hour to make the full run of four miles and 400 feet. Autos were scarce then, and many passengers took the ride for the fun of it, keeping cars full on Sundays and evenings in pleasant weather.

The cars were reliable, once the firm had replaced the original three, and breakdowns were few. But Henry True, one of the transit company's first employees, later recalled that during the winter of 1918, one of the cars stalled in a snowdrift on the Lewiston approach to the bridge. The snow downtown was four feet deep that winter, and the car stayed in the drift for five days before the crew was able to move it. It was customary after a snow storm to put a man or boy out in front of the car to throw salt on the rails for traction. A box of sand was standard equipment in each car, to be used in early mornings when the rails were wet or frosty.

Conductor E.J. Hill once recalled the time a circus was in town and he had to pack 108 men and women into a trolley car with 50 seats. As the car crawled up the incline in front of the car barns near the Lewiston approach to the bridge, Hartung ran out and in his excitement slipped into the German accent he had long outgrown.

"My God, Eddie, how many you got on?" he shouted from the front fender. On receiving the answer, he said, "for goodness sake take it easy."

"Maybe you think I haven't been taking it easy!" Hill replied.

As the years passed and the streets filled with automobiles, the trolleys attracted fewer and fewer customers. The line was already on the skids in 1925, when a motor bus began making runs on Normal Hill. Finally the competition became too severe and the Lewiston-Clarkston Transit Co. threw in the towel. The last trolley pulled into the barns on August 3, 1929. A motor bus immediately took its place.

Some of the cars were junked but several were bought by an enterprising businessman who set them up in a trailer court in Clarkston and rented them out as bachelor quarters. The tracks were removed over a period of years as the cities' streets were resurfaced, and the car barn was dismantled when the approach to the new Interstate Bridge was built in 1939. Superintendent Hartung became an orchardist and was elected to the Washington Legislature. Hill operated a bus for several years. Some of the other employees of the transit company were V.A. Bilderback, who was in charge of the mechanical department, and S.L. Fowler, Milo Gipson, William Doran, J.A. Morrow and Ed Parks.

*   *   *

A Lewiston cabbie one day in 1910 left his team and rig at the livery stables and made his rounds in a Ford instead. It was Lewiston's first taxicab. Soon after that, L.D. Fountain, Lewiston's first taxi operator, put on more Fords and called in his son, Earl, and other drivers to help him. He opened an office in a cigar store near Fifth and Main and sold his interest in the White Front livery stable. Fountain was learning first-hand that Lewiston was a good town for taxis.

In 1912 or thereabouts, Fountain sold his taxi

business to William Day. Day was not content to run about town and became one of the first to hire out for long-distance trips. He got a mail contract and began a regular stage service to Asotin. Taxis were cars for hire in those years and the drivers carried salesmen, surveyors and others as far as Boise, Spokane and Pocatello. The fare was roughly $6 to Asotin, $150 to Boise and $250 to Pocatello. Sometimes the driver would wait several days while a business errand was completed, then carry his passenger back to Lewiston.

A taxi operated by Fred Lowery, with George Parks as driver, doubled as the first Normal Hill bus. Parks made an almost continuous circuit of the hill in the early 1920s, from daylight until dark, charging a fare of eleven cents. Out of town, the roads would challenge the best driver. Parks once recalled driving the steep Shumaker grade above the Grand Ronde River during a heavy rainstorm while enroute to Enterprise, Oregon. He found that a flash flood had carried off much of the roadbed on the narrow, rocky grade, but he managed to get his car down to the bottom. Stopping at the foot of the hill, he arranged for a horse and rider to help him back up on his return trip. On returning from Enterprise, he called for the horse and rider only to be told that another flash flood had made the grade impassable. With no other route open, Parks and the rider attempted the ascent anyway. He was forced to abandon the car and climb to the top alone. Eight days later, Parks and Lowery rescued their taxi.

Taxis operated for several years before there was any requirement for liability insurance, and competition was keen. A motorcycle rider whisked his fares around town in a sidecar at fifteen cents a trip. Insurance requirements reduced the competition and the motorcyclist found that even Lloyds of London would not insure him. He dropped out of the business and so did a lot of others. One of the early taxi drivers was Walter Addison, who made a bid for the businessmen's trade with a big Buick that had cost him $1,500. The tall, slender Addison became a familiar figure at the corner of Fifth and Main, where he spent his time between fares polishing his car. No other driver was permitted that spot after his death because the traffic was so heavy there. Other taxi stands were regulated off Main to the side streets in 1925. In 1926, Parks, who by then was in the business on his own, put into service the town's first glass-enclosed taxicab, a big Dodge sedan.

Among other early Lewiston-Clarkston taxi drivers were George F. Mitchell, Cecil Humphrey, Bill Smith, Hiram Lentz, Fred Jenkins, Gene Gasser, Matt Dowd, Thomas Tabor, William Jackson, Lynn Parkins, Tom Boise, Harvey and Arlie Longeteig and Homer Turner.

* * *

Matt Dowd was not only one of Lewiston's early taxi drivers; he operated what may have been the town's first garage. And Matt's brother, Charlie, owned one of the town's first automobiles.

It was an adventuresome undertaking, to drive in the first decade of the century. There were cars rattling around the byways of the Lewiston country before there were any garages to serve them, and motorists had to be their own mechanics. That was a large part of the pleasure. A Lewiston woman, recalling an auto owner she had known in the early days of motoring, remembered that "He had the parts all over the kitchen. He had more fun with his automobile than anyone I have ever known."

The first cars were strictly for fun. Anyone who had to get there on time used a horse. Some doctors may have fooled around with autos as a lark, but they continued to make their calls with horse and buggy.

By 1905, there were a few automobiles tooling around on Normal Hill, where the mud didn't get as deep as it did downtown on the flat. Most of these were powered by two-cylinder gasoline engines, but there were a few steam-driven cars also. W.F. Kettenbach, a prominent Lewiston businessman, had a White steamer which used a gasoline fire to heat the boiler. It was quite a good arrangement in some ways, but it had drawbacks, as Kettenbach discovered one day when he was driving in the countryside with an assistant. They stopped to refill the gasoline tank, spilled some of the fuel and started a fire that came close to destroying the car and sent Kettenbach rolling down the hill. Curtis Thatcher also drove a steam-powered car, and Frank Thompson owned an early Franklin which operated with side gears. It was considered dependable enough to make the trip to Lake Waha for Sunday outings. John P. Vollmer proudly drove a Baker Electric, an elegant enclosed-cab car powered by storage batteries in front and behind. It was richly upholstered, with seats that faced each other and it was tall enough that Vollmer could sit inside with his top hat on.

The typical auto of this vintage had lights operated by a carbide generator, usually placed on the running board. Water dripping on the carbide generated a gas that was carried by tubes to the headlights. The operator would raise each headlight lid separately, strike a match, then close the lid quickly to keep the wind from blowing out the flame. Among the first primitive warning signals was the shrill whistle that was produced by pulling a cord over a hole in the spark plug. There also was a coaxle horn, which produced a loud squawk; but the standard noisemaker was the common bulb horn, which gave a sad bleat when you squeezed it.

By 1909, autos were becoming fairly common and in September of that year the Lewiston Commercial Club sponsored a two-day motor excursion into the country.

Those cars were unlicensed, of course, because autos were still not numerous enough to require regulation. And even when licensing was imposed, most drivers paid little attention to it. Lewiston's city officials complained at one point that a hundred cars were operating in town and only thirty were licensed. Most people resented having to license their cars, and some of that resentment still lingered in 1928 when Idaho plates came out with the words "Idaho Potatoes" inside an outline representation of a spud. It meant that the Idaho driver, whether he liked it or not, would thenceforth advertise the potato wherever he went even though he might be a wheat grower himself. In the wheat, pea and lentil country of northern Idaho, that doesn't sit well even now.

25

The 43rd Star

For Idaho, statehood should have come hard. The population in 1890 was still relatively small—too small, many thought, to justify two United States senators. The territory was practicing offical discrimination against a quarter of its people, the Mormons, something that offended many members of Congress. And the northern part of the territory was trying mightily to separate itself from the southern part.

But Idaho had one positive thing going for it that cancelled out all the negatives: It had voted Republican in the territorial election of 1888, and the national elections that year had produced slim Republican majorities in both houses of Congress. In the Senate, however, the Republican edge was so thin that the GOP would be unable to put together a working majority without the addition of several new Republican senators. That meant creating several new states. New Mexico had been seeking statehood for several years, and had a much larger population than Idaho, but New Mexico was voting Democratic (and would not achieve statehood until 1912). The Republican leadership could find three territories that, among them, might be counted on to send eight Republican senators to Congress after statehood. They were Washington, Wyoming and Dakota (by dividing Dakota into two states). There was also Montana, which

235

was leaning Republican but was by no means a sure thing. And there was Idaho, which was.

Idaho had not been actively seeking statehood. Quite a few Idahoans, in fact, were against it, fearing that statehood would solidify the current boundaries, which they deplored. There was a strong movement in the north, centered at Lewiston and Moscow, to make northern Idaho a part of Washington and at one point it nearly succeeded. In 1887, Congress passed a bill merging Washington Territory with the northern part of Idaho Territory. There was great rejoicing at Lewiston and Moscow, but the cheers turned to groans when President Cleveland killed it by letting it die without his signature—the so-called pocket veto. The north was one reason why there had been no serious statehood movement in Idaho. Annexation to Washington first, the northerners insisted, then statehood.

Lewiston was a hotbed of annexation activity. Since the birth of the territory in 1863, with Lewiston left hanging on the very edge, Lewistonians had been seeking what they called border reform. Committees were formed and prodded at annual citizens' meetings to pursue the goal, and it was not simply because the "Boise gang" had "stolen" the capital. The anti-southern feeling was almost as strong at Moscow, also on the Washington border and also feeling orphaned by the power centers of the south. The two parts of the territory were separated by cultural, political, economic and geographical differences that they could not seem to reconcile. The commercial centers of the south were Boise and Salt Lake City—almost inaccessible to northerners—and the commercial centers of the north were Spokane and Walla Walla, both of them familiar, comfortable, and relatively accessible by the standards of the time. The people of Nez Perce County had other reasons to feel no great affinity with the south. There was, for example, the time Boise and Ada County had supported Idaho County's attempt to alter boundaries in a way that would have eliminated Nez Perce County by putting three-fourths of its area and much of its tax base in Idaho County. R.W. Miller, a member of the upper house from Nez Perce County, attacked the measure with such fiery language that his remarks were stricken from the record. Governor Thomas W. Bennett agreed with Miller that the bill was an unfair invasion and quickly vetoed it. The Legislature sustained the veto, and the threat was passed. But the episode contributed to northern Idaho's distrust of the so-called Boise gang.

When Republicans gathered for their territorial convention in May, 1888, the northern Idaho delegates differed angrily with their fellow Republicans from the south. Mass meetings were held on June 5 at Moscow that year, on June 26 at Grangeville, on July 14 at Lewiston and on August 20 at Genesee, and at each of these the citizens reaffirmed their hopes for annexation to Washington. While that division continued, Idahoans could not think seriously about statehood. And in the south, where most of the population was by now, there was the added difficulty of the anti-Mormon laws which were sure to raise eyebrows in Congress. The Mormons were in a difficult position. They didn't want to become part of an anti-Mormon state, but they had no effective means of opposing statehood since they could not vote. The Territorial Legislature had enacted a test oath law requiring that no one could vote who had not signed an oath swearing that he did not belong to any religion that advocated polygamy—as the Mormons then did. On March 8, 1888, the Utah Legislature passed an anti-polygamy statute to help pave the way for Utah's admission as a state and incidentally to make the Idaho oath seem unnecessary. It didn't help. The oath remained even after their leaders advised Mormons to resign from the church so that they could sign the oath and vote; the Territorial Legislature answered that with a statute denying the franchise to anyone who had been a Mormon on January 1, 1888.

That November, after the Republicans had won only

a slim majority in Congress, the leadership saw the need to create two new Republican senators from Idaho. To the pro-statehood forces in Idaho they gave money, encouragement and advice. Statehood, they declared, could be achieved in a matter of months, not years as was usually the case. They would make sure that everything went smoothly, and it did.

The Territorial Legislature had created the University of Idaho in 1887 and put it at Eagle Rock, later to become Idaho Falls. Governor E.A. Stevenson had vetoed the bill because of serious technical flaws, so that by 1888, the territory had a university without a home. The Legislature gave it to Moscow, effectively defusing the strong anti-statehood, pro-annexation movement there. Lewiston, however, was not yet ready to give up. In January, 1889, the citizens of Lewiston sent a memorial to Congress declaring that the "welfare of northern Idaho depends on its becoming a part of the new state of Washington." The signers included Alonzo Leland, Samuel H. Reed, S.N. Cooper, L. Rowley, Benjamin Booth, A. Quackenbush, C.C. Bunnell, C.W. Van Pelt, Edward McConville, J.D. Kester, S.G. Isaman, L. Grostein, M.M. Williams, J.D. McConkey, N.B. Holbrook, T.H. Worden, C.A. Thatcher and J.L. Goodnight.

From eastern Washington Territory came sympathetic responses. The *Boomerang* of Palouse wrote, "It does not look humane for anyone to raise a voice against annexing northern Idaho to Washington Territory." But cool heads could see that the game was lost. At the last of a long series of annual citizens meetings in Lewiston, James W. Reid and J.W. Poe argued that there was no longer any hope of annexation to Washington since Washington was about to be admitted as a state without northern Idaho. Reid and Poe (who gave his name to Poe Grade in Lewiston) persuaded the others to adopt an Idaho admission resolution. This apparently convinced the Territorial Legislature that northern Idaho no longer was a problem and the admission process could proceed.

The Legislature authorized a constitutional convention, which Governor Stevenson called for July 4, 1889, at Boise. Reid and Poe, along with J.M. Howe, were the delegates from Nez Perce County and Reid also served as vice president of the convention. Latah County sent W.J. McConnell, later to become governor, Judge Willis Sweet, J.W. Brigham, W.D. Robins, H.D. Blake and A.S. Chaney. Idaho County's delegate was Aaron Parker. The convention produced a document that was less a constitution than a statute book, but that was typical of a time when convention delegates distrusted legislators to properly make the laws. The constitution (which contained the anti-Mormon test oath) went to the voters on November 5, 1889. Moscow area voters approved it by a large margin but in Nez Perce County where anti-Boise sentiment remained strong, two-thirds of the voters stayed home. The constitution was ratified nonetheless by 12,398 votes to 1,773. Alonzo Leland and the *Teller* had campaigned vigorously for annexation to Washington, but he was resigned to statehood within the current hated borders. "We are convinced," he said, "that most of our people prefer statehood to territorial vassalage."

To the gentiles of Idaho Territory, the anti-Mormon test oath did not seem to be a problem, and they were right. In February, 1890, the U.S. Supreme Court inexplicably upheld it and it remained a part of the Idaho Constitution, although unenforced, for many years.

When the Idaho admissions bill came up in the House, Democrats raised some objections, claiming the Idaho population was too small, that the constitutional convention had been improperly called and that the territory had disfranchised a significant number of its people. But Idaho's delegate to Congress, Fred T. Dubois, in a speech to the House declared that "Idaho in its material embodiment is large enough, rich enough and prolific enough to serve as a theater for activities of a great American commonwealth." The objections were half-hearted and the speech unnecessary because everyone knew that political considerations had guaranteed the bill would pass. It sailed through the House on April 3 and on July 1 it passed the Senate so quickly and quietly, according to Dubois, that "I hardly knew the child was born."

Federal law provides that stars may be added to the flag only on Independence Day, and President Benjamin Harrison signed the admission bill on July 3, 1890, so that the forty-third star could become part of the flag that year.

Wyoming followed Idaho into the union of states a week later. In two years and a flurry of statehood bills, Congress had created six states and increased the Republican majority in the Senate by twelve.

Most of northern Idaho evidently agreed with Leland that statehood with southern Idaho was better than no statehood at all, and they put a good face on it. Reported the *Teller* on July 10, 1890: "Idaho is in the union and the Idahoan who did not celebrate with lusty cheers amid the general rejoicing is hard to find . . . " Fifty years later, on July 3, 1940, the *Lewiston Morning Tribune* noted that at Boise the people were joyously celebrating the anniversary. Well, let them, said the *Tribune*'s editorial in effect; it had celebrated Idaho's real birthday in 1936, on the hundredth anniversary of the founding of the Spalding mission on Lapwai Creek.

26

Land!

Probably no single event had greater impact on the agricultural economy of the Lewiston area than the opening of the Nez Perce Reservation in 1895. Settlers had been eyeing these lands since the 1880s, itching to put them to the plow. To the settlers it didn't seem right that the Nez Perces should have so much good farmland when they didn't care much for farming. To the business people of Lewiston, white settlement of the reservation promised new trade. It would have been hard to find a white man or woman at the time who didn't believe that the Indians were unfairly hogging land that could be better used by white farmers.

It did seem like a lot of land, even though the original Nez Perce Reservation, as established in 1855, had been shrunk drastically by the Treaty of 1863. And it seemed also, to the whites, that the Indians weren't properly using it. In the summer of 1890, the steamer Annie Faxon made frequent trips up the Clearwater to and beyond Big Eddy, near present Lenore, to haul flax from a warehouse at Fir Bluff. A reporter for the *Teller*, after taking one of these excursions, wrote that between Lewiston and the reservation border "the whole flat of the river is rapidly growing into one immense orchard. Machines and water wheels of all descriptions line the river front and supply water for the fields about . . . ." The question the whites were asking was, why should the orchards stop at the reservation border?

The answer was simple: Give each Indian a specific allotment of land and open the rest of the reservation to white settlement. The big push came from the business leaders of Lewiston who argued that three-quarters of a million acres of land was entirely too much to set aside for some two thousand Indians. The clamor increased and Washington at length reacted by approving an Indian allotment plan drawn up by the Indian Agent at Lapwai, Charles E. Montieth.

The Indian Bureau negotiated an agreement with the Nez Perces that reduced the size of the reservation from 750,000 to 21,390 acres. The government divided the remaining Indian land among the individual Nez Perces (80 acres per man if the land was tillable, somewhat more if it was good only for grazing) and set some timberland aside for the tribe as a whole. The Indians were to be paid three dollars an acre for the land the tribe gave up, a total of $1,626,222. Part of this—$626,222—was to be paid in a per capita cash settlement and the balance in payments over a period of time. Although the Indians voted to accept the arrangement, it was clouded temporarily by charges that some of the Indians' votes had been bought with whiskey and cash; one report had it that the going rate was 50 cents per vote. These claims apparently never reached court, for payment of the first installment began in mid-August, 1895, and was completed in about two weeks. The immediate cash settlement amounted to $302.96 for each member of the tribe. The Indians' drafts were cashed at Lapwai by officers of banks at Lewiston, Moscow, Kendrick and Juliaetta.

That amounted to more than half a million dollars—a lot of money in those days—and security was tight. Each morning bank officers would take gold and silver coins from the vaults at Lewiston and load them into a two-horse buggy. Escorted by two armed guards riding in front and two more behind, the buggy driver would flip the reins and the whole entourage would race out of town at a gallop. The route lay up the Clearwater on the south side to Hatwai Creek, then by ferry to the north side and thence to Spalding where the driver and his guards would take another waiting ferry to the south side and proceed to the Indian agency at Lapwai. There the representatives of the various banks and the armed guards would preside at a table piled high with gold and silver coins. The Nez Perces would file into the room and as each presented his draft his money would be counted out.

Some of the Indians chose to take only part of their money in cash and leave the rest on deposit in the banks. That was the prudent thing to do and exactly what the Indians' white missionary teachers would have advised. However, some of the Indians never saw the money they left on deposit; for some reason, the banks proved unable to pay on demand.

Once the Indians had been paid for the land they were giving up, the reservation could be officially opened. But first a proclamation had to come from President Cleveland, and the president was slow in signing it. Several weeks passed as the whites fumed and fidgeted. Finally, on November 9, word came from Washington that the proclamation had been signed and that the reservation would be opened to settlement at noon on November 18. Hundreds of families were waiting to stake their claims on these coveted acres. "There was a hurrying to and fro," wrote the *Lewiston Tribune*, "for many had not yet settled in their minds what particular quarter section they would select and no time was to be lost in securing a choice selection." At the Lewiston Land Office, clerks worked around the clock to get everything ready for the 18th.

"The transient population of Lewiston is rapidly swelling," said the *Tribune* as the day neared, "and the rest of the week there will be a veritable rush. These are joyful days for Lewiston, but still better are in store for us!"

Although it was technically against the law, the

reservation was flooded well before opening day with homeseekers. Speculators were plotting townsites and planning a killing in building lots. A week before the opening they had located at least a dozen townsites. By the 16th, the homeseekers were arriving in battalions from every direction and whole families, in wagons filled with provisions, were out reconnoitering the land in preparation for Monday's big rush. Surveyors were doing a land office business. Ferry operators were getting rich taking people over the river to the promised land.

Finally the 18th of November arrived and noon came, but there was no stampede. The homesteaders had been there since dawn and had already staked their claims. The great land rush was not from town to the reservation but from the reservation back to town to file the claims. The urgency to file fast on choice locations inspired some heated races and perhaps a few killings as well. One lively contest developed for a nice piece of land about 40 miles from Lewiston. Jacob Pipinger and F.P. Vaughan had chosen their quarter sections there before the opening and made arrangements in advance to file ahead of any rival that might show up. On the 18th, they found that half a dozen others were after the same parcels, so Pipinger and Vaughan leaped on their horses and sped toward Lewiston. Another party also had planned ahead, however, and Pipinger and Vaughan found they were being raced to Lewiston by two men in a small boat. At the mouth of Potlatch Creek the boat was well in the lead. Pipinger and Vaughan paused there and mounted two fresh horses they had posted in advance and raced on toward Lewiston, now sixteen miles away. Near Spalding they passed the boat, which had gone aground, and sped on down the Clearwater to the Lewiston ferry—which had just pulled away from the shore. They waited seven minutes for the ferry to return, watching upstream for the boat, and rode across to Lewiston. They arrived at the Land Office door at 4 p.m., filed their claims, and the quarter sections were theirs.

According to one report in the *Tribune*, a fight erupted among six persons claiming the same quarter and four of them were killed.

Of all the towns the speculators had located in advance of the rush, only one came into existence. That was Nezperce, now the seat of Lewis County. Wrote the *Tribune:* "H.M. Jorgens, the Kamiah post trader, came in yesterday from the new town of Nezperce, located at the Big Holes. He says there was the maddest rush he ever knew all day Monday to reach the site from every direction. There were 600 men on the ground, all bent on securing town lots. An organizational meeting was held and Dr. J.B. Morris of Lewiston was elected chairman. Monday was spent in surveying and subdividing the site and Tuesday the apportionment of lots was made. It was feared there might be some trouble at that stage of the proceedings and in fact all day rumors were coming in of several people having been killed but none of the officials were notified. Before nightfall a hotel had been erected and was feeding people at 50 cents a head."

The reservation remained, but much of it was now owned by white settlers and the Indians, who had been accustomed for generations to roaming at will over a vast territory, were left with their individual allotments plus their tribal timber land and the agency land at Lapwai. Some of them invested their money wisely and prospered, but others found themselves wondering rather quickly where it had gone. Frank Corbett, the son of a prominent Nez Perce family, told a friend years later that his father, whom he described as an old-fashioned Indian in braids and a big hat, had helped to finance the construction of the Lewis-Clark Hotel in 1922—"even though, of course, he couldn't get a room there."

27

Tall Timber

When the Corps of Discovery reached the site of present day Lewiston in 1805, Captain William Clark wrote in his journal that he could see "not one stick of timber on the river near the forks, and but a few trees for a great distance." Wood floats, however, and the river that carried the explorers' canoes this far would one day carry enough logs here to supply the largest white pine mill in the world.

The Rev. Henry Spalding built the first sawmill in what is now Idaho at his mission on Lapwai Creek in 1840. Part of the trench that carried the millrace, the water that powered the big circular saw, is still there in what is now Spalding Park. Other primitive sawmills appeared at Pierce and Mount Idaho in 1862. Alonzo Leland, later to become a Lewiston newspaper editor, helped organize the mill at Pierce, where miners had been building sluice boxes of planks whipsawed by hand — a slow, backbreaking task. L. P. Brown, who had founded the town of Mount Idaho a few miles south of Grangeville, probably also established the mill there. Its lumber, the first in the region to be planed, helped build the Hotel De France at Lewiston. Starr & Atwood built the first mill in what is now Asotin County in about 1865, some eight miles from the mouth of the Grand Ronde River. Thomas Bean built a mill at Anatone in 1878 and he was joined in the enterprise by Thomas Farrish. Lumber from the Bean & Farrish mill, later known simply as the Farrish Mill, was in great demand for many years. Owners of other early day sawmills included John P. Vollmer of Lewiston, L. A. Porter, an east Lewiston Orchardist who put his orchard crew to sawing logs in the off season, and L. Rowley, who owned a planing mill near the Lewiston approach to the present Interstate Bridge. A. E. Snell and J. N. Burns operated mills at Potlatch.

Frederick Post built a water-powered sawmill at Post Falls in 1871 and in 1889, the Saginaw Lumber Co. was building a sawmill at Coeur d'Alene, the largest in Idaho at the time. Some of the early mills were powered by steam, some by water either flowing past a wheel or falling on it. All were small outfits limited in production and versatility. The first sawmill of consequence to go up at Lewiston was the Harrington Mill, operated by Jason M. Harrington and his son, E. M. They were operating a mill on one of the Minnesota lakes and had run out of trees at about the same time some civic leaders were trying to get a good-sized sawmill established at Lewiston. The elder Harrington toured the Pacific Northwest looking for a new site and found the Clearwater woods impressive. He expressed interest and the town's leaders promised him land in east Lewiston for a mill that would employ forty or more men.

Harrington returned to Minnesota, dismantled the mill there, and hauled it out to Lewiston. He reassembled it in 1893 on a site near what is now the foot of 21st Street, and at that time was considered east Lewiston. Harrington didn't expect the move from Minnesota to Lewiston would be easy, and it wasn't. Moving the machinery itself was hard enough, but there was also the need to adapt to different kinds of logging and transportation. In Minnesota, the Harringtons had skidded logs to a placid lake with teams of oxen. Oxen were strong, sure-footed in snow, and they pulled from a single chain attached to the yoke. In Idaho there were no oxen and the Harringtons would have to use teams of horses. They were not as tough, less handy in snow, and they frequently got tangled up in their harnesses. The white pine and cedar the Harringtons prized most was a hundred miles upriver from the mill in steep timber. They would have to maintain and supply that distant logging camp and then bring the logs down the river a hundred miles to Lewiston.

And they did. A crew of fifteen loggers felled the trees with hand saws (called "Swedish fiddles" because most loggers were Scandinavian) and skidded them to the edge of the river with horses. For this they got $35 to $40 a month — to be paid when they brought the logs in — plus such food and lodging as the crude camp afforded. When the spring thaw came, and high water, the men pushed the logs into the river and spent the next month coaxing them through shallows and eddies, around boulders and off beaches until they had the last of them at Lewiston.

A reporter for the *Lewiston Teller* described, in September, 1893, what was going on at the then-new Harrington mill.

"The steam whistle in the morning starts about 75 men to work. There are teamsters, loggers and wood cutters, yard men and other helpers whose work cannot be named by any general term but they are present and busy as bees in taking care of the machinery of the mill and the production. The mill is running a day and a night shift now. Monday night the lath machine was at work. Tuesday and last night the shingle machine was busy cutting some fine cedar shingles. In the daytime the saws are kept busy in getting cut boards into dimension timber. Eight saws are kept busy turning out about 30,000 feet of lumber daily . . . They have some magnificent logs. Many of their trees measured five feet on the stump and were four feet at the upper end. The Clearwater reaches back into the magnificent timber belt and with its numerous branches can be used to float the logs to this point."

Three years later, the Harrington Mill burned, as so many sawmills did. It was rebuilt, but there were other difficulties and the Harringtons sold out. The mill later suffered a second fire and was not rebuilt again.

The same incentive that brought the Harringtons to the Northwest — dwindling forests in Minnesota — brought other outside interests into Idaho as well. The chief of these was Frederick Weyerhaeuser, of St. Paul, who had founded a family timber dynasty in the Midwest and in 1906 was acquiring interests in timber and mills in Idaho. The Weyerhaeuser family bought into mills at Boise, Sandpoint, Coeur d'Alene and Potlatch as well as the Clearwater Timber Co., which had no mill of its own but purchased timber on the stump and logged it for sale to others.

Directors of the northern Idaho mills began discussing mergers in 1919 when all the companies were suffering from post-war declines. But by 1923, business had improved and the merger talk ceased. By this time, the Weyerhaeusers had become convinced that the Clearwater Timber Co. needed a mill close to its source of supply. The major stockholders asked John P. Weyerhaeuser Jr., known simply as Phil, to take charge of that project. E. C. Rettig, a trusted and experienced lumber cruiser out of Orofino, made a survey of the timber resources of the Clearwater in 1923, and on the basis of his report the directors agreed that a mill at Lewiston would be feasible. They asked Phil Weyerhaeuser, Frederick's grandson and at that time the general manager of the Rutledge mill at Coeur d'Alene, to take charge of the Lewiston project. Phil moved to Lewiston in 1925, taking with him Charles Lee Billings, his assistant, George F. (Fritz) Jewett, his cousin and then manager of the mill at Potlatch, and Rettig. They opened a headquarters in the Breier Building and Phil began dickering for land.

Lewiston's civic leaders were eager to see the mill built and helped the company acquire land in east Lewiston on the site of the Great Northwest Livestock Show. The Inland Power Co. built a dam on the Clearwater that not only produced electric power, but a millpond. At the same time, Weyerhaeuser persuaded the Northern Pacific and Union Pacific to extend rails into the timber. Construction of the mill itself began in February, 1926, and the first log went through the saw on August 8, 1927. It was a huge mill by the standards of the time, and it dwarfed the Potlatch mill, then the state's largest. Phil Weyerhaeuser, in a letter to a friend, wrote that to call the mill "colossal" seemed to him a "very conservative statement."

By 1929, none of the companies was doing well and merger talk renewed. Jewett and Phil Weyerhaeuser circulated a plan for merging three companies — Rutledge at Coeur d'Alene, Potlatch Lumber Co. at Potlatch and the Clearwater Timber Co. at Lewiston. Stockholders approved the union two years later and the emerging company, Potlatch Forests, was incorporated in 1931 with headquarters at Lewiston and with Phil Weyerhaeuser as its first president. Rudolph Weyerhaeuser, Phil's uncle, became president in 1935, when Phil was moved to Tacoma as vice president of the Weyerhaeuser Timber Co. Rudolph was succeeded in 1946 by Jewett, who served as president until 1949 and continued after that as chairman of the board. Billings, meanwhile, remained general manager at Lewiston until his death in 1948.

Billings had become expert in forestry as well as mill management, and he is credited with developing a policy, unusual at the time, of sustained yield. Instead of cutting all the trees and moving on, as the Weyerhaeusers and others had done before, he advocated selective logging and reforestation. (Billings' philosophy was not shared throughout the company, apparently; Frederick E. Weyerhaeuser, Phil's uncle, argued against maintaining a mill at Potlatch, saying the company should cut what remained of the white pine in that area and close the mill.)

When the firm decided to establish a pulp and paper mill at Lewiston, in the late Forties, Jewett was instrumental in tapping an experienced paper mill executive, William P. Davis, to be the next PFI president. The paper mill began producing in December, 1950, and Davis continued to guide the affairs of the company until his death in 1958.

The company put a heavy emphasis on product development and innovation. A PFI engineer, Robert T.

Bowling, invented the Pres-to-Log to utilize waste sawdust, and later an edge-glueing process that made it possible to turn scrap lumber into usable boards. PFI built a veneer plant in 1949 and was making plywood in 1950, then paper, and other wood products including wallboard and roofing materials.

Meanwhile, the company was using some of its profits for expansion out of Idaho. It bought mills and timber elsewhere, and eventually found its Lewiston headquarters too isolated for efficient management. It moved its chief executive offices to San Francisco and changed its name to Potlatch Corporation to reflect its varied interests, and its managers now commute by jet plane from their corporate headquarters to their far-flung plants and forest properties.

*　　*　　*

The Lewiston mill remains the region's largest single employer, although much else has changed. The dam that created the millpond is gone, as is the millpond itself along with Clara, the little iron boat that pushed the logs around. The logs that used to come down the river arrive at the mill now by truck and rail and are turned into lumber by automated machines electronically driven. And gone are the "river rats" who brought the timber down the North Fork and the main Clearwater to the wing dams at Lewiston that guided them into the millpond.

It was a hard and dangerous job. They herded the logs in rowboats, nudging them along and breaking up jams with peaveys, saws and dynamite. In the meantime, they lived in a cookshack mounted on a raft that followed the drive and ate at a long table set up between two rows of bunks. After the second or third week they would have reached Ahsahka, the first sign of civilization, and the worst would be over. After Ahsahka, the men would have fresh food and deeper water and, in a few more days, their pay.

That annual log drive began in 1893 for Harrington and Son and continued until the North Fork was blocked by construction of Dworshak Dam in the early 1970s, almost without change. At the end, the crews were work-

251

ing for a different company, they were skidding logs with tractors and powering their boats with outboard motors. They were moving more logs and using three rafts instead of one to carry the kitchen and bunkhouse. And the pay was a bit better.

They were a colorful, gallant bunch of men in their iron pants, cork boots and black suspenders, skipping among the logs as the river roared around them. On April weekends, in the last stages of the drive, people would go up the river to where the action was that day and enjoy the drama from their cars or their places on the bank. Some lucky ones would be invited aboard the wanigan to say hello to the cook or the cook's helper, and to become, in a way, a part of the last great log drive in America. For that is what it was; when this one ended, there were no more worthy of the name.

BIBLIOGRAPHY

Newspapers

The Golden Age, Lewiston
The Signal, Lewiston
The Radiator, Lewiston
The Idaho County Free Press, Grangeville
The Teller, Lewiston
The Lewiston Journal, Lewiston
The Lewiston Morning Tribune, Lewiston
The Idaho Statesman, Boise

Historical Works, Memoirs and Essays

BEALE, Merrill D., *History of Idaho*. New York: Lewis
Historical Publishing Co., 1959.

BIRNEY, Hoffman, *Vigilantes*. Philadelphia:
Pennsylvania Publishing Co., 1929.

DEVOTO, Bernard, ed., *The Journals of Lewis and
Clark*. Boston: Houghton-Mifflin Co., 1953.

DONALDSON, Thomas, *Idaho of Yesterday*. Caldwell,
Idaho: Caxton Printers, 1914.

ELLIOTT, Wallace W., *History of Idaho*. San Francisco,
1884.

ELSENSOHN, M. Alfreda, *Pioneer Days in Idaho
County*, vols. I and II. Caldwell, Idaho: Caxton
Printers, 1947 and 1951.

Idaho Chinese Lore, Cottonwood: Idaho Corp. of
Benedictine Sisters, 1970.

GOULDER, William A., *Reminiscences of a Pioneer*.
Boise, 1909.

HAILEY, John, *History of Idaho*. Boise, 1910.

BIBLIOGRAPHY (cont'd)

HIDY, Ralph W., Frank Ernest Hill and Allan Nevins, *Timber and Men; the Weyerhaeuser Story*. New York, 1963.

HOWARD, O.O., *Nez Perce Joseph*. Boston, 1881.

HUNTLEY, James L., *Ferry Boats in Idaho*. Caldwell, Idaho: Caxton Printers, 1979.

JOSEPHY, Alvin M., *The Nez Perce Indians and the Opening of the Northwest*. Lincoln: University of Nebraska Press, 1979.

LAWSON, Benjamin S., *Joaquin Miller*. Boise State University.

LINDSTROM, Joyce, *Idaho's Vigilantes*. Moscow, Idaho, 1984.

McCONNELL, William J., *Early History of Idaho*. Caldwell, Idaho: Caxton Printers, 1983.

McWHORTER, L.V., *Yellow Wolf: His Own Story*. Caldwell, Idaho: Caxton Printers, 1983.

MILLER, Joaquin, *Selected Writings*. Urion Press, 1977.

PETERSEN, Keith C., *Company Town*. Pullman: Washington State University Press, 1987.

POWELL, Barbara, *Citizens of North Idaho*, vols. I and II. Medical Lake, Washington, 1986.

SIMON-SMOLINSKI, Carole, *Clearwater Steam, Steel and Spirit*. Clarkston, Washington, 1984.

TWINING, Charles E., *Phil Weyerhaeuser, Lumberman*. Seattle: University of Washington Press, 1985.

WILLIAMS, J. Gary, and Ronald W. Stark, eds., *The Pierce Chronicle*. Moscow: Idaho Research Foundation.